Health and Social Care

NVQ 2 Candidate Handbook

Mark Walsh
Tricia Banks
Deborah Boys
Lorna Evans
Janet McAleavy

Published in 2005 by:
Nelson Thornes Ltd
Delta Place
27 Bath Road
CHELTENHAM
GL53 7TH
United Kingdom

05 06 07 08 09 / 10 9 8 7 6 5 4 3 2 1

A catalogue record for this book is available from the British Library

ISBN 0–7487–9319–4

Illustrations by Clinton Banbury, Jane Bottomley, Angela Lumley and Peters & Zabransky

Page make-up by Florence Production Ltd

Printed and bound in Great Britain by Scotprint

Contents

Mandatory units

Optional units

Introduction

This textbook has been written for care students and practitioners who are studying for a National Vocational Qualification in Health and Social Care at level 2. Students on other courses that require a knowledge and understanding of the principles and practice of health and social-care work will also find this book useful.

The contents of the book

The book is divided into 10 units each providing full and detailed coverage of the relevant unit of the level 2 NVQ Health and Social Care award. This includes coverage of the four core units (HSC21–24) and six of the optional units (HSC25, HSC27, HSC210, HSC214, HSC216 and HSC218) that make up the level 2 NVQ Health and Social Care award. The full range of units is listed below.

To gain a National Vocational Qualification at level 2 in Health and Social Care you will need to demonstrate competence in all of the four core units and any two of the optional units that are available.

Table 1 NVQ units covered in this book

NVQ unit number	Unit title
HSC21	Communicate with and complete records for individuals
HSC22	Support your own health and safety and that of other individuals
HSC23	Develop your knowledge and practice
HSC24	Ensure your actions support the care, protection and well-being of individuals
HSC25	Carry out and provide feedback on specific plan of care activities
HSC27	Support individuals in their daily living
HSC210	Support individuals to access and participate in recreational activities
HSC214	Help individuals to eat and drink
HSC216	Help address the physical-comfort needs of individuals
HSC218	Support individuals with their personal-care needs

The structure of the book

As mentioned, the book is organised and structured around the 10 NVQ units. Each unit in the book is divided into sections that follow the elements and performance criteria of the NVQ unit being covered. The beginning of an element is clearly signposted with an Element heading. There are a number of other features in each unit including the following.

The main text of the unit

The main text provides coverage of the essential knowledge base for the element being covered. That is, it tells you what you need to know and understand in order to practise competently in a particular area of care. The main text is linked as closely as possible to the expected outcomes of the NVQ unit you are studying. You will see that glossary terms are highlighted and there are a variety of diagrams, photographs, cartoons and other visual material to illustrate and support the points that are made in the main text. Each unit contains information that links to the **knowledge, understanding and skills criteria**. To help you make these links, you will find yellow stickers in the margin that tell you which criteria are covered.

KUS 3, 8, 10, 12, 13

Practical examples

This feature provides a care-focused example to make you think about how the knowledge that you have been developing could be used in practice. Each practical example provides a realistic scenario and a few questions for you to respond to. Your answers to the questions cannot be used as evidence of your competence for

Practical Example

KUS 2, 3, 7, 9

Help and support

Mrs Davies, aged 78, is being admitted to your residential home for a three-week respite period for the first time. You have been given the job of showing her around. You know that Mrs Davies has become deaf because of injuries she received in a car accident.

On arrival Mrs Davies is accompanied by her daughter and by a social worker. When you introduce yourself to Mrs Davies, her daughter answers by saying, 'You're wasting your time. She doesn't communicate any more.'

➤ *Suggest reasons why Mrs Davies may communicate less than she used to.*

➤ *What could you do to maximise communication with Mrs Davies during her brief visit?*

➤ *What kinds of extra help and support might improve Mrs Davies' ability to communicate effectively during her three-week respite break?*

the NVQ award. However, you will develop your learning further by answering the various questions that you find throughout the book.

Key points

This is a summary of the main points and themes that are covered in each unit. There is a Key Points feature at the end of each element. You can use this to reinforce your learning when you have finished reading a section. Alternatively you could use it to jog your memory if you need to clarify or check a topic quickly.

Key points – identifying the best forms of communication

- Individuals receiving care have different and particular communication needs and preferences.
- Sensory impairment, language difficulties, speech impairment or neurological and psychiatric problems can affect a person's ability to communicate effectively.
- Effective communication involves responding appropriately to each individual's particular needs and adapting your own communication to meet these.
- You should find out about each individual's communication skills, support needs and the communication aids that they use.
- Where necessary you should seek and make use of extra support to ensure that the individual is able to maximise their communication skills.

Are you ready for assessment?

This feature appears at the end of each unit. It aims to direct your thinking towards the assessment that you have to undertake in order to demonstrate your practical competence as a care worker. The assessment features encourage you to identify and think about what you will have to do to prepare for and carry out an assessment successfully.

Unit

HSC21   **Are you ready for assessment?**

Communicate with and complete records for individuals

This unit is all about how you use your skills to communicate with individuals and the key people in their lives in ways which meet their particular needs and preferences.

Check your knowledge

This feature occurs at the end of each unit. It consists of a small number of comprehension questions. These are designed to test your understanding of the material you have worked through in the unit. It is worth trying to answer all of the questions as this will improve your learning and understanding. However, completing the questions does not provide evidence that you can use to gain your NVQ award. The evidence that you use to claim competence must be produced through the work that you do in your care setting.

Check your knowledge

- Name at least three different ways of communicating in a care setting.
- Describe three reasons why individuals may need extra support to communicate effectively and identify ways that this can be provided.
- Explain what active listening involves and why this is important when communicating with individuals and other key people involved in their care.
- Give reasons why it is good practice not to discuss an individual's care when you are away from work.
- Describe how you could check your understanding when talking with individuals and other key people.
- Explain what 'being objective' involves when making entries in individuals' records and suggest reasons why this is important.

Glossary

You will find this feature at the end of the book. The glossary gives a brief explanation of important words and phrases that are highlighted in the main body of the text.

Legislation

There are legislative differences in England, Scotland, Northern Ireland and Wales relating to health and social care. Please check that you know about the regulations that apply in your area of work. Your supervisor or assessor will advise you about this.

Finally

Good luck with your level 2 NVQ Health and Social Care studies. We hope that the book provides you with interesting, supportive and motivating learning materials and helps you to succeed in your course.

About the authors

Mark Walsh is an experienced writer, teacher and registered mental-health nurse who currently works for the Open University. He has written a wide range of health and social-care textbooks, course syllabuses and examination papers for work-based learners as well as further education and undergraduate students.

Tricia Banks is a health and social-care practitioner with 10 years' experience having initially qualified as a registered nurse in learning disability. She has experience as both an assessor and internal verifier, having been centre co-ordinator of a social services NVQ care centre for three years. She currently works for an NHS Primary Care Trust as a lead internal verifier for Health and Social Care NVQ awards. She maintains occupational competence in care, working in a respite unit for children with multiple disabilities.

Deborah Boys is an advanced practitioner and lecturer at Oxford/Cherwell College (Banbury), and course leader in Health and Social Care. She originally trained as a registered general nurse working mainly in adult care and went on to First Aid Training and Examining for the St. John Ambulance Association. She has been teaching and training for 10 years having gained a Psychology degree with the Open University and Postgraduate Certificate in Post-16 Compulsory Teaching at Oxford Brookes University.

Lorna Evans has been an external verifier for care awards with City & Guilds for the last four years. She has an extensive background in nursing and during this time she has worked for both the NHS and the independent sector. She has also set up and run NVQ centres. Lorna is currently lecturing for the Royal College of Nursing.

Janet McAleavy is Head of Non-Medical Education at the Sheffield Teaching Hospitals Foundation Trust Critical Care, Anaesthesia and Operating Services. As education leader for the care group, her role involves providing educational input into a wide range of strategic developments. She works with directorate educators to plan, implement and evaluate non-medical education and lead the development of a range of innovative programmes to develop new roles within the care group. She is the quality assurance co-ordinator for the City and Guilds Assessment Centre based within the group.

Acknowledgements

The authors and publishers would like to thank their families, friends and colleagues and the following organisations for permission to reproduce materials and photographs in this book:

Chacombe House Residential and Nursing Home; Roses Nursing Agency, Cheltenham; Karen Seymour and staff at Littlemore Mental Health Resource Centre, Oxford.

British Deaf Association for the finger spelling alphabet, © British Deaf Association. Reproduced by permission; Health and Safety Commission Comprehensive Injury Statistics: Health Services (2003) © Crown Copyright 2005; Commission for Racial Equality for 'There are lots of places in Britain where racism doesn't exist' poster, © Commission for Racial Equality. Reproduced by permission; British Crime Survey 2002/2003 ONS © Crown Copyright 2005.

Clark Brennan/Alamy, p.285; Photofusion Picture Library/Alamy, p.235; OnRequest Images Inc/Alamy, p.266; Helen Broadfield, p.247; Instant Art (NT), pp. 59, 63; Photodisc 18 (NT), p.213; Photodisc 40 (NT), p.237; Photodisc 40 (NT), p.98; Photodisc 59 (NT), p.190; Janet McAleavy, p.105; mediacolor's/Alamy, p.284; Biomedical Imaging Unit, Southampton General Hospital/Science Photo Library, p.50; Martin Sookias, pp. 10, 22, 26, 35, 42, 43, 55, 84, 94, 118, 123, 140, 141, 150, 155, 162, 185, 192, 198, 205, 215, 233, 239, 276.

Every effort has been made to contact copyright holders and we apologise if anyone has been overlooked.

Assessment of National Vocational Qualifications

Before you start your National Vocational Qualification (NVQ) it is important that you are familiar with the assessment process and the way in which your NVQ is structured.

What is assessment?

In order to achieve your NVQ you will be assessed in your workplace. You will be assessed or measured against national occupational standards in health and social care. These standards outline the performance and knowledge requirements of workers in the health and social-care sector and have been developed by experts and experienced professionals from the specialist area. Awarding bodies (organisations that are responsible for awarding/providing qualifications) use these standards to design agreed nationally recognised qualifications, for example NVQ 2 Health and Social Care. This means that across the UK people will be undertaking the same qualification and this will ensure that your skills and knowledge are transferable should you change employer.

Assessment is important so that both you and your employer know that the required standard has been reached. Your assessor will observe how you go about your work and also find out if you understand what you are doing. In other words, they will assess your knowledge. It is not enough to perform well but not understand what you are doing, or to understand the theory but not be able to put it into practice. In order to obtain the NVQ you must be able to perform at the required standard and know why you are doing what you are doing. Once your assessor has seen your practice at work and found out if you have the necessary background knowledge, they will decide whether you have demonstrated that you are competent and whether there is sufficient evidence to show that you consistently meet the required standard.

The structure of NVQs

The NVQ is broken down into units. These units cover a broad range of activities. The units are numbered and they have the letters HSC in front of the number, signifying that they are health and social-care units. Some of the units are called core units. The core units cover activities that are relevant to all health and social-care workers whatever the care setting – for example, health and safety. There are only a few core units but there are several optional units because health and social-care settings can differ greatly. Your assessor and employer will guide you regarding your choice of optional units. Remember, you can only choose an optional unit which relates to the job you are doing as you have to demonstrate your competence in real work situations. Each unit of the NVQ specification contains a brief explanation of the unit followed by a section called 'Scope'. The aim of the Scope section is to provide guidance on how the unit relates to the work setting. It also helps you to identify the sort of work you might be doing with individuals. This helps to ensure the unit is relevant to your work. There is a list of terms which are relevant to the unit, followed by examples. Use this information to give you ideas about how the unit applies to your own work and also to help identify assessment opportunities. You will be expected to show evidence of any aspects of the Scope that relate to your work.

There is a statement at the beginning of each NVQ unit which summarises the values underpinning the unit. This reinforces the importance of the values and attitude of all workers in health and social-care settings. A worker would not be considered competent if they do not demonstrate these values. It is essential to apply them in all aspects of your work.

Some of the key words and concepts which appear in the NVQ are explained in the Glossary. It is important to read this section carefully to make sure you understand how the words and phrases are being used.

The units are further broken down into elements. There are between two and four elements in each unit. For example, in Unit HSC21 (Communicate with and complete records for individuals) there are four elements of competence which are numbered HSC21a, HSC21b, HSC21c and HSC21d.

Within the element there are performance criteria (sometimes called PCs). The performance criteria state what you have to do to show that you are competent in that particular element.

At the end of each unit there is a section called 'Check your knowledge'. This outlines the knowledge requirement for the whole unit.

Who is involved in the NVQ process?

Many people are involved in the NVQ process, as described below.

You are the candidate. All individuals who are undertaking an NVQ are referred to as candidates and you will have a candidate number from your awarding body.

You have an assessor. This person must be occupationally competent to assess you. In other words, they should be suitably experienced and they must also have a qualification in assessment. You may already work alongside this person, they may be in the same team as you, or you may work with them occasionally. This will depend upon the organisation that you work for and the nature of the work that you do.

You might have a peripatetic assessor. This person will not be based with you but will come into your work area to assess you.

Wherever your assessor is based, it is vital that you develop a positive working relationship with them. You should be in regular contact throughout your NVQ.

In addition to your assessor you might also be watched by an expert witness. This person must also be occupationally competent and familiar with the health and social-care standards but not necessarily a qualified assessor. The expert witness can provide proof of your practice which will contribute to the evidence presented to your assessor.

At different points as you progress to the qualification the assessment records are passed on to the next stage of the process called internal verification. The role of the internal verifier (IV) is to maintain the quality and consistency of the assessment process. The IV does this by sampling evidence, checking that documentation is completed properly, and ensuring that you have been assessed, as required, by a suitable assessor. Once the IV has sampled your work they will either agree with the decision of your assessor and add their signature or they will identify areas that need further work or clarification. The internal verifier could be employed in the same organisation as you, or if you are doing your NVQ at a college or with a training provider, they may be based there.

The external verifier (EV) is appointed by the Awarding Body. The EV monitors the overall quality of the Assessment Centre. They do this by visiting Assessment Centres, usually twice a year, and conducting a thorough audit. They will examine candidate evidence and talk to candidates, assessors and IVs.

Achieving the NVQ

You do not 'pass' or 'fail' an NVQ as such. Instead, in order to achieve your NVQ you have to demonstrate that you consistently meet the required standards of practice. To show this you must collect evidence which confirms this. Your evidence could be made up of the following:

- **Observation** – this type of evidence is *required* in all of the elements of the core units of your NVQ. It will also be required in the optional units unless your assessor has agreed that you may use testimony from an expert witness as an alternative. Your assessor will observe you as you work and check that you are working in accordance with the health and social-care units that you are undertaking. A written statement describing what was observed will be produced.

- **Expert witness testimony** – a written statement provided by an occupational expert which will give testimony to your practice when carrying out a specific activity in your workplace. This person needs to be known to your assessor and should have agreed to and prepared for their role.

- **Work products** – your assessor can examine items such as records or forms that you have been responsible for completing as part of your day-to-day work.

- **Confidential records** – records which you complete and which contain confidential information can be part of your evidence but must not be placed in your portfolio. They should stay in their usual location and be referred to by your assessor in their records. Confidential records are items such as care plans, individual plans, reviews.

- **Witness testimony** – a written statement from a person who has knowledge and experience of your work practice. This could be a co-worker or other linked professional, service users or their relatives. Your assessor will help you identify the best use of witnesses.

- **Reflective accounts, case studies, projects, assignments** – your explanation of work that you have undertaken. This is particularly useful to cover aspects of the knowledge specification or events which might happen rarely or be difficult to observe.
- **Questioning** – your assessor could ask you to answer written or oral questions which will be recorded and kept in the evidence portfolio.
- **Simulation** – a simulation could be used where it is difficult to obtain the evidence from a real work situation. This form of evidence is only permitted as part of the evidence in element HSC22c covering emergency situations.

Getting started

In order to start your NVQ you will need to be registered with an Awarding Body. You can register through an Assessment Centre. An Assessment Centre could be a college, an NHS Trust or other employer, or a private organisation. The Assessment Centre is approved by the Awarding Body to offer a particular qualification. The assessment and verification processes within the assessment centre are monitored by the Awarding Body. This helps to promote fairness and to maintain the high standard that is required of any person working within health and social care. When you have successfully completed your NVQ in Health and Social Care your Assessment Centre will give you a certificate from the Awarding Body.

Once you are registered for your NVQ, you will then be assigned an assessor and an internal verifier. You will receive a full induction to the qualification and you should then meet with your assessor and discuss your level of experience and knowledge. Depending on your existing skills and knowledge you may need to attend a training programme or to receive coaching while you work. When you are ready for assessment you will agree a plan which will outline how you will start to gather evidence relating to the units of your NVQ.

Any plan must be agreed by you and your assessor. You should agree and record target dates and specific units that you are planning to achieve. Your plan will state how you are going to obtain the evidence that you need and identify the types of evidence you are going to gather, as mentioned above.

All assessment plans will contain the following information:

- WHAT will be assessed.
- HOW it will be assessed.
- WHEN it will be assessed.
- WHO will be involved.

Once you have gathered your evidence you will place it in a folder – this is your portfolio of evidence. Some centres may use an electronic portfolio system which means your documentation will be kept on a computer rather than in an actual folder. Your assessor will advise you of the system in use at your centre and how to put your evidence together. Your portfolio should be organised and all your evidence must have a page number and show the specific unit/element/PC or knowledge point that it relates to. Once you have obtained the evidence your assessor will examine it and check that it is:

- **Valid** – the appropriate and required assessment methods have been used.
- **Authentic** – it is your own work. All signatures and dates must be included and any testimonies must be written by appropriate people.
- **Current** – the evidence indicates today's standards of practice, legislative requirements and practice policy.
- **Sufficient** – there must be enough evidence to demonstrate that you have met the required standard. You should have covered all the performance criteria, and have the knowledge and any additional evidence requirements for the unit.

Your assessor will give you feedback and review your progress to make sure that you understand how you are getting on with your NVQ. Feedback should be recorded.

At the end of each unit of this book there is a heading 'Are you ready for assessment?'. In this section there are questions relating to the unit and suggestions regarding relevant evidence. The section should help you to decide whether your understanding of the subject is clear enough, and it indicates how you might prepare for assessment in the workplace.

Conclusion

Often the most demanding part of doing an NVQ is becoming familiar with the paperwork and the way that the qualification is structured. As you progress through each unit the process becomes more familiar. Keep motivated, and if you are experiencing difficulties ask for help.

Undertaking a qualification in the workplace is hard work and requires a great deal of commitment. However, achieving a formal qualification in health and social care is very important. It is a recognition of the skill and knowledge that you need to fulfil your role and it means that individuals can have confidence in the service you provide.

Communicate with and complete records for individuals

This unit covers the communication competence that is required by all care workers. People who work in care need to be able to use a range of verbal and non-verbal communication skills and should be able to listen and contribute effectively to written record keeping.

This unit links to all of the other units that you will be studying to achieve your NVQ award and contains four elements:

⌣ *HSC21a Work with individuals and others to identify the best forms of communication*

⌣ *HSC21b Listen and respond to individuals' questions and concerns*

⌣ *HSC21c Communicate with individuals*

⌣ *HSC21d Access and update records and reports*

⌣ Introduction

Effective communication skills are essential whether you work in domiciliary, residential or community care or within a hospital setting. This unit covers the type of communication skills that you will need to use every day. The quality of your **interaction** with **individuals**, their relatives and other care staff and the effectiveness of your written record-keeping skills will depend on your ability to communicate effectively.

⌣ Types of communication

When people communicate with each other they send, receive and respond to each other's 'messages'. We communicate with (or send messages to) each other in a variety of different ways, for example verbal (spoken), non-verbal (body language), written and visual forms of communication. Each of these different types of communication are used within health and social-care settings. They all rely on the same communication process of sending, receiving and responding to 'messages'.

KUS 3, 8

Most interaction between care workers and individuals occurs through verbal (spoken) and **non-verbal communication** (body language). However, you may also need to make use of written forms of communication in your work as well as graphs and charts. This is especially important if you are involved in record

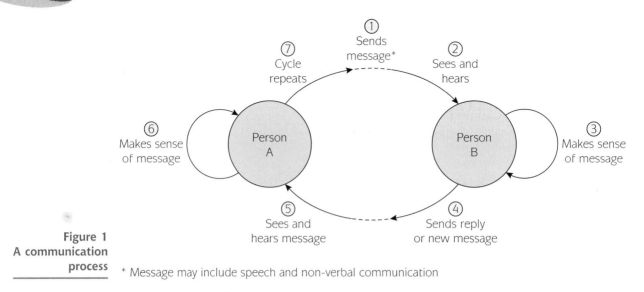

**Figure 1
A communication
process**

* Message may include speech and non-verbal communication

keeping. Even if you do not write in an individual's care plans or notes, you will often need to read and understand them. You will also need to develop your reading skills so that you can understand the policies and procedures that have been produced by your employer.

Verbal communication

Verbal communication involves the use of speech. Talking with individuals, their relatives and friends and with colleagues is a common, everyday occurrence for care workers. For example, it happens when you:

- Respond to an individual's questions and feelings of distress.
- Talk to an individual about how they are feeling.
- Speak at a team meeting.
- Break bad news to an individual, their relatives or friends.
- Answer the telephone and provide information to a colleague or an individual's relative.
- Deal with problems and complaints about care.

The quality of your verbal communication will be affected by how you speak as much as by what you say. For example, it is never a good idea to shout or to talk so loudly that the listener believes you are shouting. This is unprofessional and the listener's attention is distracted from what is being said. Mumbling, speaking too quickly, failing to complete your sentences or using a hostile or aggressive tone will also reduce the effectiveness of what you say.

Instead, your speech should be clear and reasonably paced. This will help listeners to hear and understand what is being said. A relaxed, encouraging and friendly tone of voice will also help you to convey warmth, sincerity and appropriate respect for the listener.

Non-verbal communication

Non-verbal communication is important for care workers for two reasons:

- You need to be aware of the ways that individuals and others communicate their thoughts and emotions without speaking.
- You must also be aware of how people use non-verbal communication during interactions with others and the impact that this can have.

KUS 9

Non-verbal communication is as important in the care workplace as it is anywhere else in our lives. The ways that you use posture, stance, tone of voice, facial expression and gesture, for example, will affect how individuals think about and understand you.

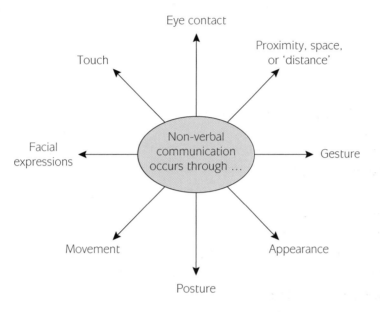

**Figure 2
Non-verbal
communication**

It is important to note that your body language is always 'switched on' and active. Sometimes you might deliberately use your body to communicate with another person – such as through a controlled facial expression or a gesture. However, there are also times when your body language is less controlled because you are under a lot of pressure or are feeling intense and powerful emotions. In these circumstances your true thoughts and feelings are likely to be revealed through your non-verbal behaviour.

Written communication in care

**KUS 3, 8,
10, 12, 13**

You probably spend a lot of time writing and evaluating care plans and documenting the care that you provide. Your care organisation may have an official record-keeping system and standard forms that you are required to complete. As a result you will need to develop clear, effective writing skills. You should know how to complete different kinds of documents (such as individuals' notes, reports and formal letters).

Many of the writing skills that you need for care work are learnt in practice and will quickly become a part of your everyday work. However, it is important to regularly

**Figure 3
Reasons
for writing
things down**

review the purpose and usefulness of the different kinds of records that you complete and to reflect on the effectiveness of your writing skills.

Whatever type of communication you use in your everyday work, you should always aim to make the individual's needs, wishes and preferences the central focus. This means that you will have to develop a good understanding of both general communication issues and the particular communication needs, preferences and problems of the individuals that you work with.

Element HSC21a *Work with individuals and others to identify the best forms of communication*

Communication needs and preferences

KUS 2, 7

Responding to each individual's particular needs and preferences is the key to communicating effectively. In this section of the unit we will consider both the range of factors that can affect individuals' needs and preferences and how you can adapt to them.

The ability to communicate plays a fundamental part in our lives. It enables us to make contact with others, to form various relationships, to express our feelings and to meet our everyday needs. Communication difficulties and problems can have a major impact on people's lives. It can have a direct effect on a person's ability to live independently, it can result in social isolation and a heightened sense of anxiety, and it can increase an individual's vulnerability.

The ability to communicate effectively is particularly important to those who require greater support and rely heavily on care workers to meet their daily living needs. As a result, you have an important responsibility to identify and respond to each individual's communication problems, needs and preferences. This means that you should:

- Develop your awareness of general communication issues and problems.
- Understand each individual's particular communication needs and preferences.
- Review and develop your own communication skills.
- Establish a rapport and a respectful relationship with each individual you work with.
- Obtain extra support to maximise communication where this is necessary.
- Promote interaction between yourself and others so that communication is two way.
- Record and share appropriately information about each individual's communication skills, needs and language preferences.

Communication problems

KUS 2, 7, 8

The people who you provide care for may be perfectly capable and confident communicators who have many communication skills that they use regularly. It is important to note each individual's communication strengths and abilities and to ensure that your colleagues are also aware of them. However, you should not take any individual's communication skills for granted – it is also quite possible that some or all of the people you work with experience communication problems. This could be because of sensory impairments, language problems or lack of confidence.

Sensory impairment

KUS 7

We all rely on using our senses to communicate. Sight and hearing are the most important senses used in communication, though touch also plays a part. It is important to be aware of any sensory problems that an individual may have as these may affect the person's ability to communicate.

Visual impairment

There is a saying that the eyes are the windows of the soul. We can tell so much about how a person is feeling by looking at their eyes for evidence of fear, pain, anxiety, humour, fun, love etc. However, conditions such as cataracts, blindness, impaired vision and a squint can make communication more difficult for some individuals. For example, visual impairment may reduce a person's ability to pick up visual cues during interactions. It may be difficult to see what emotion the individual is feeling if they do not use their eyes as a means of communication.

You should be able to identify individuals with visual impairment as they often use prescription spectacles, contact lenses or specialist equipment. Diagnosed problems should be documented in the person's records and these should be read and

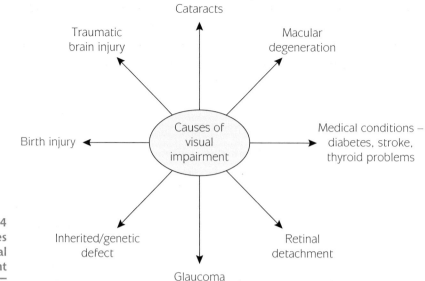

Figure 4
Some causes
of visual
impairment

understood. If the details of a report on a person's problems are technical or complex, ask your supervisor or a senior colleague to explain what they mean. The person themselves may also be able to provide a clear explanation. It is possible that you will work with an individual who develops some visual impairment after coming into your care setting or who has a pre-existing but undiagnosed problem. If you suspect that the person has a problem you should try to talk to them about it, and report it to your senior colleagues in an appropriate way.

Hearing impairment

Hearing is one of the most important senses in the process of developing and maintaining communication. Individuals (or staff) may experience a range of

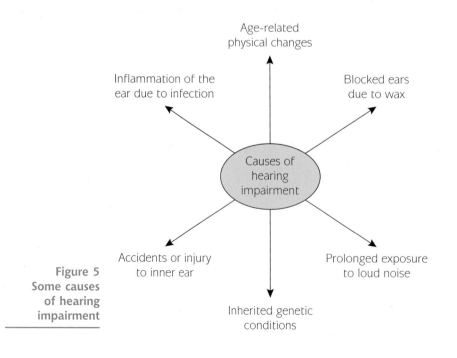

Figure 5
Some causes
of hearing
impairment

communication problems as a result of hearing impairment. For example, a hearing-impaired person may need to be able to see you in order to lip read, or they may need a hearing aid that is functioning properly. People with some limited hearing ability may also find that the background noise of a busy care setting interferes with their ability to hear when somebody is speaking to them.

As with visual impairment, some people with hearing problems may already have had their difficulties recognised and diagnosed. You should be able to find out about the causes and effects of a particular individual's problems by reading their notes and by asking colleagues and the individual about the problem. These individuals should have personal hearing aids and may use other equipment or be skilled lip readers. However, degenerative hearing loss may occur unnoticed in some individuals. In such circumstances you may suspect or notice that an individual has hearing problems before they do. Good indicators include having to repeat yourself a lot, being asked to speak louder, noticing that the individual speaks loudly but is unaware of this, or that they have the radio or television turned up very loud. Again, where you suspect the person may have some hearing impairment you should try to talk to them about it and report your concerns and observations to a senior colleague.

Language needs

KUS 1, 3

In a **multicultural** society like that of the UK, it is important to find out about each individual's language needs. If you assume that everyone can speak and understand English, you risk isolating people whose first language is not English. Where an individual prefers to speak another language, you will need to obtain extra support in the form of an interpreter, a multilingual colleague or a person who can communicate effectively with them.

You should also avoid using the technical jargon of health and social care when speaking with individuals and other **key people**. This can be confusing and meaningless even for those who speak English well but who have little or no experience or training in care.

Speech impairment

KUS 7

An individual's communication problems may also be the result of speech rather than sensory impairment or language problems. Speech impairment may occur because of injuries or conditions that have caused damage to the person's mouth.

The shapes we make with our mouth produce sounds out of which we form words in our chosen language. Developmental problems and injuries to the mouth, teeth, tongue or lips can all impair a person's ability to speak. People who experience speech impairments may be perfectly capable of understanding you but might have difficulty responding. In addition to appropriate speech and language therapy, it is important to give such people enough time and support to reply.

Neurological problems

Brain injuries caused by traumatic accidents or conditions such as **strokes** and degenerative dementia-related conditions cause some individuals to have communication difficulties. In particular, changes to the structure of the brain can damage and disrupt its ability to work in the expected way. If this damage affects the areas of the brain that are responsible for speech and language, the person may be unable to communicate temporarily or permanently.

Specialist treatment and therapy is usually offered to people who experience speech impairment as a result of **neurological** problems. This may involve relearning speech or developing new ways to communicate through the use of sign language, touch, specialist 'communicator' equipment or by adapting any remaining verbal or non-verbal skills. Make sure you are aware of individuals who have these types of communication problems. They will probably have been fully investigated, diagnosed and documented. The person's records and your senior colleagues should be able to tell you more about the individual's problems and explain how to meet their communication needs.

Psychiatric problems

An individual's ability to communicate effectively may also be affected by psychiatric or mental-health problems. Again, these may be temporary or more long term. Conditions such as depression, anxiety and mania may result in problems with concentration, disorientation and confusion, for example. Other conditions such as dementia, schizophrenia or bipolar disorder may have serious effects on the person's memory, mood or general ability to think and make sense of everyday information.

It is important that you try to understand what individuals who have psychiatric problems are trying to communicate. This means that you should pay attention to the emotions that accompany what they say as much as the words that they use. You should never dismiss a person's attempts to communicate as 'meaningless' or 'gibberish'. Instead you should acknowledge the instances when you struggle to understand or fail to communicate with an individual and you should seek support, advice and guidance from senior colleagues or staff who have received specialist training in this area.

Reviewing your communication skills

KUS 3

Your own skills and abilities are an important factor in making communication with different individuals effective. As we have just noted, you need to find ways of using your skills to the best advantage of each person you work with. This means that you will need to have a good, ongoing awareness of your own strengths, weaknesses and limitations in this area.

Hopefully your communication skills will develop as you gain experience in care work. However, if you feel that your range of skills and abilities are not sufficient to meet the communication needs and preferences of particular individuals, you should acknowledge this and seek extra support and guidance on how you can best communicate with these individuals. There will be many situations where you think that you can meet an individual's communication needs and preferences. However, when you cannot meet their needs, be realistic and recognise those instances as a learning opportunity that will help you to develop your skills and will ensure that the person receives more appropriate support.

Effective communication

KUS 6

As we noted earlier, responding to each individual's particular needs and preferences is the key to communicating effectively. As such, it is important that you gather information about each person's communication skills, problems and support needs. You can do this by reading their charts and files and by asking colleagues questions before you go to meet someone for the first time. The extra time spent in preparation is likely to improve your chances of forming an effective care relationship with the individuals you care for and may in fact save time later.

An individual's care plan and notes or records should indicate their preferred language and name. You should respect the individual's wishes and preferences where these have been indicated. However, if this information is not available, you should try to find out:

- The name the person likes to be called.
- Which language the person prefers to use if it is not English.
- Whether the person uses an interpreter or **advocate** to help them communicate.
- Whether the person has any sensory or speech impairments, neurological or psychiatric problems that affect their communication abilities.
- Whether the person uses any communication aids (such as glasses, hearing aids or communicator devices) or special techniques (such as sign language, lip reading or **Makaton**) to overcome communication problems.

As mentioned earlier, you should also note and share information about each individual's communication strengths and skills as there may be many positive features that will help the communication process.

Thinking about communication aids

Glasses:

- Do the glasses belong to this individual?
- When did the person last have an eye test?
- Are the person's glasses clean?
- Does the individual need to wear their glasses all the time or only during certain activities?
- Are the glasses labelled so that the rightful owner can be identified?

Hearing aids:

- Where does the person use their hearing aid?
- When does the person use their hearing aid?
- Are the batteries working?
- How is the hearing aid inserted?
- Is the hearing aid mould clean?

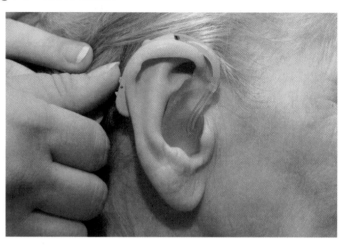

Figure 6
A hearing aid

The first step in finding an answer to each of these questions is to ask the individual. You could also check the person's care plan and ask colleagues and other **key people** if you need to. This kind of information should be documented in the individual's records so that all care workers fully understand the person's needs and how they are met.

It is important to note that individuals have constantly changing needs. If you are meeting the person for the first time, it is good practice to confirm with them the accuracy of any information about their communication needs. If the individual's needs or preferences have changed you should do your best to adapt to and accommodate them and also report these changes to your colleagues.

Obtaining help and support

KUS 2

There may be times when you require help and support to establish or maintain effective communication with an individual. A range of other people including the individual's family and friends, your colleagues and specialist support staff, may be available to help you at these times. Whenever you seek extra help, remember that an individual's privacy, dignity and confidentiality should be respected. Check any information that is given to you by an individual's family or friends to make sure that it is accurate, up to date and not simply their inaccurate opinion about the person.

An individual's children, siblings or parents may not always be the most appropriate source of extra help even where they do speak the same language as the individual or have specialist communication skills. This can be the case where an individual refuses, or finds it impossible, to discuss personal problems or intimate details of their life in the presence of people they know well. It is best to acknowledge the confidentiality issues involved and to use an independent, professional translation service in these circumstances. Translators and interpreters are available for those who speak a foreign language and for people who use sign language as their preferred form of communication.

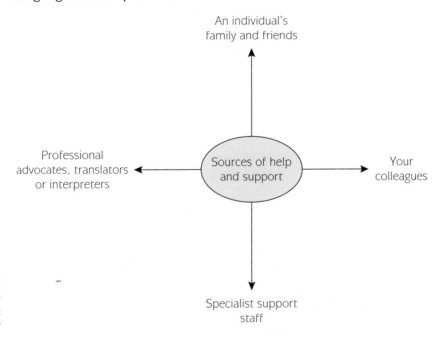

Figure 7
Sources of help and support

Help and support

Practical Example

KUS 2, 3, 7, 9

Mrs Davies, aged 78, is being admitted to your residential home for a three-week respite period for the first time. You have been given the job of showing her around. You know that Mrs Davies has become deaf because of injuries she received in a car accident.

On arrival Mrs Davies is accompanied by her daughter and by a social worker. When you introduce yourself to Mrs Davies, her daughter answers by saying, 'You're wasting your time. She doesn't communicate any more.'

➤ *Suggest reasons why Mrs Davies may communicate less than she used to.*

➤ *What could you do to maximise communication with Mrs Davies during her brief visit?*

➤ *What kinds of extra help and support might improve Mrs Davies' ability to communicate effectively during her three-week respite break?*

Recording and sharing information appropriately

KUS 10, 11, 12, 13, 14

Many individuals report that one of the most annoying things about receiving care is the fact that they have to tell different members of staff the same thing over and over again. This is easily avoided through the appropriate recording and sharing of individual-related information.

You will need to become familiar with the record-keeping systems in your organisation and should be clear about your responsibilities for record keeping. Individuals' records should contain relevant and appropriate information about each person's communication needs. They should also identify any extra help, support or communication aids that an individual requires. Ideally this will all appear prominently and may even be incorporated into the individual's care plan.

If you obtain new or additional information when working with and observing a particular individual, you should ensure that it is noted in a clear and accurate way in the appropriate place in the person's records. It is likely that each individual's communication needs will change, not least because everyone is going to get older and their health will alter over time.

Key points – identifying the best forms of communication

- Individuals receiving care have different and particular communication needs and preferences.
- Sensory impairment, language difficulties, speech impairment or neurological and psychiatric problems can affect a person's ability to communicate effectively.
- Effective communication involves responding appropriately to each individual's particular needs and adapting your own communication to meet these.
- You should find out about each individual's communication skills, support needs and the communication aids that they use.
- Where necessary you should seek and make use of extra support to ensure that the individual is able to maximise their communication skills.

Element
HSC21b

Listen and respond to individuals' questions and concerns

This element focuses on the important skills of listening and responding to individuals. The ability to listen and respond appropriately to the individuals you work with is an essential part of providing effective, sensitive care. In this section of the unit we will consider how these skills can be used in your interactions with individuals, their families and friends and with your colleagues.

Care settings are busy, often complex and pressured places to work. The pace of work and the need to get things done may result in your actions becoming almost unconscious as you **multitask** your way through the day. Does this sound familiar? You might have cleared dishes from breakfast tables while also checking that some individuals have had enough to eat at the same time as finding out who has outside appointments and who has visitors due. The fast pace of care work can sometimes leave little time for thinking. On the other hand, the regular, everyday tasks that are part of care work can also become mundane and routine. This can sometimes lead care workers to 'switch off', to go on 'automatic pilot' or to respond to people without thinking about what they are saying. In these situations care workers stop listening properly.

Active listening

KUS 9

Care workers are encouraged to use **active listening** techniques to avoid the problems described above and to maximise communication with individuals. When a person listens actively they will deliberately focus their attention on:

- The content of what the speaker is saying.
- The way in which the person speaks (for example the volume, pitch, speed and tone of the person's voice).
- The non-verbal behaviour the person uses.

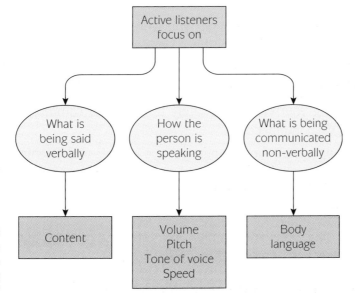

**Figure 8
An active approach to listening**

As a listener it is not easy to achieve all of this at once! The skill of active listening certainly takes practice and effort to achieve, but it is worth it. The quality of care and the emotional support you can offer to individuals will be improved by your careful use of active listening techniques. Listening actively to an individual who you are caring for will help the person communicate their views, needs, wishes and preferences more effectively.

Questions for active listeners

- What is being said?
- How is it being said?
- What is the person's body language and behaviour saying?
- What is not being said?

Becoming an active listener

There are a number of things that you can do to become an active listener and to maintain high standards of practice in this area. Before we consider these, it is useful to note that you should make a continual effort to present yourself in a positive way to the people you work with. This will increase the likelihood that they will actually want to communicate with you and will not feel anxious about doing so when they really need to. For example, you should:

- Make time for people, even if it is only to say hello at the start of a shift or goodbye before you leave.
- Be approachable and behave in ways that make individuals feel able to talk to and trust you. Wearing your uniform in an appropriate way, having your ID badge available to show that you are who you say you are and being presentable all help to establish trust.

Let us assume that the individuals you work with do trust you and are happy to communicate with you. You can be a more effective, active listener by:

- Providing each individual with the support they need to communicate their views, wishes and preferences.
- Positioning yourself appropriately to maximise communication and listening during each interaction.
- Using appropriate body language, eye contact and listening skills during your interactions.
- Responding appropriately to any questions or concerns that an individual expresses.
- Recognising your own limits and referring matters outside your area of competence to appropriate people.

Supporting communication

People who require health and social-care services may have a range of communication support needs. The precise nature of the support required will depend on the individuals' particular situation. However, you should always check and take appropriate action to ensure that the individuals you work with have access to:

- Adaptive equipment or communication aids, such as glasses, hearing aids and electronic communicator devices if they normally require or choose to use them.

- Specialist support staff such as interpreters, advocates and speech and language therapists if they have speech or language problems or if they are unable to communicate or express their views independently.

The use of appropriate support will increase the possibility of achieving effective communication and interaction with the individual.

Body language

Your non-verbal behaviour, such as your posture and positioning, is important when you have to listen and respond to individuals' questions and concerns. Also, you should be aware of the importance of your facial expression, eye contact and how you respond to individuals.

- Facial expression is closely monitored by the people you are communicating with.

- The human face is an important source of non-verbal communication.

- Facial expressions reveal a person's feelings.

- Eye contact provides some insight into your feelings and level of interest.

- You should make and maintain good eye contact to indicate interest and respect for the individuals with whom you are communicating.

- Good eye contact can also generate trust and reassurance.

- Long, unbroken eye contact may be interpreted as hostility or attraction, depending on the context of your communication.

- The use of eye contact is influenced by a person's cultural background.

- You should monitor individuals' reactions to check that what you are doing is socially appropriate.

- People from European cultures tend to interpret broken, or avoidant, eye contact in a negative way (mistrusting the person). People from non-European cultures tend to avoid direct eye contact and this shows respect and deference.

Positioning and body posture

Where and how you position yourself in relation to an individual and any other people involved in an interaction will affect the communication that occurs. It is important, for example, that the individual can see you clearly and that you do not intimidate them with your body posture or **proximity**.

Body posture is an important aspect of non-verbal communication. Standing with your hand on your hip may be comfortable for you but it could convey impatience; having your hands in your pockets may keep them warm but it could look lazy. Being too close to an individual could also make them feel uncomfortable. Sitting

**Figure 9
SOLER behaviour**

on their bed without asking could be seen as disrespectful. However, if you stand too far away it might look like you are frightened or uninterested. Therefore, it is good practice to check that your positioning allows the individual to see you and that they feel comfortable with it.

As well as thinking about where you position yourself in relation to the individual you are providing care for, you should also think about how your behaviour can improve communication. Using SOLER behaviour can help. This stands for:

S face the other person **S**quarely

O adopt an **O**pen posture

L **L**ean towards the other person slightly

E maintain good **E**ye contact

R try to be **R**elaxed whilst paying attention

These tips provide useful guidance. However, you might have to adapt them to suit the circumstances you work in and an individual's particular communication needs. They are not unbreakable rules.

Responding to individuals

KUS 2, 3

It is important that each different individual you work with feels valued and respected and that their needs and wishes are taken into consideration. Responding clearly and appropriately to an individual's questions and concerns is one way of achieving this. Key points to think about include:

- Think before you speak.
- Be clear in what you are saying.
- Speak loud enough to be heard.
- Speak slowly enough to be understood.
- Consider the words that you use.

It is important to give individuals the time, support and encouragement to raise questions and express their concerns. How you respond during an interaction can influence whether the person actually gets to say what they want to. Good practice points include:

- *Respecting silences* if an individual pauses to think or is struggling to express themselves. Do not jump in too quickly with your own response or ask questions that will distract the individual from what they are trying to say.

- *Using **minimal prompts*** to show that you are focused on and actively listening to the person. Try to use an appropriate variety of these prompts without overusing them.

- *Not interrupting* an individual when they are speaking. You will remember more of what has been said if you listen more and say less. The individual will also have a better chance to speak.

- *Maintaining an even and respectful tone of voice.* Humour, anger and sarcasm are all displayed through our tone of voice. There are some circumstances where humour is helpful and appropriate. Shouting and being sarcastic to people is never appropriate or acceptable.

- *Providing privacy.* Do you discuss your health or personal problems in public when surrounded by strangers? Probably not. However, care workers sometimes put the individuals they work with in this situation. You should avoid doing so by discussing such matters in a private room or area of your care setting. This will enable you to preserve confidentiality and it is more respectful. It will also reduce the kind of interruptions that occur in busy care settings.

Adapting communication for special needs

KUS 7

Depending on the particular needs of the individuals you work with, you may need to develop specialist communication skills. For example, it is helpful to gain some additional communication training and support if you work with people with dementia, mental-health or learning disability problems.

You will also need to think carefully about how you can adapt and develop your current communication skills to meet the particular needs of people who experience sensory impairment, speech and language difficulties or neurological problems. By listening to what individuals say helps them and watching how they respond to your efforts to communicate, you should learn how to adapt to each person's communication needs and preferences. However, there may be some situations where you require extra support to communicate with and understand the needs and wishes of particular individuals. You should always seek extra support when necessary.

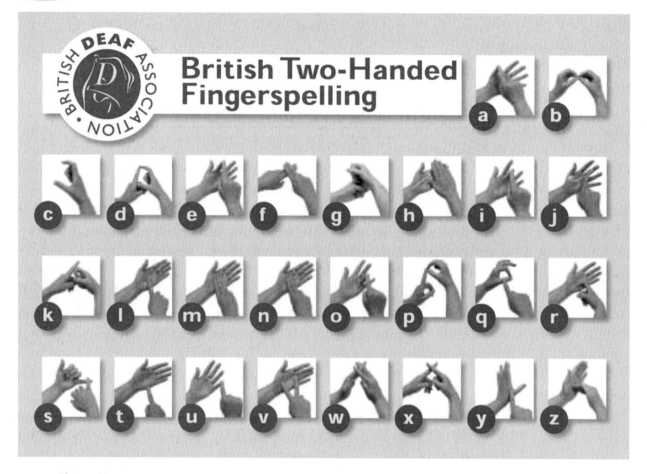

**Figure 10
Fingerspelling**
Source:
www.learntosign.
org.uk/fingerspelling

Communication

Danielle, a 27-year-old woman with learning disabilities, was admitted to your workplace during the night. She was confused and disorientated following a series of epileptic seizures. Since waking early this morning she has been concerned about her money. She thinks that you have forgotten to put it in the office safe. Every time you pass her chair she calls you over and says, 'You have remembered to put my purse away haven't you?'

➤ *How could you respond to Danielle's repeated questions?*

➤ *What could you do to demonstrate that you were listening actively and taking Danielle's concerns seriously?*

➤ *Explain how you would position yourself and what body language you would use whilst communicating with Danielle.*

Using advice and support

You may need to seek advice and extra support to enable you to communicate effectively with some individuals. You may need to do this:

- *Before* you try to interact with a particular individual for the first time. This might occur, for example, when you are aware that a person does not speak English, or communicates through sign-language, or has a limited ability to communicate because of learning disability or a degenerative brain disorder.

- *During* an interaction. This might be the case, for example, where you are supported by an interpreter, advocate or specialist care worker who is able to guide the individual's communication and can suggest ways of overcoming some of the difficulties that you face in communicating effectively.

- *After* an interaction. This might be the case, for example, when you have had a difficult or problematic interaction with an individual and want to discuss it and get some advice on how you could communicate more effectively in the future. Colleagues, specialist care workers and the individual's relatives may all be able to provide help and guidance. However, you should always ensure that you maintain confidentiality whilst discussing a person's particular needs with other people.

Key points – listening and responding to questions and concerns

- Listening is a vital communication skill in care work.
- To be effective in your communication with individuals and key people you should develop and use 'active listening' skills.
- 'Active listeners' focus on the verbal and non-verbal features of an individual's communication.
- You need to be aware of your own body language, posture and positioning when listening to others as these can influence communication.
- Avoid interrupting individuals when they are speaking. Think before you respond and always try to respond to individuals in a clear, unambiguous way.
- You should give individuals the time, support and encouragement that they need to enable them to communicate their needs, wishes and preferences effectively.

Element
HSC21c

Communicate with individuals

This element deals with the skills and knowledge that you will need in order to communicate effectively with individuals in your care setting. The effectiveness of your communication with different individuals will depend on your understanding of:

- The individual's particular communication needs.
- The different communication situations that occur in care settings.
- Common barriers to communication and ways of overcoming them.

Individual communication needs

Above we covered a number of the issues that can affect an individual's ability to communicate effectively (see page 5 for more details or a reminder). One of the key things that you learnt was that it is always necessary to assess and respond to an individual's particular communication needs and preferences and to any particular requirements that they may have for extra support. Briefly, this means you should ensure that the individual has:

- Any communication aids or equipment they need.
- The support of an advocate or interpreter if they require or want one.

We have also covered issues relating to active listening and the use of non-verbal forms of communication. All of these points should have helped you to appreciate that you need to focus on:

- Identifying and providing **active support** for individuals' communication needs.
- Listening actively and paying attention to individuals' verbal and non-verbal communication.

In this part of the unit we will focus on ways that you can promote and support individuals' efforts to communicate with you.

Giving and receiving information

KUS 3, 8, 14

Care workers give and receive information in both one-to-one and group situations. For example, information exchange happens when:

- An individual asks you about their treatment or about possible sources of support.
- A relative phones you to find out about the progress or condition of an individual.
- A colleague explains how the particular individuals you care for have been during the night.
- A care team meets to discuss the care required by one or more individuals receiving care.

The main issues that you need to think about when giving information are:

- *The pace of your speech*. For example, most people struggle to retain information that is delivered very quickly. Breaking your message into manageable sections and speaking in a clear, unhurried way will help your listeners.

- *The manner in which you provide the information.* In particular, your tone of voice and the complexity of the words that you use will affect what the listener hears. An angry, hostile, irritated or sarcastic tone of voice is never appropriate. Keeping your language clear, simple and jargon free will also help people to understand what you are saying.

Being objective

When you provide information about individuals to other people you should ensure that what you say is **objective**, well informed and factual. You should avoid presenting your views and opinions as 'facts'. There are times when you might be asked to make a judgement or to express an opinion. This might be the case, for example, when you or one of your colleagues are assessing an individual or are asked to comment on an individual's condition or progress. Where possible, base your comments on evidence or your direct experience of the person. It is not good practice to offer your opinions to individuals or their relatives.

Individuals and other people who might require information from you will find it easier to understand information that is given in a clear, straightforward way. Avoid overloading them with details or complicated choices. Choose your words carefully to maximise understanding and avoid jargon and technical terms that may confuse people.

Helping people to communicate

Care practitioners have an important role to play in helping individuals and their relatives to talk about personal matters and issues that concern them. Key skills include:

- Being able to establish a rapport.
- Encouraging two-way interaction.
- Using open and closed questions appropriately.
- Checking understanding.
- Using **empathy**-building statements.

Establishing a rapport

Effective communication begins when a **rapport** is established. This involves establishing a basic communication 'connection' with the other individual. The rapport that you establish provides a basic platform on which to build your care relationship. It is the first step in getting to know the individual better.

Encouraging interaction

Effective communication with another person involves *two-way* **interaction**. Communication does not happen just by giving information. This is why speaking *and* listening are both equally important. The turn-taking pattern of speaking and

Figure 11
Patience and a
close relationship
are needed to
promote
effective
interaction

listening is one of the factors that allow the communication to flow. You can encourage interaction by:

- Not interrupting an individual when they are speaking.
- Listening carefully to what the other person says.
- Using straightforward words that are easily understood.
- Speaking clearly and at an appropriate pace.

Using open and closed questions

Open and closed questions should be used in a normal conversational way to maintain communication with an individual and to obtain information from them. It is best to avoid using them in a way that makes the person feel that they are being interviewed or, even worse, interrogated!

Open questions give the chance for a personal, detailed or long answer. 'Can you describe the pain that you are feeling?' and 'Is there anything I can do to make you feel more comfortable?' are open questions. In contrast, 'Is your pain level okay today?' and 'Would you like another pillow?' are closed questions that can be answered with one or two words. The use of more open questions will encourage communication with the person. It also gives them an opportunity to express themselves. If you use too many closed questions the individuals you are speaking to may not have a chance to express their thoughts, feelings or perhaps their personal concerns.

Checking understanding

When you talk with individuals or other key people you should do your best to gain an accurate understanding of what they are saying. People who are under pressure, confused, in pain or emotional in some way, for example, may not be able to present their thoughts clearly and logically. Even where a person can, it is best to check that what you think they have said is the same as what they meant to say. You can do this by using a few simple checking techniques. These include:

- *Reflecting*, or repeating, some of the person's words directly back to them. This is often done to check and summarise what the person has said. A good way of picking up and exploring the key points is to focus on the things that they seem to emphasise.

- *Paraphrasing* is similar to reflecting but involves putting what a speaker says into other words. This is done to both clarify and summarise what somebody says to you. For example, you might say something like, 'Can I just check that you meant ...' and then paraphrase in order to clarify that your summary or understanding is correct.

Checking what has been said will help you to avoid making incorrect or inaccurate interpretations. It is important not to reflect too much or paraphrase too often in a conversation. This will interrupt the speaker's flow and might cause them to feel that you are 'parroting' or repeating their points too directly.

Building empathy

If you want to communicate that you understand an individual's situation and viewpoint, you should use empathy-building statements. An empathy-building statement shows the individual that you appreciate what they are saying. Comments such as, 'It sounds as though you are unhappy about that' or 'You seem to find the idea of surgery quite frightening' would indicate that you appreciate the speaker's feelings and viewpoint. You may have noticed that these two empathy-building statements are phrased in a tentative way. This is because empathy-building statements that begin with phrases such as 'You seem to be ...' or 'It sounds as though ...' indicate empathy but also leave room for the person to correct any misinterpretation or misunderstanding that occurs.

Confidentiality issues

KUS I, 13, 14

When you are asked to provide information you should think carefully about **confidentiality**. This issue affects how much information you should reveal about an individual. It is something that you need to think about when a colleague or somebody from outside the care team asks you for information about an individual.

Confidentiality refers to the appropriate protection of personal information. The word 'appropriate' is important here. Confidentiality is definitely not about keeping information secret. It is about sharing, transmitting and storing information about individuals in ways that are appropriate to their care needs. This means that confidential information can be shared between other care team members who also need to know about and use it. Beyond this, you must consult the individuals you work with and respect their wishes about who should be informed or given access to information about them. It is not acceptable for you to reveal an individual's personal details or to comment freely on their care or treatment without gaining the approval of the individual or other **appropriate people** before you do so. You should obtain and read a copy of your local policies and procedures on confidentiality in order to be clear about the expected approach within your care organisation.

There is a limited range of circumstances in which you cannot keep information confidential (see Figure 12). As a result, you should ensure that the individuals you work with know that you cannot ever promise them 'absolute confidentiality' but that you will only use their personal or private information in ways that are legally and ethically acceptable.

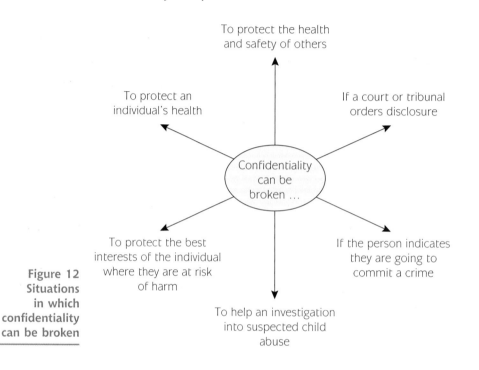

To protect the health
and safety of others

To protect an
individual's health

If a court or tribunal
orders disclosure

Confidentiality
can be
broken ...

To protect the best
interests of the individual
where they are at risk
of harm

If the person indicates
they are going to
commit a crime

To help an investigation
into suspected child
abuse

**Figure 12
Situations
in which
confidentiality
can be broken**

Ensuring that individuals maintain confidentiality between themselves is often a lot harder than ensuring that care workers observe confidentiality. The person in room or bed 1 has no right to know what the individual in room or bed 2 has been admitted for. However, when individual 1 starts to disclose information to individual 2, confidentiality is broken. You cannot stop people from doing this, but you should not discuss one individual with another even if they already appear to have some information that you consider confidential.

Good practice points in communication

- Respond to all forms of communication from the individuals you care for. This values the person as an individual.
- Use individuals' preferred means of communication, whatever these may be. If you were spoken to in sign language and did not understand it, how useful would this be to you?

- Communicate at a pace (speed), in the manner and at the level appropriate to the person who you are communicating with. In some circumstances you may have to adapt the speed at which you speak and the language you use.
- Workplace and technical jargon can be confusing and unhelpful to some individuals. An individual may get used to statements such as 'PU'd' or 'BMs', but they should not have to.
- If necessary act as an advocate for an individual by speaking on their behalf when they are not able to do so.
- You should try to actively involve people in discussions and decisions that affect them. It is important that they are able to contribute and have a chance to communicate their needs and preferences.
- Make sure that individuals have access to interpreters and communication aids if they require them.
- In professional meetings it is important that your focus remains with the individual even when there is input from their family or other sources.
- Adapt and change the way you communicate so that you can meet the changing needs and preferences of each individual you work with.
- When communicating always check your understanding of what the person is saying.
- If a misunderstanding occurs you must correct this. You may need to involve senior staff to ensure that they are informed and make accurate records of what has happened and how it has been dealt with.

Key points – communicating with individuals

- Identify and adapt your approach to each individual's particular communication needs, skills, wishes and preferences.
- Adapt the pace, volume and clarity of your speech to ensure that you communicate effectively with different individuals.
- Establish a rapport and encourage two-way interaction when communicating with individuals and key people in the care setting.
- Developing an empathetic approach, using open and closed questions and checking understanding will all enhance the effectiveness of your communication.
- Confidentiality is a key issue when communicating with individuals and key people in care. An individual's private and personal information must not be disclosed to people outside the care team without the individual's permission.

Access and update records and reports

Information about the care activities and communication you are involved in at work may need to be recorded in an individual's records. In this final section of the unit we will consider a number of issues relating to the use of individuals' care records and other reporting documents.

Reasons for record keeping

A variety of different types of records are produced and maintained in care settings. These include individuals' general health records, medical files, drug sheets, nursing notes, care plans, continence charts and activity reports. Your care setting may give these records slightly different names and you may have other records too.

Effective records make it easy for care team members to record and share information about individuals receiving care, file important reports and test results, and make entries to individuals' care plans and activity records. Producing and using a few different care records for each individual makes the information-management process much more efficient and accessible. Where there is a good record-keeping system you should be able to obtain a clear picture of an individual's care needs and an understanding of their current condition (their physical and mental state) fairly quickly and easily. This is helpful in team-working situations where everyone needs to share information and have a similar approach to providing appropriate care.

Good record keeping ensures that an individual's particular needs are identified and can be met appropriately by all members of the care team. This may involve recording vital information about drug doses, dietary needs or post-operative care

**Figure 13
Effective record
keeping is vital
in care practice**

procedures, for example. However, a simple note on an admissions sheet stating that 'Mrs Hastie prefers to be known as Ali not Alexandra' may make a big difference to how the person feels she is being treated, and this is equally as important.

Your record-keeping role

KUS 1, 4, 5, 10, 11

The record-keeping role that care workers have is defined by their employer's policies and procedures and by local practices. Hopefully these will have been explained to you during your workplace induction. Whatever your role in record keeping you should remember a number of important legal points in relation to accessing and completing individuals' records. These are outlined in Figures 14 and 15.

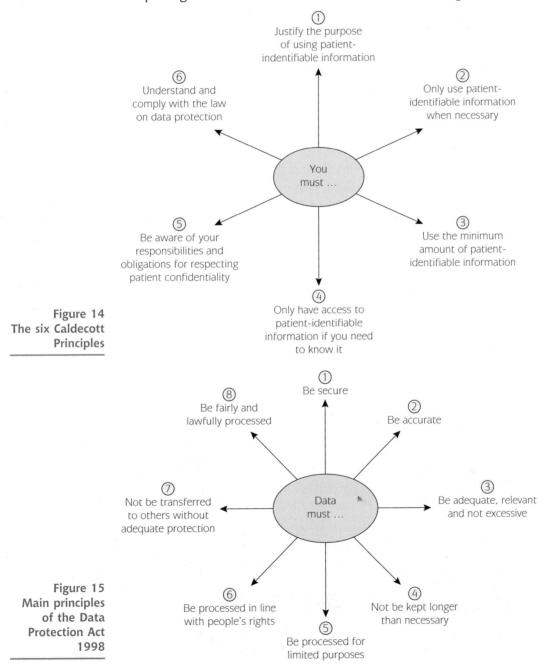

**Figure 14
The six Caldecott Principles**

**Figure 15
Main principles of the Data Protection Act 1998**

In some care settings record keeping is something that only the registered nurses and other qualified staff have responsibility for. Care workers who do not fit into these categories then tend to make only verbal reports to the senior, qualified staff. One of the reasons for this approach is that registered nurses and other qualified staff can be held accountable to their registered body for their record-keeping practice.

Writing up individual records and reports on the basis of second-hand, verbally reported information can be difficult and problematic. If you are familiar with the childhood game of Chinese Whispers you will understand how verbal messages can get changed as personal assumptions and interpretations are added and judgements are made as the message is passed between people. By the time it gets to the end of the line, a verbal message can have a totally different meaning compared to when it started. The same thing can happen where there are too many stages of reporting information about individuals receiving care. This may mean that the individual's records do not provide an accurate reflection of a care worker's original observations and comments.

To avoid the Chinese Whispers problem and also to ensure that all care workers participate fully in the care process, many organisations give employees a record-keeping role. This usually involves recording physical observations on appropriate charts and in care plans and writing up progress and care plan notes. Whilst registered and qualified members of staff may supervise and monitor this kind of record keeping, care workers should still develop a good understanding of the range of issues involved in effective record keeping.

Recording and reporting information

KUS 10, 12, 14

The Caldecott Principles underpin the way that care workers should record 'patient-identifiable information'. The six principles should be considered whenever you make a record. Remember that the individuals you care for have a right to see their records, so think about what you are doing each time you put pen to paper.

The Caldecott Principles state that you must:

- Be able to justify the purpose of the record.
- Only use patient-identifiable information when absolutely necessary.
- Keep patient-identifiable information to a minimum.
- Only have access to patient-identifiable information if you have a legitimate need to know.
- Be aware of your legal responsibilities before accessing patient-identifiable information.
- Understand and comply with the law when making records.

KUS 1, 4, 5

Legal considerations

Care records are legal documents. They can be used in court in cases where individuals suffer harm, neglect or other adverse outcomes whilst they are receiving care. So what you write should be factual and accurate. It should be able to stand up in court. You should also be aware that individuals have legal rights to access their care records.

Individuals' rights are protected by a number of pieces of legislation that have an impact on information-gathering and record keeping. For example:

- Article 8 of the Human Rights Act 1998 states that 'everyone has the right to respect for his private family life, his home and his correspondence'. This does not change once someone enters a care setting. You have to be aware of the legal responsibility to respect an individual's privacy when gathering and using personal information.
- The Data Protection Act 1998 applies to all care records. The Act requires that you obtain and hold only relevant information and use it only for the purpose it was intended for.
- The Access to Medical Records Act 1988 provides a legal right to access our own medical records. This has been further developed with the Freedom of Information Act 2000. This Act sets out to ensure that the public can access the information held about them by public authorities. So you should only write factual information about people in their records and you should be able to justify everything you write. If you cannot, the individual (and your employer) can take legal action to remedy this.

Verbal or written reporting?

You are likely to obtain, and will need to pass on, a huge amount of information during your working day. As a consequence, you will need to make judgements about the importance of different pieces of information and whether it is necessary to write it down or pass it on verbally. When you pass on information verbally you should ensure that your colleagues understand and take responsibility for dealing with it. Where information is significant and relates to a particular individual you should write it down in the appropriate records.

What to record

KUS 12

How much of the care that you provide and the observations that you make should be written down? This is an ongoing dilemma for many care workers and is often not clarified by organisational policies and procedures.

Care records should be accurate and sufficient. Accuracy is essential. It means that you must make sure that you record information:

- about the right individual
- in the right file
- at the right time

and that the information is factual.

You should provide sufficient information without going over the top or missing out important facts. In normal, everyday circumstances it is not necessary to compile a detailed log of exactly what you have done on a minute-by-minute basis for every single individual. Instead you should normally report on the care given as per the care plan, detailing individual progress, deterioration or other responses as well as commenting on anything else that is particularly significant about an individual's condition or behaviour.

You should use clear and concise language, write legibly in either black or blue pen not pencil (check your employer's policy and the practice in your workplace). Correction fluid, crossings out and writing over mistakes should not feature in individuals' care records. If you make a mistake, this needs to be crossed through with a single line and initialled by you. It is also essential that you write in an objective not a **subjective** way.

When to record

How good is your memory? Is it good enough at the end of a seven-hour shift to enable you to remember what happened at the start of the shift? Many people would find it difficult to recall lots of pieces of information. It is better practice to record observations and key points in progress notes as soon as possible after the event. This reduces the chance that you will forget information. You might need to write in individuals' records (or in your own notebook) a few times during a shift as well as at the end.

Silently writing up records in front of an individual can be intimidating and uncomfortable for the person. It is better to let the person know what you are writing and, if they ask, to show them any charts or progress notes that you have completed. You should look at your organisation's policies and procedures on record keeping to find out whether this is encouraged. If it is, ask colleagues and senior staff whether there are any exceptions to this general approach. If it is not encouraged, it may be a good idea to find out why.

Where to record

Your workplace probably has an extensive record-keeping system made up of a huge number of files. These will contain a variety of different kinds of information which vary in importance. Key points on recording information appropriately include:

- Develop a general awareness of the range of records that exist so that you can contribute to them appropriately.
- Make sure you are adding information to the appropriate file.
- Always check that you are writing in the records of the right person.
- Be careful about individuals' surnames as some may have the same or a very similar name.
- Only write in records where you have the correct authority to do so – writing on drug charts, for example, is usually restricted to registered nurses and medical staff.

Some records need to be updated on a regular basis. These include, for example:

- *Daily progress or 'activity' records* – these provide a log of what has happened to the individual, what they have done and other day-to-day information.
- *Charts* – these may include dietary monitoring, medication, fluid balance, temperature, pulse and respiration charts for an individual or be related to the organisation where you need to keep a record of fridge temperatures, vehicle mileage or timesheets, for example.
- *Reports* – it is likely that at some point in your working life you will be required to fill in an accident or incident report. This provides information for your workplace and may also be relayed to the government. These records must be accurate, concise and legible.
- *Care plans* – if you are responsible for a particular individual's care you will need to write monitoring and evaluation notes on care-plan goals and objectives.
- *Letters* – in some circumstances you may be required to write letters, either for the organisation or for an individual receiving care if they are unable to do this for themselves.

Confidentiality issues

KUS 13, 14

Confidentiality is always a very real issue in care and applies to all communication we have with the individuals we care for and with other key people. Individuals using care services often have to provide personal information, and this can seem intrusive and unnecessary at times. People provide this information on trust. They trust that care workers will not disclose or use the information inappropriately and will ensure that it remains confidential. So it is important that you assure the people you provide care for that, wherever possible, their personal and private information is carefully and objectively recorded and that their confidentiality is maintained (see page 23 for further details on this area).

Recording and reporting

Practical Example

Hassan, aged 42, woke at 10 a.m., refused breakfast but then ate a banana and yoghurt before he left the drug rehabilitation unit to go to an outside, personal appointment. He returned half an hour later and rested on his bed, missing two of his group sessions, until lunchtime. After eating lunch on his own in the dining room Hassan went into the day room and enthusiastically joined in the activities of the music group before you left at the end of your shift.

➤ *Which aspects of this individual's activity should you record?*
➤ *How would you decide what was sufficient information in this case?*
➤ *What, if anything, could you tell Hassan's relatives about his day?*

Storage and security of individuals' records

All records must be stored securely and accessed only by people who have a right to see and use them. Generally this means that individuals' records should be stored in a lockable cabinet and that access to and use of them is monitored. Individuals' files should not be left lying around and they should not be removed from their usual location unless **appropriate people** (such as a manager or shift leader) are aware of this. You should never make copies of an individual's records or take them home.

Filling out records in the middle of the day room at the end of a shift may be an acceptable practice in your care setting. However, if you are called away, you or another authorised person must deal with the records in order to maintain confidentiality and ensure that they are safely stored away. When records are in your possession they must remain secure.

Problems with record keeping

It is important that you recognise any problems that you may experience in creating and maintaining records. It is possible that an individual's records may go missing from the appointed storage area or that another member of staff has failed to make a record. You should report any errors that you see or make in an individual's records. You should also report any breaches of confidentiality or security, or instances where files, documents or letters have not been stored securely. Action should then be taken by senior staff to ensure that the matters you report are rectified and do not occur again.

Key points – accessing and updating records and reports

- Accurate and timely record-keeping is an important part of care practice.
- Your record-keeping role should be clarified, defined and monitored by your employer.
- Individuals' care records are legal documents. You must complete them in a clear, accurate and objective way.
- You should understand and always follow your employer's policies and procedures on what, when and where to write in individuals' care records.
- Observing confidentiality and the appropriate storage and security of records should ensure that information relating to individuals' care and personal circumstances is only seen by appropriate people.

Unit HSC21

Are you ready for assessment?

Communicate with and complete records for individuals

This unit is all about how you use your skills to communicate with individuals and the key people in their lives in ways which meet their particular needs and preferences. It is about how you adapt your means of communicating in ways that respect and acknowledge individual concerns. It is also about how you record and pass on appropriate information to other people whilst recognising the boundaries of confidentiality and privacy.

Most of the evidence you need to cover the performance criteria and knowledge specification can be gathered during your assessment in other units from your qualification, especially the optional units and also unit HSC24. You should consider this when planning these other units with your assessor.

Your assessment will be carried out mainly through observation by your assessor and should provide most of the evidence for the elements in this unit.

Since this NVQ is all about how you work directly with people, there will be ample opportunities for observation by your assessor. The Scope of the NVQ unit is a helpful reminder of all the different aspects of communication that you are likely to use and will be helpful when planning your assessment. However, if observation by an assessor could intrude on the privacy of individuals, then some performance criteria may require alternative sources of evidence of your work practice, such as expert witness testimony, in addition to other observations by your assessor.

Direct observation by your assessor

Your assessor will need to plan to see you carry out the performance criteria (PCs) in each of the elements in this unit.

The performance criteria that may be difficult to meet through observation are:

- **HSC21a PC 4**
- **HSC21b PCs 6, 7**
- **HSC21d PC 4**

usually because the activities do not occur routinely.

Preparing to be observed

You must make sure that your workplace and any individuals and key people involved in your work agree to you being assessed. Explicit, informed consent must be obtained before you carry out any assessment activity that involves individuals or which involves access to confidential information relating to their care.

Before your assessments you should read carefully the performance criteria for each element in the unit. Try to cover as much as you can *during your observations*.

►

Remember that you and your assessor can also plan for additional sources of evidence should full coverage of all performance criteria not be possible.

Other types of evidence

You may need to present other forms of evidence in order to:

- Cover criteria not observed by your assessor.
- Show that you have the required knowledge, understanding and skills to claim competence in this area of practice.
- Ensure that your work practice is consistent.

Your assessor may also need to ask you questions to confirm your knowledge and understanding of this unit.

Check your knowledge

1 Name at least three different ways of communicating in a care setting.

2 Describe three reasons why individuals may need extra support to communicate effectively and identify ways that this can be provided.

3 Explain what active listening involves and why this is important when communicating with individuals and other key people involved in their care.

4 Give reasons why it is good practice not to discuss an individual's care when you are away from work.

5 Describe how you could check your understanding when talking with individuals and other key people.

6 Explain what 'being objective' involves when making entries in individuals' records and suggest reasons why this is important.

Support your own health and safety and that of other individuals

*T*his unit covers all aspects of your health and safety and that of individuals and other people within the care environment. Health and safety focuses on the assessment of potential risks, actions to reduce accidents and control hazards, and ways of dealing with emergencies.

This unit contains three elements:

⌒ *HSC22a Carry out health and safety checks before you begin work activities*

⌒ *HSC22b Ensure your actions support health and safety in the place you work*

⌒ *HSC22c Take action to deal with emergencies*

⌒ Introduction

Health and social-care services are provided in lots of different care settings. These can include an individual's own home, residential and nursing homes, day-care centres, community-based surgeries, health centres, hospitals and hospices. Every

**Figure 1
Simple
adaptations and
forms of support
can often reduce
the risk of
health and
safety hazards in
care settings**

care setting is different. Bedrooms, bathrooms, kitchens, corridors, stairs, recreational rooms, gardens and perhaps lifts are familiar elements of care settings. Specialist care settings may also have clinical and treatment rooms or other less common facilities. All of these facilities, and the work that goes on in any care setting, should enable care practitioners to provide high-quality care for individuals. However, care settings are also places that contain hazards that present dangers to those who live and work in them.

Working in any environment that has people, equipment, illness, disease and disability and a lot of work pressures can be risky! One of the golden rules of care work is that the health and safety of individuals, colleagues and anybody else present in a care setting should be the main concern. People should not be at risk of injury or harm in a care setting. Care practitioners should, at least, do no harm. So awareness of health and safety issues and principles is a basic competence required of all care practitioners.

Health and safety responsibility

You and your employer share responsibility for health and safety in your place of work. Your employer is responsible for providing:

- A safe and secure work environment.
- Safe equipment.
- Information and training about health, safety and security.

In short, your employer must provide a work environment that complies with expected health and safety standards. They must make it possible for you to practise safely.

Your responsibility is to:

- Work safely within the care setting.
- Monitor your work environment for health and safety problems that may develop.
- Report and respond appropriately to any health and safety risks.

Health and safety legislation

The health and safety responsibilities of employers and employees result from the wide range of legislation, or law, that governs health and safety in workplaces generally. A number of laws also exist covering health and safety issues that are specific to care settings. Legislation is necessary to ensure that safe working practices are followed when caring for individuals and these should also protect the carer. Important examples of this legislation are described in Table 1.

Putting legislation into practice

Health and safety law provides a legal framework that both employers and employees must work within. In effect, you and your employer have to ensure that

Table 1 Legislation relevant to care

Legislation	What the law says
The Social Security Act 1998	All organisations have a responsibility to supply and provide a means of recording and reporting any accidents or injuries. This is usually an Accident Report Book or Accident Report Form.
The Health and Safety at Work Act 1974 (HASAWA)	Everyone has a responsibility to ensure their own health, safety and welfare, as well as that of their colleagues. Employers have an additional responsibility to ensure that employees have the correct training and safety clothing and equipment appropriate for the job they are doing.
Management of Health and Safety at Work Regulations 1999	Employers must assess the risks to employees and make arrangements for their health and safety.
The Manual Handling Operations Regulations 1992	These regulations require an employer to carry out risk assessments that take into account whether it is reasonable to automate or mechanise lifting in the workplace. The employer must provide equipment to avoid the hazardous manual handling of loads. The regulations apply wherever things or people are moved by hand or bodily force.
The Food Safety Act 1990	This Act provides the main framework for all food law in Great Britain. It makes it an offence to provide food that is injurious to health because it is contaminated or not fit for human consumption.
The Reporting of Injuries, Diseases and Dangerous Occurrences Regulations 1995 (RIDDOR)	Employers are responsible for reporting to the appropriate authority any serious accidents in connection with the workplace (which includes any resulting in more than three days' absence from work), dangerous occurrences and specified occupational diseases.
Control of Substances Hazardous to Health 1994 (COSHH)	All employees should follow safety guidelines and take precautions recommended by their employer who has identified and assessed the risk from hazardous substances with regard to storage, handling and first aid in the workplace.
Health and Safety (First Aid) Regulations 1981	Employers need to make sure their employees have access to first aid.
Data Protection Act 1984 and 1998	This covers the confidential storage, retrieval and handling of verbal, written and electronic information to protect the rights of the individual. It sets out guidelines and identifies good practice on the disclosure of information and breaching of confidentiality where this serves to protect the individual or others from harm.

the various pieces of legislation are put into practice in your care setting. Employers carry out their legal responsibilities by:

- Producing health and safety policies.
- Developing and implementing health and safety systems and procedures.
- Carrying out workplace risk assessments.
- Providing health and safety training for staff.
- Responding constructively and positively to lapses, breaches or problems in health and safety systems and practice.

Care practitioners carry out their legal responsibilities by:

- Developing an awareness of health and safety law.
- Working in ways that follow health and safety guidelines, policies and procedures.
- Monitoring the care environment for health and safety hazards.
- Dealing directly with hazards that present a health and safety risk where it is safe to do so.
- Reporting to a supervisor or manager any health and safety hazards or the failure of safety systems or procedures.

Risks and hazards in the workplace

In order to work safely, and avoid becoming an accident statistic, you need to become hazard conscious and risk aware.

A *hazard* is anything that can cause harm. For example, chemicals, electricity, care equipment and ill-fitting carpets are all hazards in a care setting. A *risk* is the chance of harm being done by a hazard. **Risk assessment** is the process of evaluating the likelihood of a hazard actually causing harm.

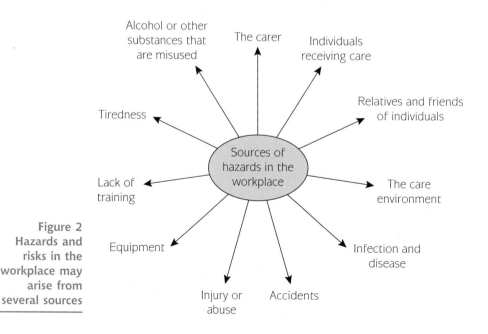

Figure 2
Hazards and risks in the workplace may arise from several sources

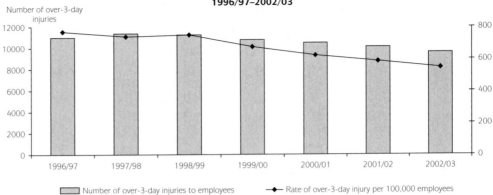

Number and rate of over-3-day injuries to employees in the Health Services
1996/97–2002/03

- 8% of all over-3-day injuries reported to HSE occur in the Health Services.

- In 2002/03, there were 9,551 reported over-3-day injuries to employees in Health Services, compared with 10,077 in 2001/02.

- The rate of over-3-day injury to employees decreased by 7% to 543.2 in 2002/03 from 582.2 in 2001/02. The rate of over-3-day injury has decreased by 29% between 1996/97 and 2002/03.

- Note: Employment data for 1996/97–2000/01 is on a 4 digit SIC basis; that for 2001/02–2002/03 is on a 3 digit SIC basis.

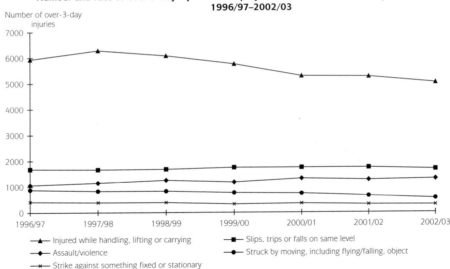

Number and rate of over-3-day injuries to employees in the Health Services by kinds of accident
1996/97–2002/03

**Figure 3
Workplace
injuries**
Health and Safety
Commission
Comprehensive
Injury Statistics:
Health Services
(2003)

- About half of all over-3-day injuries in the Health Services are due to injury whilst handling, lifting or carrying. Handling accounts for 48% of both major and over-3-day injuries combined in 2002/03.

- Slipping and tripping injuries were the second most common kind of non-fatal accident and have fluctuated only slightly in the past 5 years. There were 2,314 in 2002/03 compared with 2,389 in 2001/02.

- Over-3-day injuries caused by assault and violence have generally risen in both number and percentage share to 14% (1,293) in 2002/03, compared with 9% (1,034) in 1996/97.

One way of developing your awareness of health and safety hazards is to think about your own work environment, the equipment that is used there, the people who are present in the workplace and, importantly, how you actually carry out care work.

Carry out health and safety checks before you begin work activities

Element HSC22a

Health, safety and security procedures

The Management of Health and Safety at Work Regulations 1999 place a legal duty on employers to carry out risk assessments in order to ensure a safe and healthy workplace. The risk assessments that are produced should clearly identify:

- Potential hazards and risks to the health and safety of employees and others in the workplace.
- Preventive and protective measures that are needed to minimise risk and improve health and safety.

As a result of the Management of Health and Safety at Work Regulations 1999, employers must establish health and safety procedures to be followed by employees. Workplaces with five or more employees must have a written health and safety policy that provides details about:

- The hazards that exist in the workplace.
- The names of the people responsible for managing these hazards.
- The procedures that should be followed to minimise the risks associated with each hazard.
- Procedures for dealing with health and safety-related accidents and incidents at work.
- Accident and incident reporting procedures.

It is essential that you understand the health and safety procedures that apply in your workplace. You should obtain and read a copy of the health and safety policy for your own work area so that you are fully aware of the hazards and risks. The policy, as well as guidance and information provided by your senior colleagues, your supervisor or manager, will tell you about the health, safety and security procedures that you should follow whilst working.

Making your own risk assessments

Effective health and safety standards are achieved through employers and employees working together to fulfil the legal responsibilities that they have in this area. Your employer is responsible for providing a safe working environment and a safety system to manage hazards and risks within the workplace. You must work in ways that minimise risks. You must monitor and implement the safety systems and procedures that your employer has provided. Making your own **risk assessments** is an important part of this.

The Health and Safety Executive (HSE) has identified the five basic steps involved in making a risk assessment in the workplace. These are:

- Step 1: Look for and list the hazards.

- Step 2: Decide who might be harmed and how.
- Step 3: Evaluate the risks arising from the hazards and decide whether existing precautions are adequate or whether more should be done.
- Step 4: Record the findings.
- Step 5: Review the assessment from time to time and revise it if necessary.

Your employer may have followed a similar approach when carrying out a risk assessment process for your care organisation. You should read and gain a good understanding of any risk assessment documents that your employer has produced. These documents will alert you to the main hazards and risks in your work area. The knowledge that you gain will then enable you to carry out your own ongoing risk assessments in your everyday work. You should:

- Be alert to possible hazards.
- Understand the risks associated with each hazard.
- Report any health and safety concerns that you identify.

You can make risk assessment a regular and ongoing part of your work by focusing on the potential hazards and risks associated with the:

- Equipment used in your care setting.
- Care environment itself.
- Activities and techniques of care practice.
- People who are present in the care setting.

Practical Example

Risk assessment

Robbie George, aged 21, has recently moved to Denbigh House, a residential home for physically disabled young adults. He has found living at home with his parents increasingly difficult. Earlier this week Robbie asked Dennis, the deputy manager of the home, whether somebody could be with him if his brother Stephen came to visit. He told Dennis that Stephen is verbally abusive and threatening at times and that this frightens him. Dennis has since found out from a social worker that Stephen George has a history of threatening care staff and has also punched and kicked his brother in the past causing him minor facial injuries. Stephen's behaviour is related to his alcohol problems and is much worse when he needs money.

➤ Identify reasons why a risk assessment is necessary before Stephen George visits his brother.

➤ What are the main hazards and the potential risks involved in a visit from Stephen?

➤ What policies and procedures exist in your workplace that could provide guidance on the best ways of dealing with this kind of situation?

Checking equipment

Care settings contain a variety of items of equipment that can be extremely helpful in terms of saving time, reducing physical effort and improving the quality of care practice. However, care equipment needs to be in good condition and should only be used by people who have received appropriate training. Examples of equipment hazards that present health and safety risks to individuals and care practitioners include:

- Mobility aids that are the wrong size or which do not work properly.
- Faulty or damaged lifting equipment.
- Brakes and hydraulics that do not work properly on beds.
- Computer display screens and keyboards that are badly located, poorly serviced or over-used.
- Blades and syringe needles that are stored or disposed of incorrectly.
- Unlabelled, incorrectly labelled or leaking bottles and containers.
- Old and faulty electrical and gas-fuelled appliances.
- Excessively full or faulty waste-disposal equipment.

Before using any equipment you should always check that it is safe, hazard free and in full working order. You should not use equipment that is faulty or which you have not been trained to use. You should only use equipment for the specific tasks for which it is designed and in the way it should be used. Modifying equipment or using it inappropriately is likely to increase the risk of accidents and injury. If you identify a fault or problem with a piece of equipment, you should tell a supervisor and report it in writing if necessary. You should use an alternative piece of equipment, find another way of completing the work task, or tell your supervisor that you cannot perform the task with unsafe equipment. You should not take an unacceptable risk with faulty equipment.

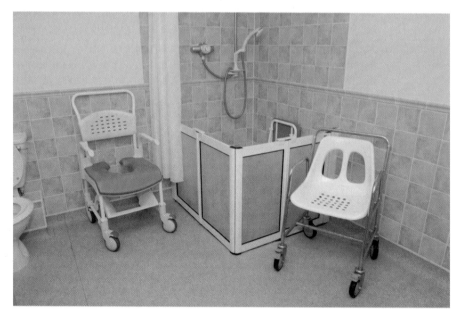

Figure 4
Example of
an adapted
bathroom

Checking the work environment

You are probably very familiar with your own workplace and you may know about likely hazards. Health and safety awareness is partly based on close observation and familiarity with environmental hazards. Examples of environmental hazards that present health and safety risks to individuals and care practitioners include:

- Wet, highly polished or slippery floors.
- Furniture and equipment that blocks access.
- Cluttered corridors or passages.
- Worn or ill-fitting carpets, rugs or other floor coverings.
- Exposed wires or dangling electrical flexes.
- Steep stairs or unexpected steps.
- Loose banisters or grab rails.

Figure 5
Health and safety signs should always be used where the environment is hazardous

You should always check that the environment where you work is safe and appropriate for the work that you are expected to do. Lack of space that affects your ability to move and manoeuvre, or changes (either temporary or permanent) to the layout of work areas should be a cause for concern. Before carrying out any care activities you should check the safety of your work environment. You should also report any problems and concerns and you should refuse to work in conditions that you assess as hazardous and potentially dangerous.

Being a safe practitioner

The activities and techniques that are a regular part of your care practice should also be assessed for health and safety risks. For example, you are likely to face a health and safety hazard when:

- Moving and supporting individuals who are frail or immobile.
- Using equipment such as hoists, commodes and waste-disposal units.
- Using electricity when, for example, operating microwaves, cleaning equipment or hairdryers.

- Stacking and storing equipment, laundry and food deliveries used for care practice or for individuals' everyday living needs.
- Working in small spaces with large items of equipment, such as wheelchairs.
- Working in crowded living and social areas.
- Handling waste materials and sharps such as needles, knives and other blades.

The risk of an incident or injury occurring during any of these activities is significantly reduced if appropriate health and safety procedures are in place and are followed when you carry out the activity. You should only carry out tasks and activities that you have been trained to perform and which you feel confident to do. You should not try to work beyond your level of competence.

Gaining the confidence and agreement of the individual who you are working with is likely to reduce the risk of accidents and injuries occurring during care practice. You should always take account of each particular individual's needs, wishes and preferences before performing any care procedure. Whenever possible you should speak with the person and talk about what you would like to do. This will prepare them for any subsequent movement or touching that could otherwise frighten and unsettle them. It is also good practice to talk to an individual during a care procedure. This keeps them fully informed of what you are doing, or are about to do, and allows them to say if they are feeling uncomfortable or unsafe or that they do not wish to continue. You should also monitor the individual's non-verbal behaviour and respond appropriately to any signs of discomfort, distress or displeasure.

People hazards

Generally, care practitioners and individuals get to know how their care setting functions and become familiar with it. However, a person who is unfamiliar with a care setting can be a health and safety hazard either because of their inappropriate behaviour or because they do not appreciate the effect that their presence may have on established safety and security systems. Examples of people hazards that present health and safety risks to individuals and care practitioners include:

- The presence and behaviour of visitors, including individuals' relatives or friends and maintenance workers.
- The unexpected wandering and confused behaviour of disorientated individuals.
- An individual's illness, disability, hearing or visual impairment that prevents them from appreciating the presence of, or risk associated with, an environmental hazard such as a step or set of stairs.
- Visitors who smoke cigarettes in non-smoking areas containing medical gases or other flammable substances.
- Aggressive and violent behaviour from individuals or visitors.
- The unexpected presence and aggressive behaviour of an intruder.

Some people-related hazards are easily dealt with by way of a quiet, polite word or by redirecting the person to a safer and more appropriate part of the care environment. Sometimes, particularly when people are uncooperative, aggressive or abusive, you will need to seek additional help and support to resolve a health and safety or security problem.

If you are alone you should not try to tackle intruders or people behaving aggressively. Instead you should alert other colleagues to the situation and you should put your organisation's safety and security procedures into operation. You should know the security policies and procedures for managing aggression in your care setting. These may include phoning emergency numbers, using a bleep system or setting off security alarms.

Reporting concerns and incidents

Reporting accidents and dangerous incidents that occur in your workplace is part of your health and safety role. Your employer is under a legal duty to keep a record of the accidents, injuries and 'near misses' that occur in your workplace. Usually this will be achieved through the completion of accident and incident forms by care workers and their managers.

You should always report an accident, incident or near miss if you witness or are involved in one. Reporting ensures that:

- Any pattern of accidents and incidents in a workplace can be easily identified.
- Managers can respond appropriately to any incidents, perhaps by improving or changing health and safety procedures.

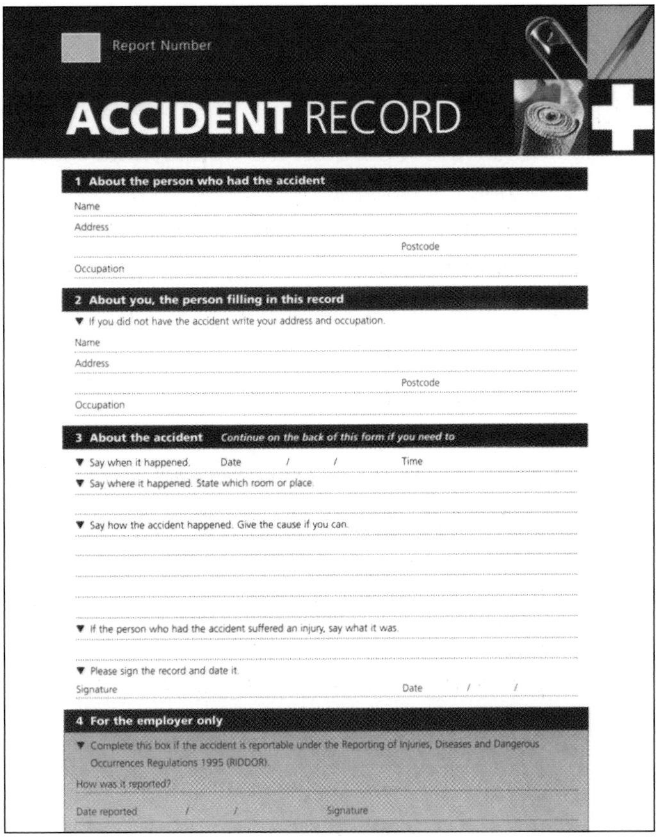

Report Number

ACCIDENT RECORD

1 About the person who had the accident

Name
Address
Postcode
Occupation

2 About you, the person filling in this record

▼ If you did not have the accident write your address and occupation.
Name
Address
Postcode
Occupation

3 About the accident *Continue on the back of this form if you need to*

▼ Say when it happened. Date / / Time
▼ Say where it happened. State which room or place.
▼ Say how the accident happened. Give the cause if you can.
▼ If the person who had the accident suffered an injury, say what it was.
▼ Please sign the record and date it.
Signature Date / /

4 For the employer only

▼ Complete this box if the accident is reportable under the Reporting of Injuries, Diseases and Dangerous Occurrences Regulations 1995 (RIDDOR).
How was it reported?
Date reported / / Signature

Figure 6 An accident report

- A record of the causes and types of any injuries suffered is available to those treating the people involved. This can be helpful if the physical or psychological effects of the accident or injury take some time to emerge.
- The people involved have evidence that they can use in any legal or insurance proceedings that are taken.

Key points – health and safety checks

- Familiarise yourself with the health and safety policies and guidelines that apply to your workplace. Your organisation will produce them and will expect you to read and understand them.
- Carry out a hazard check and risk assessment before you undertake a care task or activity.
- Ensure the working environment is free from clutter and obstructions before you work with an individual.
- Carry out care activities in the way specified by the health and safety policies and procedures of your workplace.
- Only carry out tasks and procedures that you are competent in or for which you have the support and assistance of a competent colleague or supervisor.
- Ask for help and advice if you are uncertain of any procedures, or if the task is new to you.
- Ensure that you know how to summon help in an emergency or urgent situation.
- Always report, on the appropriate form, any accident, incident or near miss.
- Carry out and participate in regular fire drills, evacuation procedures and training events to deal with specific incidents, such as abusive behaviour and burglary.

Ensure your actions support health and safety in the place where you work

Actions to support health and safety

As you will now be aware, you have a personal responsibility for ensuring that your actions support and promote effective health and safety in the workplace. To do this you will need to:

- Ensure that your own health and hygiene does not pose a threat to the health and safety of others and that you manage your personal safety at work.

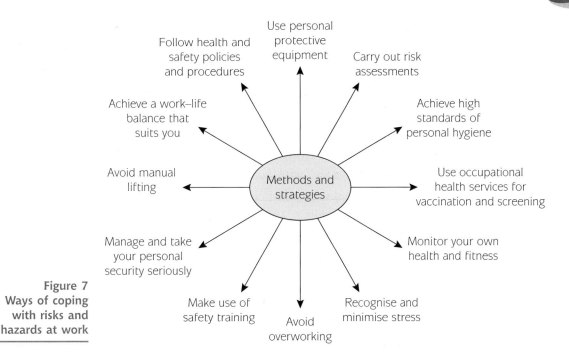

**Figure 7
Ways of coping
with risks and
hazards at work**

- Follow the infection control, moving and handling, accident and waste-disposal procedures set out in your employer's health and safety policies.
- Make and use risk assessments during your work to minimise health and safety hazards.
- Respond appropriately to security risks in the workplace.
- Report health and safety and security issues to the relevant people.

Personal health, hygiene and security

Personal health

Managing your own health, safety and personal security is important if you are to become a safe care practitioner. As a care worker you may be exposed to all sorts of risks and hazards during the course of your working life. The individuals you are caring for, for example, may present biological hazards to your own physical health. If you do not take the appropriate infection-control precautions it is possible to contract infectious diseases such as hepatitis and tuberculosis through direct contact with individuals who are already infected, and are perhaps ill, with these conditions.

You should make use of occupational health services such as screening, vaccination and other health checks. Care practitioners should be immunised against diseases such as polio, tuberculosis and hepatitis B. You should also receive information and advice on back care and ways of coping with stress.

Avoiding overwork

- The Working Time Regulations 1998 state that you should not work more than 48 hours per week.
- Daily rest for adult workers should include 11 hours of consecutive rest between each working day.
- Weekly rest for adult workers should be a minimum of one day off per week.
- In-house rest breaks for adults should be 20 minutes if the working day is longer than six hours.

You should always take your own health as seriously as that of the individuals you are caring for. Often care workers accept that long hours, physically hard work and high stress levels are all part of the job. However, failure to find a satisfactory work–life balance, to maintain a reasonable level of physical fitness and take regular breaks from the emotional and physical stresses of care work may lead you to experience burnout, chronic fatigue and an increased vulnerability to personal health problems. If work starts to cause changes in your behaviour and mood patterns, is making you restless, anxious or too fatigued, it may be time to consider your own health and consult your General Practitioner (GP). In order to survive as a care worker you must know and respect your own limits.

Managing hygiene

Personal hygiene and hygiene practices in the care workplace are both sensitive and important issues for care workers. Nobody would like to have their personal hygiene standards questioned by colleagues or individuals they are caring for. Everybody working in care is expected to have clean and tidy hair, nails, skin and work clothing. As well as achieving this socially expected level of appearance, care workers are also expected to maintain high standards of hygiene in their work activity. This issue is covered in more detail in the section on infection control and hand washing below (see page 50).

Managing personal security

Personal safety and security at work are increasingly becoming issues for care workers. Care settings are typically thought to be safe environments where people are cared for, not harmed. However, care workers are subject to increasing levels of aggression and violence in the workplace (see Figure 8). Bearing this in mind, you should take precautions to manage your own safety and security when at work. Basic precautions include:

- Understanding the security and incident policies and procedures that apply in your care organisation.

Employees who are victims of assault once or more	Percentage
Protective service occupations	12.6
Health and social welfare associate professionals	3.3
Transport and mobile machine drivers and operatives	1.9
Managers and proprietors in agriculture and services	1.8
Health professionals	1.4
Caring personal service occupations	1.3
Leisure and other personal service occupations	1.1
Teaching and research professionals	1.0
Elementary administration and service occupations	0.9
Corporate managers	0.8
All	**0.9**

1. Source 2001/02 and 2002/03 BCS.
2. Based on adults of working age, in employment.

Employees who are victims of threats once or more	Percentage
Protective service occupations	3.0
Health and social welfare associate professionals	2.3
Health professionals	2.3
Managers and proprietors in agriculture and services	2.2
Skilled agricultural trades	1.6
Leisure and other personal service occupations	1.5
Sales occupations	1.3
Transport and mobile machine drivers and operatives	1.3
Teaching and research professionals	1.2
Business and public service professionals	1.0
All	**1.0**

**Figure 8
Statistics on
aggression
and violence in
care settings**
British Crime Survey
2002/2003, ONS

1. Source 2001/02 and 2002/03 BCS.
2. Based on adults of working age, in employment.

- Knowing how to operate any alarms or security systems that are provided.
- Wearing your identification badge and carrying any security alarms that are provided for security purposes.
- Asking visitors to identify themselves and show some official identification badge or letter before you let them into clinical areas of the care setting.
- Locking doors and windows that are supposed to be locked for security purposes.

- Letting people know where you will be and what you will be doing.
- Not putting yourself at risk by being alone with people you do not know and who cause you to feel concerned.
- Signing yourself in and out of work if your organisation uses a sign-in book for employees.

Minimising infection risks

The control of infection and the maintenance of acceptable standards of hygiene are increasingly important health and safety issues in care settings. Hospitals and other residential care settings have made infection control a high priority because of the increasing problems and potentially fatal consequences that infections pose for users of care services.

The bacteria and viruses that cause infections are present in everyday life (see Table 2). In most cases people build up immunity to common infections and suffer only minor illnesses in the process. However, people who are physically frail or who are suffering from significant health problems tend to be more vulnerable and susceptible to common infections. Also, hospitals and residential care settings are places where new and more unusual infections may be present and can be contracted.

Table 2 Methods and modes of infection

Method of transmission	Mode (How it is spread)	Example
Airborne	Droplet	Coughing, sneezing
Instilled	Liquid	Splashes to eye
Ingested	Contaminated food/water	Eating raw or undercooked meat, eggs, unprocessed cheeses
Insects	Injected	Mosquito or flea bites
Direct contact	Touching; absorption	Not covering open wounds; incorrect disposal of waste products
Indirect contact	Animals	Worms
Infestation	**Fomites**	Scabies in bed linen

The risks of infection and **cross-infection** are reduced by correct hygiene and infection control techniques. These include:

- Good hand hygiene. This is the single most important infection control measure. Washing your hands thoroughly with a decontamination agent and drying them before and after working with each individual is recommended. Research carried out by the National Patient Safety Agency shows that infection rates are reduced by between 10 and 50 per cent when healthcare workers clean their hands regularly.

- It is good hand-washing practice NOT to use the individual's own soap or towel when cleaning your hands.

- Using personal protective equipment (PPE) and the correct equipment for the task you are performing. PPE includes disposable gloves, masks, aprons and goggles or visors. You should always use PPE when attending to dressings, performing **aseptic techniques** or dealing with bodily products such as blood, faeces, urine and vomit.

- Tying your hair back if it is long and keeping your jewellery to a minimum to avoid the risk of cross-infection between yourself and the individuals you are caring for.

- Disposing of waste, PPE and protective clothing correctly (check your waste disposal policy and see page 57 below).

- Covering cuts, grazes, sores or wounds on your own hands with an impermeable protective dressing. A blue plaster should be used if preparing food as this will be more visible if it becomes detached.

- Dealing with blood and body-fluid spills immediately by following your local policies and procedures on spillages (see page 56 below).

- Equipment such as commodes and non-disposable bedpans should be cleaned thoroughly with detergent and hot water after use.

- Clothes and bedding should be bagged and machine-washed in accordance with your local policy and procedures.

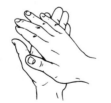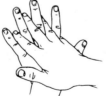

**Figure 10
Effective
hand-washing
technique**

Dealing with MRSA

Methicillin-Resistant Staphylococcus Aureus (MRSA) is an infection that has become a serious problem in care settings, both nationally and globally. The overuse of antibiotics is one of the main reasons for this bacteria's resistance to some antibiotics. However, low standards of hygiene and poor use of infection-control techniques in care settings have also played a significant part in the spread of MRSA.

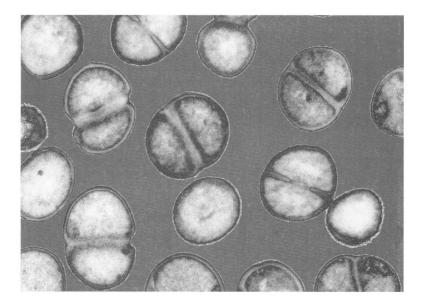

Figure 9
The MRSA
bacteria under
an electron
microscope

The MRSA bacteria can cause tissue damage resulting in pimples, boils and wound infections. It has also been known to cause pneumonia. MRSA has serious clinical consequences because it is expensive to treat and wounds that are infected with it take longer to heal. MRSA infection can be fatal for individuals with weak or compromised immune systems. Individuals who are hospitalised, have intra-vascular lines, indwelling urinary catheters, pressure ulcers and/or underlying immune-system problems are the most at risk from MRSA infection.

Minimising the risk of MRSA infection

Ineffective hand washing by health-care workers before and after dealing with MRSA-positive individuals is the main cause of MRSA infection in care settings. Studies show that hand decontamination with alcohol disinfectant is effective in combating MRSA, especially when supported by health education on good hand hygiene practice.

If basic good hygiene precautions are followed (see page 51), MRSA-positive individuals are not a risk to other individuals, staff, visitors or members of their family, including babies, children and pregnant women. In 2002 the Department of Health stated that 'there is no justification for discriminating against people who have MRSA by refusing them admission to a nursing or residential home or by treating them differently from other residents'. Individuals with MRSA should be helped with hygiene if their mental or physical condition makes it difficult for them to manage these areas independently.

Risk assessment and good hygiene practices are the key to managing MRSA-positive individuals and minimising the risks of cross-infection to staff and other individuals. Good practice points include:

- The nurse in charge should carry out a risk assessment to identify how MRSA will affect the individual and what the risks are to other people due to cross-infection.

- Information about an individual's MRSA status and management should be clearly written in their care plan.

- All care staff should be familiar with the infection-control policy, local procedures and agreed care plan approach to MRSA infection in a care setting.

- Practising effective hand washing and following general hygiene precautions (see page 51) are the basis for dealing with MRSA in practice.

- The Department of Health also advises the following:

  - MRSA-positive individuals may share a room as long as neither they nor the person with whom they are sharing has open wounds, drips or catheters;

  - MRSA-positive individuals may join other residents in communal areas such as sitting or dining rooms, as long as any wounds or sores are covered with an appropriate dressing which is changed regularly;

  - MRSA-positive individuals may receive visitors and go out of the home, for example to see their family or friends.

- Staff with eczema or psoriasis should not perform intimate nursing care for MRSA-positive individuals.

- Staff should complete any procedures on other individuals before attending to dressings or carrying out other nursing care for MRSA-positive individuals.

- Staff should carry out any clinical procedures and dressings on an MRSA-positive individual in the person's own room.

- Staff should seek and follow expert infection-control advice from the consultant in communicable diseases control and/or an infection-control nurse for any MRSA-positive individual who has a post-operative wound, drip or a catheter.

- MRSA-positive individuals with open wounds should be allocated single rooms if possible.

Safe moving and handling

Poor moving and handling techniques are the most common causes of absence due to injury and sickness in care workplaces. It is vital that you undertake training for this type of work before you move or handle individuals. Using safe moving and handling techniques is an important way of contributing to the health and safety of your care setting. Employers and employees share responsibility for ensuring that moving and handling activity is carried out safely.

It is the *employer's* responsibility:

- To provide an induction and training course in current manual-handling practice with compulsory yearly updates.
- To produce and implement a manual-handling policy.
- To provide equipment that meets both the specific and collective needs of the individuals concerned.
- To employ a competent person to monitor manual-handling practice or seek advice from an expert, such as a back-care adviser.
- To minimise risks in the workplace environment by providing adequately trained staff, clear guidelines and support and an appropriate uniform or clothing policy.
- To ensure that members of staff are fit to carry out work and that there are sufficient reporting mechanisms in place if injuries do occur.
- To investigate any injuries and aim to prevent any reoccurrence through risk assessment and clear policies and procedures.

It is the *employee's* responsibility:

- To be accountable for their own actions and to seek advice if unsure of safe practice.
- To undertake manual-handling training and update practice at least once yearly.
- To report any manual-handling concerns regarding individuals, equipment or staff to a manager or supervisor.
- To use moving and handling equipment appropriately and responsibly.
- To request and receive assistance regarding individuals with special needs or requirements.
- To carry out a personal risk assessment to consider their own safety and that of the individual and equipment.

Your care organisation should have produced an organisational policy on moving and handling. It is important, and it is your responsibility to find out what this says and to follow the practices and procedures that it sets out. The moving and handling policy should incorporate all of the latest moving and handling regulations and laws. You will not be covered by your employer's insurance policies, and may not have any legal comeback, if you fail to follow the moving and handling policy and subsequently get a back injury due to unsafe practice.

Using moving and handling equipment

The majority of health and social-care settings have a policy of no manual lifting. This ensures that individuals are assisted to move with the aid of equipment or

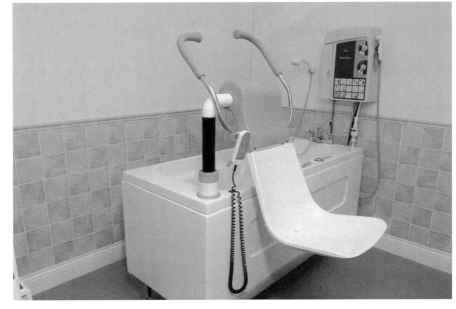

Figure 11
Specialist and
adapted
equipment may
be provided to
improve the
health and
safety aspects of
care procedures

support aids. However, when there are staff shortages and equipment is lacking or defective, many care practitioners will continue to lift or manually handle individuals. In doing so they are putting themselves at risk of sustaining a musculoskeletal injury and may also be endangering the safety of the individuals they are caring for.

The term 'no-lifting policy' can be misleading. It does not mean that you should not assist individuals with movement. Rather, it is used to imply that lifting all, or most, of a person's weight is not permitted. It is acceptable to give individuals some support or to perform horizontal moves with sliding aids if this is done according to agreed safe handling principles. However, only individuals who require light assistance should be helped in this way.

Risk assessment will determine what constitutes safe handling practice in any situation. The starting point for risk assessment should be that lifting an adult's weight is likely to be unacceptably hazardous to an individual worker. The Department of Health also advises that certain moves, such as the shoulder or 'Australian' lift, are now considered to be unacceptable from a risk control point of view.

You should seek detailed advice on safe moving and handling practice in your workplace from a specialist practitioner or adviser responsible for this area of work. You should also consult the safe moving and handling policy and any in-house training guidance that your employer provides on these matters. Remember that no one working in a hospital, nursing home or community setting should need to manually lift patients any more. Non-weight bearing individuals should only be moved using appropriate equipment and safe techniques.

Manual handling – good practice guide

- Before attempting any moving or handling, explain to the individual what you need to do and obtain their assistance where appropriate.
- Prepare the area first so that it is free from clutter and objects on the floor.
- Confirm that the equipment to be used has been checked and is safe to use. If this is not the case, do not use it.
- The correct sling or hoist should be used to suit the weight and size of the individual.
- Sufficient time and space must be allowed when carrying out the manoeuvre so that the individual does not feel rushed.
- The individual's dignity must be maintained throughout and they should not be unduly exposed or made to feel vulnerable.
- The hoist should be placed in a suitable position near to the person's bed, chair or bath, for example. At least two people should support the individual during the procedure: one person to operate the device and one to support the individual so that no injuries occur.
- If the individual is being transferred to another area it is advisable to transport them in a wheelchair first and then to use the hoist in the transfer area, such as a bathroom.
- The individual should never be left alone whilst in the hoist. Therefore, before you begin take all of the necessary equipment, toiletries, clothing and belongings to the area where care will be provided.

Dealing with spillages

Spillages should be treated as health and safety hazards. This may be because the substance that has been spilled is a potentially infectious or harmful body fluid, a chemical or a toxic substance. Alternatively, it may be because the spillage causes a floor or other work surface to become wet and slippery. Wet and slippery floors are the cause of many accidents in care settings.

Your employer should have produced organisational policies and procedures that set out the process for dealing with different types of spillage. You should read and understand these procedures. It is best to ask a senior colleague to explain or provide guidance on any areas that you do not fully understand. The actual procedure used for any particular spillage is likely to depend on the substance involved and the level of risk associated with it.

In some care settings cleaning and portering staff are responsible for dealing with certain types of spillage because they have received special training to do so. In other situations care workers may be directly responsible for dealing with spillages.

When there is confusion or disagreement about who is responsible for dealing with spillages, hygiene standards and infection-control procedures may break down and cause health and safety problems. You should know what spillages you are and are not responsible for dealing with in your care setting. You should also know the procedure for contacting cleaning or portering staff when you need their assistance.

Dealing with waste

The various kinds of clinical, food and everyday waste that are produced in care settings present an infection hazard unless dealt with correctly. Your care organisation should produce a detailed policy for safe waste disposal. You should read and understand it. Again, ask a senior colleague or supervisor for more guidance on any aspect of the policy or procedures that you are unsure about.

The waste-disposal policy should detail the procedures that you are expected to follow in order to deal with the different kinds of waste that you will encounter in your workplace. This should include colour coding of the bags used for waste (see Table 3 overleaf). You should always wear protective gloves when handling waste that carries an infection risk.

There may also be other procedures in your workplace to deal with specific forms of waste such as aerosol canisters, glass or empty medication bottles. You should find out what these local procedures are and you should follow them consistently.

One of the basic principles of safe waste disposal is that you should not take the waste any further than you need to. For example, it is better to bring the correct bag to the bedside or treatment area rather than to take clinical waste through the care setting. Use the same good practice that you would employ for the disposal of bed linen and towels. This will reduce the risk of cross-infection in different areas of your workplace.

Practical Example

Safe disposal of waste

Laura Henry is a first-year student nurse. She also does part-time work at Pine Lodge, a hospice that provides end-of-life care for people with terminal illnesses. This is Laura's first ever night shift. She is working with two qualified nurses and two other experienced care assistants. Whilst Doreen, her qualified supervisor, is on her break Laura realises that Mr Domingues, a 52-year-old man with motor neurone disease, has been incontinent of faeces and needs cleaning and changing. Laura has never dealt with this situation before.

➤ *Identify reasons why Laura should get some help from her colleagues in this situation.*

➤ *Describe the potential hazards that need to be dealt with in order to provide care for Mr Domingues.*

➤ *How can Laura maximise health and safety and minimise the risk of infection when dealing with Mr Domingues' soiled linen and night clothes?*

Table 3 Waste disposal

Type of waste	Method of disposal
Linen	Soiled sheets, towels and clothing should be kept separately from other used linen and clothing. In many care settings they are placed in a red bag to indicate that they are soiled. In home-care and other non-institutional settings soiled linen should be washed separately from other linen and should be dealt with as soon as possible. Non-soiled linen should be placed in an ordinary laundry bag according to local policy and procedure in care institutions or using the individual's preferred method in home-care settings.
Sharps	Sharps such as used needles, cannulas and blades should be disposed of in a yellow sharps bin. This should not be over-filled as it must be sealed before incineration.
Body products	These include body fluids such as blood, urine and sputum as well as other waste products such as vomit and faeces. Spillages should be cleared up and flushed down a sluice or toilet or sink as appropriate. The spillage area should be cleaned and disinfected as directed by local policies and procedures.
Clinical waste	This includes used dressings, bandages and swabs, for example. In residential care settings it should be disposed of in marked clinical waste bins that contain a yellow clinical waste bag. Each bag should have a label attached detailing its contents and the care area it came from before being sent for incineration. In home-care situations clinical waste should be dealt with according to the policy and arrangements put in place by your care organisation.
Recyclable equipment	Clinical equipment that is designed to be reused should normally be returned after each single use to your Central Sterilisation Services Department (CSSD) in the bags (usually blue) or packaging that CSSD provide for this purpose.
Household waste	This should normally be disposed of as domestic rubbish in black bags or using the waste disposal system provided by your local authority.
Leftover food	Food that is left over from individuals' meals should be disposed of in a kitchen bin immediately after the meal is finished. Staff employed to work in the food preparation and serving areas should normally receive food-hygiene training which covers ways of dealing with food waste.

Care and control of materials and equipment

A range of substances commonly found in the care workplace are hazardous to health. The law recognises this and the Control of Substances Hazardous to Health (COSHH) Regulations set out what these are and how the employer should act to minimise the risk to people.

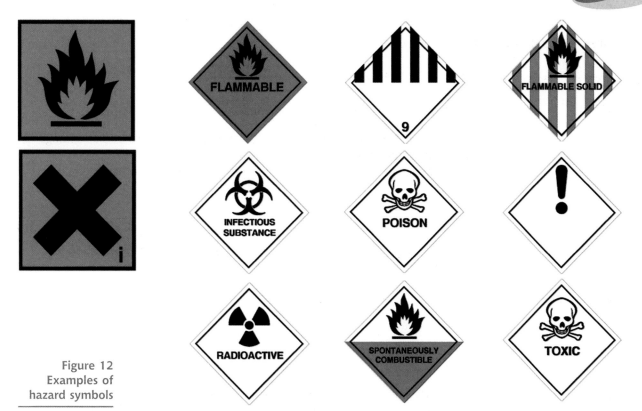

Figure 12
Examples of
hazard symbols

Hazardous substances include:

- Substances used directly in work activities, such as cleaning fluids, medication and hand cleaners.
- Substances generated during work activities, such as bodily waste products, soiled dressings and soiled linen.
- Naturally occurring substances, such as dust and animal hair from pets.

The effects of hazardous substances can include:

- Skin irritation or dermatitis as a result of direct contact.
- Asthma as a result of allergy to irritant substances used at work or in the individual's home.
- Loss of consciousness as a result of being overcome by fumes.
- Cancer, which may appear long after exposure to the chemical that caused it. For example some cytotoxic (i.e. cell-destroying) drugs increase the risk of cancer in users.
- Infection from bacteria and other micro-organisms.

It is important for your own health and safety as well as that of the individuals who you are caring for, that you know about the products you use and which you are exposed to in your daily working practice. Advice and guidance can be obtained through appropriate training and from the COSHH file that should, by law, be available in your workplace. The COSHH file should contain a list of all the hazardous substances and their location in the workplace. It should also provide safety details about the effects and exposure risks of each hazardous substance as well as information on how to deal with them in an emergency.

A number of good-practice measures can also be used to protect your health and safety. These include the following:

- Wear gloves and an apron if dealing with hazardous substances.
- Wipe up spillages of hazardous substances immediately and follow safety guidelines to dispose of them accordingly.
- Always store chemicals and medication in the appropriate, labelled container.
- Read the labels on any products that you use.
- Report and do not use unlabelled products that you find.
- Check safety information and expiry dates for all products.
- Store potentially hazardous materials in a locked cupboard after use. Do not leave products unattended in case confused or infirm individuals misuse or trip over them.
- Ask for advice and guidance from a registered nurse, your supervisor, a General Practitioner or a pharmacist if you are unsure about using anything listed in the COSHH file.

In addition to using and storing hazardous substances correctly, you should also be aware of local policy and procedures relating to the use and storage of equipment in your care setting. You should only use equipment that you have been trained to use and which you feel confident to use. To avoid creating hazards in the workplace, all items of equipment should be stored appropriately and should be returned to their usual place immediately after use. Equipment that clutters or blocks an area of an already busy and possibly overcrowded workplace may cause you or your colleagues, an individual or a visitor to trip and fall.

Reporting problems

It is important to know how and to whom you should report any concerns regarding health and safety so that they can be dealt with swiftly. This issue has been dealt with above (see page 45). The key points are that:

- Your employer is under a legal duty to keep a record of the accidents, injuries and near misses that occur in your workplace.
- You should always report an accident, incident or near miss if you witness or are involved in one.
- If you have a health and safety concern, you should tell a supervisor or manager as soon as possible and, where necessary, put your concerns in writing.

Key points – supporting health and safety in your workplace

- Health and safety in your workplace starts with your personal health, hygiene and security. You should take care to minimise the health and safety risks to, and from, yourself.

- Good personal hygiene and hand washing are vital for effective infection control.
- The risks of infection and cross-infection can be minimised by using personal protective equipment, through following infection-control policies and procedures and by effective hand washing.
- Back injury can be avoided through training in manual-handling techniques and the appropriate use of manual-handling equipment.
- You should undertake manual-handling training and always use manual-handling equipment appropriately after carrying out a risk assessment of each moving and handling situation.
- Plan and prepare all necessary equipment, belongings and toiletries before starting a personal-care activity so that the individual is not left unattended or exposed.
- Spillages and waste are health and safety hazards in any care setting. You should understand and follow policies and procedures on how to deal with different types of waste.
- Health and safety issues and problems should always be reported as soon as you become aware of them. You should not take an avoidable risk by carrying out activities or working in situations where health and safety problems exist.

Take action to deal with emergencies

Health and safety at work is generally achieved through preventive measures such as risk assessment, safe care practice and the correct use of safety systems and procedures. Despite this, emergencies do occur where an immediate response is required. In the final part of the unit we will consider ways of dealing with first-aid emergencies, fire situations and security breaches by intruders.

Dealing with emergencies

During the course of your job you may need to provide emergency assistance. This could happen if you are first on the scene of an accident or the first person to notice a fire. In other situations a colleague may ask for your help. Whatever the scenario, you will be better able to help if you follow a structured emergency response procedure (see Figure 13 overleaf).

Using the emergency response procedure will enable you to approach any emergency situation efficiently and effectively without overlooking your own safety or the safety of others. It is important that you put safety first in emergency situations. Becoming a casualty yourself or creating additional casualties through unsafe or reckless action simply makes the situation worse.

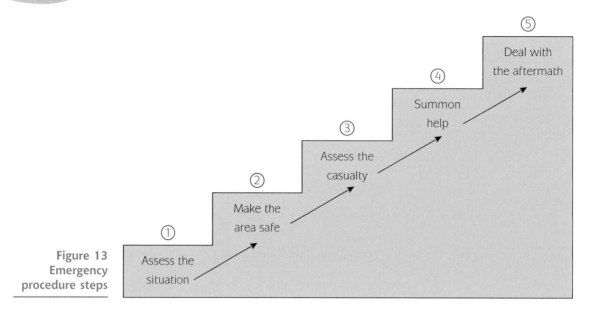

Figure 13
Emergency
procedure steps

In some emergency situations you may need to summon help before you do anything else. Your employer's first-aid and emergency response policy should provide details of the agreed procedures to be used in your care setting. You should read and develop a clear understanding of this. Alerting a colleague and phoning for help may be the most practical thing to do in some situations. However, if you are on your own it is better to quickly assess the cause of the problem. Then you can tell the emergency services or senior staff exactly what the problem is so that they can bring appropriate equipment.

If you are in a situation where senior colleagues or emergency services are able to respond and take over quickly, it may be best for you to support other individuals. Accidents and unexpected incidents can provoke a lot of anxiety and fear. Calming and reassuring others whilst keeping them away from the scene is helpful to all of those involved in and affected by the incident.

People (including yourself) who may be shocked, upset or unsettled by an accident, incident or first-aid emergency should be given an opportunity to talk through their thoughts and feelings. This kind of debriefing may be supportive and helps some people to deal with the aftermath of emergency situations.

Fire emergencies

Fire emergencies are frightening and can be very dangerous. Your employer should have a detailed fire and evacuation policy and you must be familiar with this. Fire drills and familiarity with evacuation procedures should be part of induction and update training for all care workers. Drills and training should be carried out on a regular basis so that all members of staff have the opportunity to practise working with different colleagues and with different individuals for whom they are caring. Good practice will include real-life evacuation simulations and scenarios involving

Figure 14
Fire classification
signs

KNOW YOUR FIRE EXTINGUISHER COLOUR CODE

WATER CO/2	DRY POWDER	FOAM	CO/2 CARBON DIOXIDE	VAPOURISING LIQUIDS
RED	BLUE	CREAM	BLACK	GREEN
WOOD, PAPER TEXTILES etc.	FLAMMABLE LIQUIDS	FLAMMABLE LIQUIDS	FLAMMABLE LIQUIDS	FLAMMABLE LIQUIDS
UNSAFE ALL VOLTAGES	SAFE ALL VOLTAGES	UNSAFE ALL VOLTAGES	SAFE ON HIGH VOLTAGE	SAFE ON HIGH VOLTAGE

the fire brigade. Many lessons can be learnt by taking part in this and it is reassuring when everyone knows exactly what to do and what their roles are.

In your workplace you should know how to:

- Raise the alarm.
- Alert emergency services and your colleagues.
- Evacuate individuals from the building.

Once a fire alarm has been raised and the emergency services are on their way, the evacuation of individuals should proceed calmly and promptly and in line with the agreed procedure and action plan. You should know where all of the fire exits and the outside evacuation points are. Individuals who are nearest to the fire should be moved first to the fire safety area. The person in charge should consult the bed state (i.e. the list of residents and their location) and staff register or signing-in book to find out who is on the premises. However, all rooms should be double-checked before leaving to ensure that nobody is left behind during the evacuation.

You should not enter a room if the door is hot when you touch it. Opening the door could cause any fire behind it to explode outwards. To restrict the progress of the fire you should close doors behind you as you evacuate the building.

Where residents cannot be moved easily, any doors between them and the fire should be closed as this will offer them some form of protection (up to 20 minutes if it is a regulation fire door). The individual must then remain inside with the door closed until the emergency services arrive. In practice this is extremely difficult as it will mean leaving a vulnerable person in a building that is on fire. However, the emergency services always recommend that you protect yourself first so that you can assist and protect others later.

If individuals and staff are requested to wait outside the building in a fire emergency, it may be advisable to have a stock of space blankets available. These should be stored outside or near to exit points so that people can be kept warm while waiting for the all clear or to be moved to safer premises.

If you care for individuals in their own home it is wise to have a fire action plan that has been discussed and agreed with them and which can be implemented easily. As a basic measure, exits and entrances should be free from clutter. Smoke detectors and fire alarms should also be fitted and should be checked regularly.

Security problems and intruders

It is important to consider the security of the care setting where you work and also that of the individuals who are cared for there. This is particularly important if individuals are disorientated and confused or disabled by illness, accident or disease.

Doors and windows must be secured but the individual must be able to open and close these as appropriate. Sometimes adjustments to door handles and windows may be necessary. Where there is a keypad or card entry system, you must not lend your entry card or give the keypad code to other people. This may be a disciplinary offence and will compromise security. Staff should make regular checks of ground-floor windows and doors to ensure that they are safe and secure and that they have not been tampered with or left wedged open. You should always report to the senior person in charge any concerns that you have about visitors and any apparent attempts to break into the building or inappropriately enter your care area.

Intruders can be a problem for some care organisations. Unfortunately some people do prey on those who are unable to look after or defend themselves. It is appropriate to politely challenge any unfamiliar people that you see on the premises, and you should alert your colleagues to the presence of any suspicious or unexpected person. However, personal safety is important and if you have any serious suspicions or become aware of an intruder it is advisable to seek help quickly and call onsite security staff and/or the police.

Common emergency aid problems

First-aid emergencies are best dealt with by care workers who have received appropriate training. Ideally there should always be a trained first aider on duty in your workplace. The aim of first aid is to provide a prompt response, to do the casualty no further harm and to summon help. We have already covered the basic emergency response procedure (see pages 61 and 62). We noted that obtaining help and supporting casualties and others are important aspects of your role in any emergency situation. However, there may be times when you can provide direct first aid to a casualty.

The information that follows should raise your awareness of different first-aid situations. Reading and understanding this section of the unit will not make you a competent first aider. If you wish to achieve competence in first aid you will need to complete a full first-aid course where your practical skills will be fully assessed. The information in the rest of this unit should make you more aware of the different kinds of first-aid emergencies that may occur. It is important that you accept the limitations of your own ability in this area and do not try to act beyond your level of competence in treating other people's injuries.

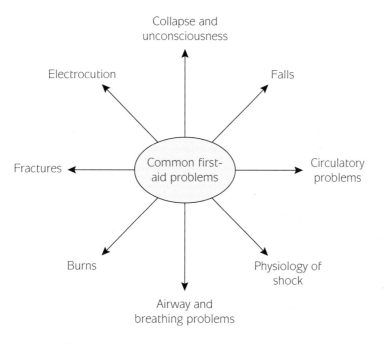

**Figure 15
Common first-aid
problems**

Whatever the first-aid emergency you should initially follow the emergency response procedure described above (see pages 61 and 62). The following explanations describe some of the basic measures that can be taken in each specific emergency situation.

Unconscious casualties

Loss of consciousness can occur for many reasons. Whatever the cause, you should follow the emergency response procedure. Step 3 involves carrying out an initial assessment. When a person is unconscious, you should first check their ABC (airway, breathing, circulation) (see Figure 16 overleaf).

If the person is not breathing you must raise the alarm immediately and alert the person in charge. Medical aid is vital and artificial ventilation must be given quickly. If you have been trained to do this then you should proceed once you know that it

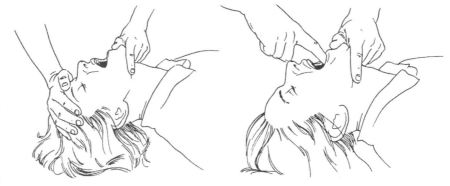

Figure 16
Opening and
clearing the
person's airway
is vital to allow
them to receive
oxygen

is safe for you to do so. The person's brain function will begin to deteriorate without oxygen after three minutes and other organs will also be affected. Delays in treatment can lead to death.

If the person is breathing, they should be placed in the recovery position (see Figure 17). Again, you should do this if you know how to. If not you should get help from somebody who does and alert the person in charge. However, if you suspect that the person has also suffered a head, neck or back injury, they should not be moved unless they are at risk of choking. This could occur, for example, in the case of an overdose or poisoning.

Figure 17
Put a breathing
but unconscious
casualty in the
recovery position

The recovery position is used to prevent a casualty from choking as a result of their airway being obstructed. This position is also useful if you need to turn someone who is in bed when they become unconscious. You should always support the casualty in the turn and move them towards you not away from you. This allows you to control the person's movement and gives you a better observation point. Moving the person away from you may result in them rolling out of bed and suffering further injury.

Airway and breathing problems

The human airway starts at the nose and throat and ends in the lungs. It is important that the airway is always kept clear. If the airway is blocked, oxygen cannot enter or exit the lungs. The airway can become blocked by mucus, vomit, swelling, foreign objects and by the tongue relaxing against the back of the throat.

When the jaw is tilted slightly this will move the tongue forward and keep the airway clear.

A blocked airway will cause a person to choke. So they are likely to have difficulty in speaking and breathing and may also be coughing or spluttering. In severe cases of choking the casualty may turn blue (i.e. the colour drains from their skin) because an obstruction in their airway is preventing them from obtaining oxygen. This can lead to loss of consciousness. The emergency aid for choking is to:

- Reassure the casualty.
- Sit the casualty, leaning forward.
- Encourage them to cough hard to remove any blockage from their airway.
- If this fails, give up to five sharp slaps on the person's back between their shoulder blades with the flat part of your hand whilst taking care to support the person's head. Stop if the obstruction clears.

If back slaps fail to clear the obstruction, then five abdominal thrusts should be given, and the procedure repeated until help arrives. If the person becomes unconscious the emergency services should be called and the first aider should attempt artificial ventilation.

Figure 18
Back slaps and the abdominal thrust/Heimlich manoeuvre

Non-specific breathing problems

The normal respiratory rate in adults is usually 14–16 breaths (respirations) per minute. The person's skin should look fresh and oxygenated and the correct colour for that person. If the nail bed is gently pressed, after blanching (going pale) the colour under the nail will immediately return. The person's chest should move evenly and rhythmically and there should be no wheezing or excess noise whilst breathing.

Clear signs of breathing difficulty are when a person's breathing appears to be very fast, their normal colour changes, their lips look blue (cyanosed) and they are in obvious distress and perhaps also in pain. Help should be summoned immediately. The person's breathing problems may indicate another serious health emergency such as a cardiac arrest or stroke (cerebrovascular accident). If the person is conscious you should position them sitting up and leaning forward as this will help their breathing. If the person is unconscious, place them in the recovery position but monitor their ABC and, if you know how, be prepared to carry out artificial ventilation if their breathing stops.

Dealing with an asthma attack

Asthma is an allergic response to **allergens** that cause irritation and inflammation in the lower respiratory tract (in the bronchi – large air passages in the lungs). The bronchi become obstructed with mucus and inflamed as a result of the irritants. Usually a person's bronchial inhaler will help to reduce swelling and if the allergens (such as dust, animal hair, pollen or aerosols) are no longer present the casualty should recover.

Where a person's inhaler has little or no effect, help should be summoned immediately. The person should be asked to sit leaning forward, preferably with their arms and upper body supported against a table and/or a pillow. They must be given plenty of space so that they do not feel crowded. You should try to identify the allergen if possible and ensure that it is not near the casualty. It may be a good idea to open a window. You should also help the casualty to use their inhaler whilst waiting for help to arrive. If the person loses consciousness then the ABC procedures will become a priority and the casualty should be dealt with accordingly.

Circulatory problems

The heart pumps blood around the body through the arteries and veins. The working of the heart can be measured through a person's pulse rate and their blood pressure. Age, lifestyle and disease can cause deterioration in the action of the heart and blood vessels and will affect pulse and blood pressure. Raised blood pressure and an increased pulse rate put extra strain on the heart as it attempts to move oxygen-carrying blood around the body. Over time, a blockage may occur in the circulatory system. This can cause a heart attack (myocardial infarction), a blood clot in the lung (pulmonary embolism) or a burst blood vessel (haemorrhage) which may in turn lead to a cerebrovascular accident (known as a CVA or stroke).

Dealing with a cerebrovascular accident (CVA)

A CVA is sometimes difficult to recognise as the range of symptoms can vary depending on the nature of the 'stroke' (as it is sometimes called). Common signs and symptoms are heavy, noisy breathing, weakness down one side of the body, unconsciousness or semi-consciousness, difficulty with speech, a severe headache. First aid will be carried out according to the findings on assessment. Due to the paralysis down one side of the body, it is good practice for the person to be placed in the recovery position. This will protect breathing and keep the airway open. The medical staff should be summoned immediately and the GP informed. In severe cases, the individual may need to be admitted to hospital.

Dealing with a heart attack (cardiac arrest)

A heart attack (also called a cardiac arrest) can occur quite suddenly and without warning. It is important that the carer recognises the signs and symptoms and acts immediately. When the heart stops working it can cause other problems within the body that require medical treatment that first aid will not be able to provide. After initial assessment, the emergency services should be called. Clear instructions should be given over the telephone to the emergency services and it is helpful if someone is available to meet the ambulance crew at the door. If you are working in a hospital setting, you should call for the emergency 'crash' team. Give clear details of the individual's bed number and ward.

The carer's role is to carry out first aid until the medical team arrive. This may include removing pillows so that the individual is laying flat and ensuring that they are on a firm surface. Remove any clutter around the bed so that the team can have direct access. The priority is to carry out first aid to ensure that the individual receives oxygen. Mouth-to-mouth resuscitation may be necessary, in which case you should also carry out chest compressions to ensure that the oxygen is circulated.

There is no substitute for up-to-date first-aid knowledge, especially in emergency situations such as a heart attack.

The aftermath of a cardiac arrest can be quite stressful for all concerned and relatives will need to be comforted and supported. It is important for you to talk about the incident so that you can receive reassurance and guidance from your colleagues. If there is another incident you will be able to act with confidence.

Dealing with bleeding

Cuts and lacerations to the body, or the opening of surgical wounds, may result in significant bleeding. Loss of blood from the circulatory system is more dramatic and serious where the bleeding is from an artery. Blood will spurt out because it is being pumped by the heart at high pressure. Arterial blood loss must be stopped very quickly. Cuts or wounds that involve loss of blood from veins and tissue may also be alarming and should be dealt with quickly.

First-aid action to deal with bleeding is confined to limiting the loss of blood from the casualty's circulatory system. You should summon help and get a first-aid kit as soon as possible. The casualty should be treated lying down as they may faint. It will also be easier to elevate their wounds from this position.

On an external wound the immediate first aid is to apply direct pressure to the wound, unless there is an object embedded in it. If there is an object in the wound, pressure should be applied either side of it. The object should not be removed as it may be acting as a plug that prevents further bleeding. To minimise the risk of infection, you should either wear protective gloves or ask the person to apply pressure with their own hand to the top of the wound. The wound should then be elevated (raised so that it is physically above the heart) if possible. This will help to reduce the blood flow and help to slow down blood loss. Dressings can be applied

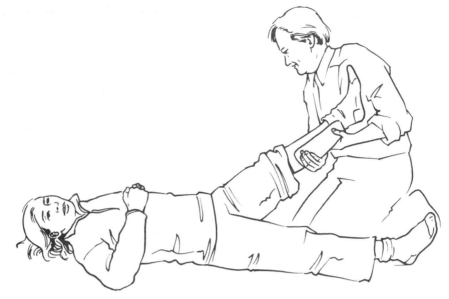

Figure 19
Elevating a
wound above
the heart will
help to slow
down blood loss

where appropriate and if the first aider is competent at this. The casualty should then be taken for further emergency treatment as necessary.

In the event of an amputation occurring, the limb, finger or toe should be wrapped in plastic then padding and kept as cold as possible. It may be possible for a surgeon to reattach it if the blood vessels are preserved as a result of swift action.

Shock

You should always treat accident casualties for **physiological** shock, especially if they have suffered bleeding. Shock occurs when a person's store of oxygen and their blood supply are redirected by their body to their essential internal organs. In severe cases the blood supply to some organs may shut down. Someone who is in shock may become pale, cold and clammy. They will also have a fast pulse that could be weak, they will feel cold and may complain of feeling extremely thirsty. Shock is dangerous but can be prevented and managed.

The first thing to do if you suspect shock is to lay the person down and then place their legs in an elevated position (if possible). This will assist blood flow to their internal organs. Keep the person warm with blankets or clothing but do not give them anything to eat or drink as they may need further emergency treatment. You should continue to observe and monitor the person, checking their ABC and responses, and provide reassurance until help arrives.

Fractures and falls

Fractures are broken bones. They tend to occur more easily in older people because their bones become less dense and may be affected by osteoporosis, arthritis and general wear and tear due to the ageing process. The symptoms of a fracture are swelling, pain and difficulty with movement. There may have been an obvious snapping noise when the fracture occurred. The bizarre angle of a person's fractured limb may also indicate what has happened. If the individual is very pale and clammy they may be in shock.

You should first make an initial assessment using the emergency response procedure and summon help as soon as possible. It is better to support a casualty's affected limb in a comfortable position rather than trying to move them. You can pad and support a fractured limb with anything that is soft. Pillows, rolled-up blankets, coats and clothing are all suitable. Do not try to splint the limb or move the person unless they are in danger as this can cause considerable pain and further distress.

If the fracture is an open fracture the bone will be visible. A light dressing pad should be applied to stop any excess bleeding. Remember to also treat the casualty for shock by keeping them warm. Do not give them anything to eat or drink as they will probably need further emergency treatment.

Emergency first aid

Victoria Cook is an 84-year-old lady with a dementia. She is cared for in a nursing and residential home (imagine that is where you work). Lately she has been prone to falls. When checking the residents during the night, the night staff note that she is restless and that the cot sides have been put on her bed but are not in use. The nurse in charge decides that they should be left down tonight as if she decides to climb over them she could hurt herself quite badly. After settling her for the night they continue on the rounds. Later there is a crash. When you go to Miss Cook's room with the night staff, you find her on the floor. Her leg is at an unusual angle to her body and she is in obvious pain. You cannot see any bone or blood protruding but she indicates that she cannot move at all. Miss Cook is very pale, cold and clammy and she is quiet (something very unusual for her).

➤ *In order of response to this accident, list your roles as carer.*
➤ *What are the priorities here?*
➤ *In dealing with the aftermath what should you remember to do in order to meet health and safety requirements?*

Burns and electrocution

The skin of older people and the very young is particularly susceptible to burns. It is known, for example, that a hot drink can scald a vulnerable person's skin up to 30 minutes after it has been made. Hot baths and showers, hot-water bottles and sitting too close to direct heat sources are also potential causes of burns in older people and the very young.

Immediate first aid for burns involves cooling the wound with water for at least 10 minutes and for 20 minutes if the burn is a chemical burn. This may be too long if the skin is very thin and fragile, so monitor the situation. You should then apply a clean, dry dressing that is lint free. Cotton wool should not be used as it can get into the wound and provide a place for bacteria to thrive. You should not apply any lotions or creams to a burn unless a qualified medical practitioner has prescribed them. Any burn that is larger or deeper than a ten-pence piece must be seen and treated by an expert burns practitioner.

Electrocution

Electrocution can cause burns too. It can also lead to altered heart rate and death. You should bear this in mind before acting in a situation where electrocution is occurring or has happened. To ensure your own safety, switch off any appliances at the power source or socket and then make the area safe. You should follow the emergency procedure guidelines and apply a dressing to any wounds that you find (usually at entry and exit points of the electrical current).

Ensuring that all electrical appliances are regularly checked and that sockets are not overloaded will reduce the risk of electrocution. Electrical appliances should never be used in bathrooms or around water, although this may still happen in the houses of some individuals. This is a serious health and safety risk.

Key points – dealing with emergencies

- In the event of an emergency in your care setting you should follow the emergency response procedure.
- Do not take risks or act beyond your level of competence and expertise in an emergency situation as this may make the situation worse.
- Emergencies may relate to fire, security or first-aid situations. You should know and understand the policies and procedures of your workplace for dealing with each of these types of situation.
- Raising the alarm, getting help and protecting people from harm are the immediate actions that you should take in an emergency situation.
- Emergency first aid should only be attempted if you have the knowledge and training to provide it competently.

Unit

HSC22

Are you ready for assessment?

Support your own health and safety and that of other individuals

This unit is all about how you keep yourself and others safe and secure in your workplace. It is about how to implement health and safety procedures and adopt good and safe working practices in all your activities. It is also about your skills when responding to various emergencies such as fire and security alerts, accidents and health emergencies.

Most of the evidence you need to cover the performance criteria and knowledge specification in the first two elements of the unit can be gathered during your assessment in other units. There should be ample opportunities for you to demonstrate safe working practices, especially in the optional units covering your activities and work with individuals. You should consider this when planning these optional units with your assessor.

Your assessment will be carried out mainly through observation by your assessor and should provide most of the evidence for the elements in this unit. However, the element relating to emergencies may require your assessor to observe you in a simulation of an emergency. The simulation will need to be as real as possible and all of the performance criteria and related knowledge should be covered. It is also possible to use alternative, additional sources of evidence showing how you dealt with actual emergencies. Witness testimony, questions or your own account of how you dealt with an emergency in your work setting could be helpful.

Direct observation by your assessor

Your assessor will need to plan to see you carry out the performance criteria (PCs) in each of the elements in this unit.

The performance criteria that may be difficult to meet through observation are:

- **HSC22a PC 5**
- **HSC22b PC 4**

usually because the activities do not occur routinely.

Preparing to be observed

You must make sure that your workplace and any individuals and key people involved in your work agree to you being assessed. Explicit, informed consent must be obtained before you carry out any assessment activity that involves individuals or which involves access to confidential information related to their care.

Before your assessments you should read carefully the performance criteria for each element in the unit. Try to cover as much as you can *during your observations*. Remember that you and your assessor can also plan for additional sources of evidence if full coverage of all performance criteria is not possible. ▶

Other types of evidence

You may need to present other forms of evidence in order to:

- Cover criteria not observed by your assessor.
- Show that you have the required knowledge, understanding and skills to claim competence in this area of practice.
- Ensure that your work practice is consistent.

Your assessor may also need to ask you questions to confirm your knowledge and understanding of this unit.

Check your knowledge

1. Describe the legal responsibilities that you have for health and safety in the workplace.
2. Identify examples of health and safety hazards that are present in your workplace.
3. Explain how you would go about making a risk assessment as a part of your everyday care work.
4. Describe ways of minimising the risk of infection and cross-infection in the care workplace.
5. Explain your responsibilities with regard to safe moving and handling in the workplace.
6. Outline the main stages of the emergency response procedure.
7. Explain what you would do if a fire occurred at your workplace.

Develop your knowledge and practice

This unit covers all aspects of learning and developing yourself at work and is linked to all of the other units of your NVQ. You will gather evidence for this unit from the very start of your NVQ programme. As you work through the various units you will be demonstrating how you are developing your own knowledge and practice.

This unit contains two elements:

⌣ *HSC23a Evaluate your work*

⌣ *HSC23b Use new and improved skills and knowledge in your work*

⌣ Introduction

The phrase **lifelong learning** is useful in care situations because it emphasises the fact that it is not possible for a care worker to reach a point where their learning and development is complete. After working in care for 30 years, a care worker may have a lot of knowledge and understanding, but that does not necessarily mean they are up to date or practise effectively. There is always more to know and care skills need to be developed on a continual basis to maintain competence. Society's knowledge and understanding of illness, disease and disability is continuously evolving. People's values and expectations of care and treatment also change over time. As a result, care workers need to develop and update their own practice to keep up with change as it happens. This is how you avoid becoming an outdated and inefficient dinosaur.

Making the most of work-based learning

Learning can occur at any age, at any time and in any place. When we think of learning we often think of formal education such as school lessons and college lectures. However, learning at work or in other informal situations can be just as important for personal and professional development. The formal and informal learning that you achieve at work, for example, is necessary for you to become a competent care worker and achieve a National Vocational Qualification (NVQ) level 2 award in care.

The first step in developing your skills and knowledge through work-based learning is to assess your existing strengths, skills and levels of competence. You need to

Figure 1
You need to
keep on top of
all aspects of
practice

identify what you already know and are good at before you can develop yourself beyond that point. The next step is to identify knowledge or skill areas that require further development. You can then look at ways of achieving any new development goals that you set.

Perhaps you only know that you are doing a good job because you have not been told you are doing a bad job! However, for your own personal development, self-esteem and job satisfaction it is better to have a clear idea of what you can do and how well you are doing at work. The first half of this unit looks at ways of evaluating the knowledge and skills that you currently use in your care work.

Element HSC23a   *Evaluate your work*

⤷ Reflecting on your work

KUS 1, 2

Some of the questions in Figure 2 may have sprung to mind when you first looked at this unit. It is now essential that you understand what developing your own practice involves and why **continuing professional development** is relevant to all care workers. This does not just involve looking at the practical aspects of your job. It involves considering your whole approach, including your values and belief systems, as well as how you can use your current knowledge and past experiences to help your further development.

Figure 2
Questions that you might have about developing your knowledge

Evaluating your job

When you evaluate, you measure or judge the value of something. The judgements that are made can be personal. **Evaluation** in a work setting may involve finding out whether you:

- Have strengths in some areas of work.
- Have areas of your skills which could be improved.
- Are doing what you should be doing.
- Have achieved what you set out to achieve.
- Are meeting the required standards of your care organisation and work role.

It is not easy to examine your own practice and identify your strengths and weaknesses. Saying 'I am good at this' is not something that comes naturally to everyone and may be as hard as admitting to areas of difficulty or weakness. Admitting that you do not understand something or cannot master a skill at work can make you feel uneasy if you think that this will be held against you. However, evaluating and acknowledging your strengths and weaknesses is an important part of personal learning and development. Thorough and honest evaluation will provide you with a baseline or starting point from which you can improve and develop your care practice.

The first evaluation question that you need to answer is, 'What should I be doing?'. You can find this out by:

- Obtaining and understanding your job description.
- Completing an organisational induction.
- Using and understanding organisational policies and procedures.
- Being aware of, and working to, national service standards, national occupational standards and codes of practice.

Understanding your job description

All employees should have a job description that summarises the responsibilities and duties of their job. Your job description tells you what you should be doing when you are at work. For example, the job description for a care worker based in a day centre might state that the role is 'to support senior care workers, whilst enabling individuals to participate in activities at the centre and assist with personal care and mobility as necessary'.

Job Description: Healthcare Assistant

As a healthcare assistant you will work with patients, ensuring basic needs are met. The role will include:

- helping patients with mobility
- helping patients with basic care such as eating, dressing and toileting
- carrying out regular monitoring of patients, e.g. taking their temperature, blood pressure and urine samples

You should always aim to help patients feel at their ease and to help speed their recovery.

The standard working hours are 37.5 hours per week.

You will be required to work a shift rota.

You must display:

- a commitment to patients care
- a warm and friendly nature
- an ability to get on with all kinds of people
- the patience and sensitivity to help patients with intimate tasks
- a general interest in personal health issues.

Figure 3
A typical job
description

If your job description is vague, too general to be helpful or too complicated for you to understand, you should ask your supervisor or line manager to explain it. You might also find it helpful to translate what it says into the kind of everyday language that you understand. It may help to add examples to the points it includes as this can help to illustrate what you are expected to do. If you work in the NHS, in addition to your job description you will also have a Knowledge and Skills outline for your post. This document will be used by your manager as a guide to ensure that you have the essential skills and knowledge required to do your job. The NHS Knowledge and Skills Framework (NHS KSF) has recently been introduced for all staff working within the NHS (except doctors, dentists and very senior managers).

Learning from an induction

As a new member of staff, by law you should have received an induction to your new workplace and work role. During your induction you should have been introduced to individuals receiving care, other staff and the working environment. Important information about the care workplace should be provided, such as policies and procedures on health and safety, infection control and confidentiality. Specific information on the day-to-day activities and procedures of the workplace may also be provided in some care settings. New and inexperienced members of staff may work under the close supervision of experienced staff during their induction period.

You may want to reflect on your own induction and review any notes or information that you received at this time. Consider what you learnt about your care organisation and how it has helped you to do your job. Induction should provide plenty of useful information and an opportunity for new employees to clarify what their work roles are. Your induction should also help you to understand how you fit into the bigger picture of the care organisation.

Understanding local policies and procedures

KUS 1

You should have learnt about the policies and procedures of your care organisation during your induction. These provide both general and specific information on the ways you are expected to deal with a range of care issues. You should understand the different policies and procedures and be able to put them into practice. If you do not do that you are not doing your job in the way that is expected.

National standards and guidelines

KUS 2

Care workers are expected to practise at a level that meets national standards for care. These **standards** are set by regulatory bodies such as the Commission for Social Care Inspection (CSCI), the General Social Care Council (GSCC), the Healthcare Commission (HC) and the care sector skills councils such as Skills for Care and Skills for Health in England, Wales, Scotland and Northern Ireland. The NVQ award that you are undertaking incorporates many of the standards of best practice that these bodies monitor. Your employer is likely to have a system of monitoring and internal checks to ensure that appropriate standards of practice are achieved and maintained. Your care organisation will be subject to external monitoring and inspection as a way of maintaining general standards of care.

As a professional care worker you should know what the good practice standard involves in your area of care work. You should always seek to achieve and maintain such standards in your own practice.

KUS 9, 11, 12

Evaluating your work role

- Do you have a copy of your current job description?
- Do you understand what your job description says about your work role?
- Have you read the organisational policies and procedures that apply to your place of work?
- Do you make sure that you follow these policies and procedures when working with individuals and colleagues?
- Do you know what good practice is in your area of care work?
- How do you try to achieve and maintain high standards of practice in your own work?

Evaluating what you are doing

Once you have obtained information on what you should be doing and are clear about the standards of practice that you are expected to achieve, you should evaluate what you are currently doing in your work role. This requires an honest, open-minded and objective approach. Do not assume that you are automatically working at the required level just because you are doing your job every day. There may be areas of practice that you could improve upon – even if nobody has complained or said that you could do better. The important point is to actively find out how well you are working.

Use different sources of information to evaluate your work performance effectively. You should note that:

- Different people will offer you different opinions on your work because they have differing relationships with you and may look at situations from varying viewpoints.
- You should avoid relying solely on your own or one other person's opinion.
- Some sources of information are more reliable than others.
- People's opinions and views of your work can change over time (both positively and negatively).

If you base an evaluation of your work skills and performance on a number of different sources of information and they all indicate similar things, you probably have an accurate assessment of your current practice at work. You should obtain more evidence (ideally from neutral sources) if there are big differences in the way people evaluate your work. Using a variety of sources of information will give you a truer picture of your own performance than if you simply rely on your own opinion, ask colleagues who are also friends or consult people who you supervise or manage.

You can examine your practice at work by:

- Increasing your self-awareness and using **reflection** to produce an honest and balanced self-evaluation of your skills, strengths and weaknesses.
- Obtaining feedback from others, including your manager or supervisor, colleagues, the individuals you care for and any other key people involved in their care.
- Having your skills and performance formally assessed.
- Reviewing the results of audits and inspections carried out in your care setting.
- Reviewing and learning from reports on incidents and accidents that occur in your care setting.

Self-awareness

We are all unique individuals with our own values, beliefs and personal experiences. These factors have an impact on us and often shape the way we are and how we behave. When you work closely with people it is important to understand that they can have extremely different views and attitudes to your own. It is also important to recognise that your own values, beliefs and experiences do influence the way you behave and the expectations that you have of other people. Conflict resulting from a difference, or clash, of values and beliefs does happen in care settings. These events can be difficult and distressing for everyone involved and can affect the quality of care that an individual receives. Conflicts are less likely to happen if you are aware of your own values and beliefs and the effect that they may have on your behaviour and on other people. This is called developing your self-awareness.

Our upbringing and our past experiences influence the way we are. It can be difficult, or even impossible, to get rid of attitudes, values and beliefs that we have acquired through our past experiences. Despite this, you have a responsibility to acknowledge and respect the attitudes, values and beliefs of every individual you care for and the key people involved in their care. Imposing your viewpoint on others is not usually appropriate or acceptable. It is normally advisable to step back from situations where you might get into disagreements or conflict with individuals or their relatives.

If you do not develop sufficient self-awareness you will not understand how your personal values and attitudes may influence your day-to-day practice. This in itself could become a major barrier to your learning and professional development.

Reflection

People who are reflective are likely to be self-aware. Reflection involves looking inward, or contemplating, and is an important way of examining your own practice. Reflection can involve thinking about what you have done and the reasons why. This might lead you to consider your actions and general practice from a number of different angles.

Being able to look critically at particular experiences or areas of your own practice is now accepted as an important way of learning and achieving professional development. You should be able to reflect on both positive and negative aspects of your practice as a care worker. Where things are not going so well, or you feel

**Figure 4
Reflective
questions**

you need support, you could follow up your reflections by talking any issues through with your colleagues or a supervisor. This kind of action leads us to learn from our mistakes and from difficult experiences. Similarly, where a situation has gone extremely well you can learn from it by reflecting on just how and why it went right. Learning lessons from success is as important as learning lessons from failure.

Making a self-evaluation

Self-awareness and reflection may be useful in a self-evaluation. When you make a self-evaluation you should be honest without being too self-critical. Table 1 provides a simple model that you can follow to carry out a self-evaluation of your care practice. To complete it you will need to draw on your own self-awareness and think reflectively.

Table 1 Carrying out a self-evaluation

Reflective question	Reflective response
What happened?	
What went well?	
What did not go so well?	
How do you know?	
What were you happy with?	
What would you change?	
What did you learn from this situation?	

If you have a mentor or supervisor it may be helpful to discuss and share your reflections with them. Regardless of whether you share your reflections with anyone, simply writing a few brief points about a situation or experience that you have thought about can be very useful. Try completing a self-evaluation using the questions provided in Table 1. It is a good way of evaluating how your attitudes, values, skills and knowledge are contributing to your practice as a care worker. This can help you to find out what you do well and what you need to improve on.

Obtaining and using feedback

Feedback can come in different forms and from different people (see Table 2).

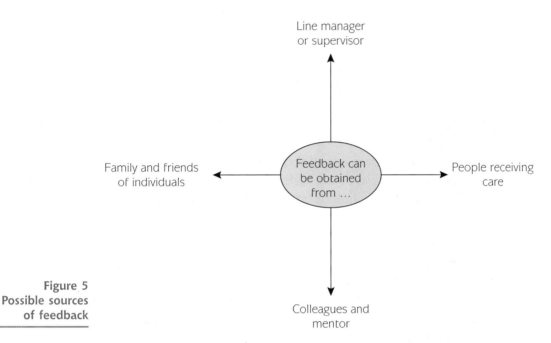

Figure 5
Possible sources of feedback

Table 2 Sources and forms of feedback

Source of feedback	Form of feedback	Example
Line manager or supervisor	Formal and written	An appraisal
	Informal and verbal	Supervision session
Colleagues	Formal and written	Comments in individual's notes on care delivered
	Informal and non-verbal	The way that colleagues behave towards you
Individuals and their family	Formal and written	A letter of thanks or of complaint
	Informal	The way that people respond to you

Figure 6
Feedback should
be given in a
constructive and
supportive way

Feedback is all about giving and receiving information about how you are doing, what you are doing well and what you need to improve on. It should help to motivate you to develop or maintain high standards of practice. However, if feedback is not given (or received) well, it can damage your motivation and confidence. Effective feedback depends on everyone being open and honest. Feedback should not be presented, or received, as a form of criticism. It should be given in a supportive way whether it offers a positive or negative view of a person's abilities and performance. This is important regardless of the person's level of experience or **competence**.

As well as your work being the focus of other people's feedback, you also have an important role to play in supporting others to give you feedback on your work. This means that you should adopt a positive and open approach in situations where people may want or need to provide you with feedback. Using your communication and interaction skills (see unit HSC21) effectively will enable and encourage others to speak to you openly and honestly. Avoid being defensive. Encourage people who provide feedback to make positive suggestions about how you could develop and improve your everyday care practice. It is good practice to establish a system of regular reflection and feedback opportunities in order to obtain the views of other people about your care practice.

Feedback that is given during **supervision** sessions with a senior colleague or supervisor provides a regular and ongoing source of information that can be used to evaluate your work performance. Supervision is generally used to give care workers a chance to reflect on their work performance and discuss any concerns they have. The outcome should be that standards of care are either improved or maintained at a high level and that care workers gain a good insight into how well they are performing at any particular point in time.

KUS 4

Appraisal involves a more formal evaluation of a care worker's performance and progress. These meetings usually happen once a year.

The aim of an appraisal and performance review is to discuss past and present performance in the job and to plan for future development. Usually, appraisal sessions begin with a discussion of current performance. Then they look forward to the next 12 months and agree new performance goals, targets or objectives that will be achieved during that time. At this point support and training needs are usually discussed. Because appraisals are formal evaluation sessions, a few documents are usually produced. These are a written agreement between the care worker and their manager outlining the discussion, the goals agreed for the next year and a written action plan for achieving them. Any new goals need to be realistic and manageable. It is useful to break goals down into achievable chunks rather than to have an enormous goal that is difficult to achieve in one go.

What is appraisal?

Appraisal is:	Appraisal is not:
● Time to discuss.	● Time to be disciplined.
● Time to listen.	● Time to moan.
● Time to plan.	● Time to be surprised or shocked by what is said.

Formal assessment may also provide you with a source of feedback on your work performance or on your level of competence in specific parts of your job. For example, your moving and handling skills, your ability to use specialist pieces of equipment, your health and safety knowledge and food hygiene skills may all be the focus of formal assessment at some point in your care career. You can use formal assessment results from areas of practice like these in an evaluation of your level of skill, knowledge and performance.

In addition to obtaining direct feedback about your own work performance you can also make use of feedback from a variety of other sources that may have a bearing on the work you do as part of a care team. These sources include the results of inspections and audits carried out in your workplace and reports on accidents and incidents that may have occurred.

Inspections and audits

All care organisations are now subject to regular inspections and **audits** of their standards. You may have heard of the Healthcare Commission (HC) and the Commission for Social Care Inspection (CSCI). You may have come across people auditing standards of care in your own workplace. Audit and inspection provides a systematic way of checking that all aspects of care practice have been carried out to the required standard. For example, when auditing hand washing, the auditor would observe members of care staff over a period of time and note whether they washed their hands and whether they followed the correct procedure.

When an audit is completed a formal report containing specific feedback details and action points is usually given to the manager(s) of a care setting. The key points found in the audit should then be explained to all staff. This can be an important source of feedback for members of the care team whose work has been the focus of the audit. For example, you may be able to use recent inspection and audit results to guide and improve your own practice in areas of care that the inspectors commented upon.

Accident and incident reports

When accidents or near misses occur in a care setting they should be documented on the relevant form in accordance with local policy and procedures. There may also be some informal, and even formal, discussion and review of an accident or incident, especially where it is considered to be serious or critical. Whilst accidents and incidents may not provide direct feedback on your own care practice, they may highlight areas of care practice that could be improved by the whole care team in order to minimise the risk of further incidents.

Therefore, you may be able to use accident and incident reports to identify areas where you need additional training and development. For example, if there is a series of incidents relating to injuries with a piece of equipment, then further training in the use of the equipment may be necessary. If there is a pattern to the particular type of accidents or incidents that you are involved in, you should reflect on your need for training and development in the areas of practice or skills concerned.

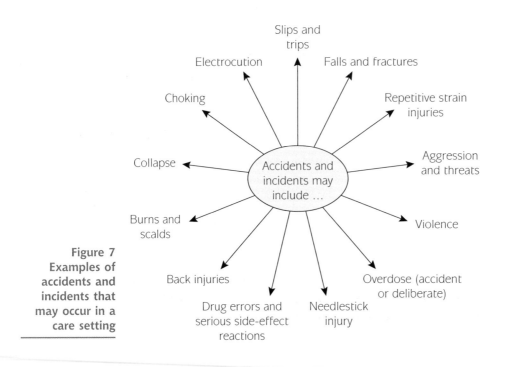

Figure 7
Examples of accidents and incidents that may occur in a care setting

Various methods will be used to measure how you are doing at work. Imagine you are the manager of a residential care home and you have been asked to write a reference for Sally, who is applying for promotion. Look at the list of evidence relating to Sally's work performance in Table 3. What does each piece of evidence tell you about Sally? Is some evidence better than other evidence?

Table 3 Assessment of work

Evidence from the workplace relating to Sally's performance	What does this tell you about Sally?
Sally has an action plan with goals. She is well on the way to achieving her goals	This is positive; she has agreed a plan and set goals. The fact that she is achieving her goals shows she is using the plan and is motivated.
Sally attended mandatory/compulsory training sessions for fire, moving and handling, and food hygiene	Sally has evidence of completing training which is required by UK law. It requires commitment from both Sally and her employer.
Sally is working towards NVQ 2 Care and is making good progress	This shows commitment and motivation. There will be regular assessment in the workplace so this is a good indicator of Sally's performance.
Sally gets on well with team members (peers, managers) and the individuals she provides care for. People ask her to do things and rely on her	Good interpersonal skills are essential. Colleagues and individuals receiving care are indicating that they like and trust Sally.
Sally has not had to complete any incident forms in the past 12 months	This could mean many things: • She may be very careful. • She may be fortunate not to be involved in an incident/accident. • She may not have documented any incidents/accidents.
Sally has not been disciplined, there are no complaints about her practice	Formal disciplinary action or complaints would be a serious concern.
Sally is occasionally late for work	Punctuality is important. If lateness persisted it could alter how Sally is viewed by the team. Senior care workers are role models. Problems relating to punctuality would not be viewed positively.
Sally has had 14 days off sick in the past year	Were all the days together or were they separate occasions? Were they legitimate episodes of sickness or is there a pattern – one or two days off every month?

No single item of evidence is enough on its own to measure workplace performance. Knowledge, skills and attitude are all equally important and they can be demonstrated in very different ways.

Dealing with feedback information

Being open to feedback is one of the hardest aspects of working and studying, especially when you receive negative comments or feel criticised. When this happens you may feel defensive, have dismissive thoughts or switch off as a way of protecting yourself. Instead, you should listen carefully, keep any feedback in perspective and try to respond constructively. Ask for clear examples of any areas of weakness or under-performance, for ideas about how you could improve in these areas and for suggestions about who could help you to improve. This will all help you to progress.

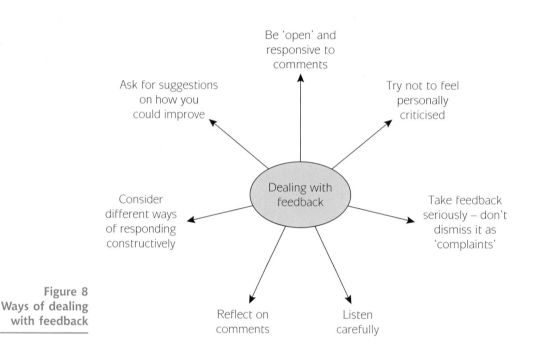

**Figure 8
Ways of dealing
with feedback**

Feedback from your colleagues can help you to develop your knowledge and skills quickly. This is especially helpful when you are settling into a new role. However, you should remember what we said earlier about the reliability of evaluation. You should be wary of reading too much into comments from your friends at work or from those who encourage you to take short cuts to reduce time and effort. Possible sources of feedback from colleagues include comments in team meetings, communication books or diaries and in informal conversations. Good team spirit, people asking for your help or advice and people wanting to work with you are also good indications that you are contributing positively to care practice.

Identifying ways of improving performance

KUS 5

The purpose of making a self-evaluation and obtaining feedback is to work out how you can develop and improve your abilities. To do this you will need to review the information that you obtain and compare it with a set of skills and knowledge that you would like to achieve. Set yourself some targets to achieve that will take you beyond your current levels of ability and performance.

You may be able to do this through your organisation's appraisal and performance system, particularly if you are still working towards meeting all of the requirements of your current job description. Alternatively, you could work with your organisation's staff training and development department to identify new skill and knowledge areas that could be included in a personal development plan (see page 94). Your targets could be based on a job description for a post that is different or has a higher grade than your current one. Whatever method you use, you will need to respond to the evaluation information that you have obtained by:

- Building on current skills, knowledge and areas of competence.
- Addressing areas where your skills, knowledge or competence are weak or lacking.
- Looking for ways to extend your current abilities and performance levels.

Using support and information to improve performance

KUS 9

As mentioned above, there are various potential sources of support and information that you could use to improve your performance (see Figure 9).

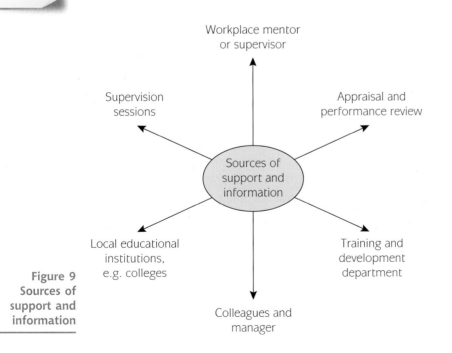

**Figure 9
Sources of
support and
information**

Wherever possible you should use all of the sources of support that are available to you to work out what your development options are and what might be the best ways of achieving your goals. This means that you will need to take responsibility for your own professional development. You should have a considered and structured plan to work through. We will consider how you can develop a personal development plan below (see pages 92–96).

Evaluation and development tips

- Know what you should be doing.
- Evaluate and compare what you are doing against what you are expected to do.
- Use different sources of information to make sure your evaluation is accurate.
- Take responsibility for your own learning and development.
- Obtain support where you need it.

Key points – developing your knowledge and practice

- Care work involves lifelong learning and a continuing commitment to developing knowledge and skills for practice.
- The first stage of developing your knowledge and practice involves evaluating your current skills and the standards of your practice.
- Evaluation involves obtaining information about what you should be doing and the standards that you are expected to achieve, reflecting on this and comparing it with what you actually do.
- Feedback from colleagues, supervisors, the individuals you provide care for and their families is an important source of evaluation information.
- Many care organisations use supervision and appraisal systems to provide care workers with feedback on their work performance.
- A positive, constructive response to feedback and appraisal is necessary to enable you to develop and improve your care practice.

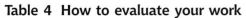

Table 4 How to evaluate your work

Tool of evaluation	Advantages	Disadvantages
Reflection	• Can do it yourself. • Do not have to rely on anyone else. • Helpful to work out what happened in certain situations.	• Can be difficult. • Effort is needed to write something down. • Need to ensure confidentiality of information.
Appraisal or performance review	• Structured and formal. • Should happen annually with review.	• People feel nervous, anxious. • Relies on skill of the appraiser.
Supervision session	• One-to-one time with supervisor. • Able to raise questions and discuss issues.	• Could be intense. • May not feel comfortable to talk freely.
Feedback from individuals receiving care	• Information from the people who are receiving care is extremely important. • Can be immediate and boost morale.	• A formal complaint may be hard to deal with. It may alter the relationship with the individual. • Could be unreliable. Individuals not wishing to upset staff.
Feedback from peers	• Easy to obtain. • People understand the job.	• Can be unreliable.
Assessment	• You know exactly what you have achieved.	• Anxiety about assessment may affect performance.
Audit/ inspections	• Not personal. • Useful to have external view of service.	• May happen on a busy day. • May not be accurate picture.
Accidents and incidents	• Can be powerful learning experiences.	• Confidence could be damaged for people involved in the incident.

Use new and improved skills and knowledge in your work

Evaluation of your work, skills and knowledge is the first step to making improvements. In this part of the unit we will focus on how you can use what you have learnt about yourself to improve your work activities. We will focus on:

- Ways of identifying the new skills and knowledge that you need to improve your work activities.
- Ways of accessing additional training to support your development.

- Using appropriate support and supervision to ensure that any new skills and knowledge are used effectively, safely and legally and by agreement with your managers and supervisors.
- Ways of monitoring and evaluating the impact on your work of your new and improved skills and knowledge.

Personal and professional development

Development – issues to consider

- How you are going to *identify* the new skills and knowledge that you need?
- How you are going to *obtain* these skills and this knowledge?
- How you are going to *check* that you have acquired the skills and knowledge?
- How are you going to *use* your new skills and knowledge when you have them?
- How are you going to *keep* these new skills and knowledge and stay up to date?

The list of points above, and the questions about professional development, suggests that work-based learning is an ongoing process. This means that it involves a repeating pattern of building on what you know and can do at a particular point in time, putting any improvements into practice, then building on this again with the development of further skills and more new knowledge.

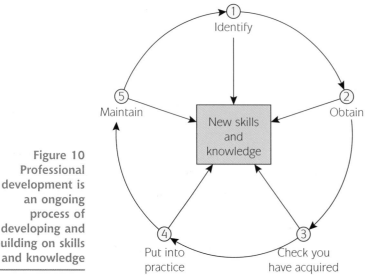

Figure 10
Professional development is an ongoing process of developing and building on skills and knowledge

However, it should be clear that just going on courses will not automatically result in you learning or developing your skills and knowledge. You will need to think and do things differently before you can claim that you have learnt something new.

A real process of learning should improve your professional competence and boost your confidence in the short term and the long term. Learning is very satisfying and really helpful when you are able to see or appreciate some instant changes. This can happen if you learn a new skill or significantly improve an existing skill. However, change and personal development may be a far more gradual process. Therefore, it is important to accept that lifelong learning is a continuous and worthwhile process that will result in your development as a care worker even though you may not experience instant change.

PERSONAL DEVELOPMENT – RECORD AND EVALUATION

Objective	Learning and development activity	Hours and dates	Has the learning activity been a) completed and b) effective?	How will you apply this learning to your work?	Who else could you share this learning with?

Signature of individual .... Date .... Name of individual ....

Signature of reviewer .... Date .... Name of reviewer ....

**Figure 11
An example of a personal development evaluation form**

Obtaining new skills and knowledge

KUS 3, 8

So, how can you obtain new skills and knowledge? The best way to do this is to produce a plan that maps out your development needs and then match these needs to realistic ways of achieving them.

Although much learning happens without planning, a **personal development plan** will focus your own learning and development process much more effectively. Your work skills and career development are likely to progress much quicker if you set improvement targets and focus on ways of achieving them. Leaving your professional development to chance or assuming that you may benefit from future opportunities will result in you drifting along and only achieving part of your potential.

Personal development plans

KUS 6, 7

Earlier in the unit you learnt about the role that appraisal and performance review systems play in evaluating care workers' performance (see page 85). Ideally your care organisation will have an appraisal and performance review system in place. If this is the case you should have some evaluation feedback with which to begin your personal development plan. If you have not had an appraisal yet or your employer does not offer a formal performance review system, you may need to ask a supervisor to offer support and **mentorship** before you begin your own personal development plan. The first step is always to get an idea of your strengths and weaknesses.

Having discussed your performance at work and received feedback from your manager or supervisor, you need to do something constructive with this feedback. Remember that the aim is to use it to help you to improve and develop further. At this stage, you could write some goals or objectives that you want to work towards over the next year. Sometimes the development plan may look further ahead than a year, especially if you have a master plan to become a senior carer, to complete a professional care training course or to remain in the same role but to keep up to date and teach new staff, for example. Whatever your overall aims are, the development plan should identify how you will achieve your annual objectives and your overall aim. The plan should include details of:

- Study you might need to undertake.
- Projects that you might be working on.
- People that you might work with.
- Specific skills that you might need to master.

Even at this early stage you might be thinking, 'Why do I need a plan? I know what I am doing this year and how to do it. I intend to come to work, do my job and finish my NVQ.' This type of reaction is understandable. There is no suggestion that only people who are unmotivated or inefficient need to have personal development plans. In fact, the opposite is often the case. Those who are more motivated, who already have a good sense of their own ability and a sense of career direction may be

Figure 12
A motivated
and efficient
care worker

more likely to take personal development plans seriously. Despite this, everybody should have a development plan whatever their role within the organisation.

Identifying development goals and making plans is valuable because it can help you to break your progression down into more achievable chunks or stages of development. Establishing realistic and achievable goals is very important. Often when people do not achieve their goals or start to feel stressed by them it is because they are overwhelmed by the size of the tasks.

Personal development plans provide information, a way of focusing, a 'road map' for getting you where you want to go. So, the plan should be useful to you. If you think about going on a journey you would not set off without some sort of plan about how to get there. If the plan is too vague or too detailed it might not work. It needs to suit you as an individual. This means that it has to be written in a way that is meaningful to you. Your personal development plan should be seen as an agreement between you and your manager. It should not be imposed upon you by your manager. If you do not agree with it or do not understand any aspect of it you should say so at the time.

As well as identifying the key areas for your ongoing development, your personal development plan should identify the support you will need to obtain additional skills and knowledge and achieve your goals. This is a crucial part of the plan. You should have information or written instructions that tell you how to get the skills and knowledge you need and how you are going to use those skills.

Assessing your strengths and weaknesses

Use evaluation feedback as the basis of your personal development plan. Your own assessment of the strengths and areas of weakness in your current practice should

PERSONAL DEVELOPMENT PLAN

Goals	What is the development need/interests?	What will I do to develop myself?	How will I know I have done this?	What is the date for planned completion?	What support do I need and where will I get it?	What are the barriers and how can I overcome them?

Signature of individual .... Date .... Name of individual ....

Signature of reviewer .... Date .... Name of reviewer ....

**Figure 13
An example of
a personal
development
assessment form**

be your starting point. However, make sure that you also obtain other people's assessments of your strengths and weaknesses. Compare your own views with those of others. Are they similar to yours or have very different things been identified? The practical example below shows how an individual's view of themselves can differ from outsiders' views.

Assessment of strengths and weaknesses

Sabina, aged 43, is a support worker based in a hospital. She works on the stroke unit and has been in the job for five years. This is Sabina's list of her own strengths and weaknesses.

Table 5 Sabina's assessment of her strengths and weaknesses

Strengths	Weaknesses
Good communication skills	Do not always feel confident
Know what to do in emergency situations	Sometimes get bored at work
Can cope under pressure	Cannot always get down on paper what I want to say

This is a colleague's list of Sabina's strengths and weaknesses.

Table 6 A colleague's assessment of Sabina's strengths and weaknesses

Strengths	Weaknesses
Great with individuals receiving care, visitors, staff – she can talk to anyone	Can be a bit disorganised on a daily basis
Calm in a crisis	Not very good on the computer
Very helpful and friendly	Is so keen to help other people that she leaves her own work

Sabina thought that her computer skills were satisfactory because she did use it occasionally. However, her colleague's comments made her realise she could do better. It was something that was becoming more important in the workplace and for study. She also thought that she was organised, but is able to admit that work routines do sometimes get to her. She would rather go and help colleagues as she finds the interaction is more rewarding than working on her own.

➤ *What are the main sources of feedback here?*
➤ *How can the differences between these lists help Sabina?*
➤ *What can Sabina do to improve on her weaknesses?*

So what should Sabina do with this feedback? If she took it negatively, she might not want to use the computer any more. She may feel she is being criticised for not being very good. However, if she was more constructive Sabina would take notice of the feedback and set herself a goal to improve her computer skills. If Sabina copes well when under pressure, this could be something to build upon. Perhaps she is ready for more challenges and should make a developmental goal in this area. Sabina's alleged lack of organisation and inability to stick to the daily routine may require her to work with a more experienced member of staff or to arrange to spend a morning in another department to see how they do things. Either of these strategies could help her to develop greater insight into the importance of routine tasks and may provide sources of guidance that will help to improve her performance in this area.

Obtaining and using feedback on your own abilities and performance can be worrying. However, if your colleagues and supervisors are constructive and you talk through any points that you do not understand or disagree with, you are likely to arrive at a mutual understanding. Often people do not realise how much they agree on issues until they have been able to talk about their apparent differences of opinion.

Writing development objectives

Evaluating your strengths and weaknesses should enable you to identify your development needs. The next issue that you need to consider is how to set yourself some development goals or objectives. The goals or objectives that you set yourself should be SMART – Simple, Measurable, Achievable, Realistic and Time limited.

Table 7 SMART goals

Quality of goal	What does this mean?
Simple	The goal or objective should be clear, unambiguous and easy to understand.
Measurable	The goal or objective should identify how you will be able to judge your progress. For example, it should clearly identify the point at which you have succeeded by stating exactly what you need to do (by how much, by when, in what way) to achieve it. You can then measure your actual performance against the goal.
Achievable	The goal should be something that, with appropriate effort, experience and training, you can actually reach in the time that you anticipate and with the resources that are available to you.
Realistic	This is related to the above point. You should set improvement goals that are a step or two on from where you are now rather than put yourself under pressure to achieve dramatic, extensive improvements that may well be unrealistic given the time and resources that are available to you.
Time limited	It is best to set some form of deadline or evaluation point for achieving your goals. This provides you with a timetable and more clearly focuses your efforts to improve and achieve your goals. A time limit will also help you to work out whether the goals that you set are realistic and achievable.

Working towards achieving personal development goals

Once you have worked out some goals for your personal development plan you need to identify ways of achieving them. The following examples of fictional but realistic development goals illustrate how to do this. Imagine these goals are yours:

- Complete training on vital-signs monitoring.
- Set up a relatives support group.
- Find out more about dementia.

How could you go about meeting these goals?

Figure 14
Monitoring
vital signs

Objective one is to become competent at **vital-signs monitoring**. If you have never done this before you should attend a training course and then have supervised practice, followed by an assessment of your knowledge and skills. Your manager should advise you and may be able to organise the training. This might be work based or may require you to go on a study day. Table 8 gives you an example of how you might plan your training.

Table 8 Objective and action

Objective one	Action
To be able to monitor vital signs of patients/individuals	• Attend study day. • Practise under supervision in the workplace. • Complete assessment on vital-signs monitoring.

The actions listed should enable you to progressively develop your knowledge and skills and build on these through supported practice.

Objective two is to set up a relatives support group. This could be achieved by consulting and spending time with someone who has done this in another area of your care organisation. Arrange to meet, and perhaps work with or shadow, this person in their support group. Ideally this person would also be able to explain how they went about establishing such a group. This situation provides a good example of how development goals can be achieved by learning from others. This strategy would give you an opportunity to observe what others have done. It also enables you to benefit from their experiences, thereby avoiding some errors.

The final objective in our list is for you to increase your knowledge of dementia. If this was one of your development goals, your manager might ask you to find some information on the subject. You might also be asked to produce a list of possible study days or other ways that you could gain this knowledge. If you have never done this before, the task could be difficult. Useful starting points could include:

KUS 7

- The internet – to carry out a general information search.
- A library – to conduct a more specific search for books or other literature on the subject.
- Learn Direct – this is a web-based service offering advice on learning and specific online programmes (www.learndirect.co.uk).
- Your local NHS Trust – the education and training department may run a short course or have information about where courses are available.
- A local College of Further Education – this may run short courses or have library-based resources on dementia.
- Contact with your local GP practice – to speak with specialist social-work, nursing and health-visiting staff to obtain brief information or an indication of where this can be found locally.
- Voluntary and support groups – they may have specialist knowledge, skills and interests in this subject that they would share with you.

Preparing for learning

KUS 10

After you have identified your learning and development needs and have established some goals for development, you will have to look for opportunities to gain new skills and knowledge. Courses and update training sessions may seem to provide ideal opportunities for development. However, make sure that they also offer positive learning conditions. You may be familiar with training sessions and study opportunities where the learning goals just could not be achieved (see the Practical Example below). You should do your best to avoid such situations.

Training days

Damian, aged 31, went on a training day to learn how to use a new hoist that his employer had recently bought. He attended the session on a warm, Friday afternoon in a hot, stuffy training room. For long periods of the tutor's talk, Damian found himself thinking about the weekend.

A tutor demonstrated the hoist and gave everyone a chance to use it and also to be moved in it. Damian thought the experience was quite useful but felt a little self-conscious moving the others in the group. He was glad to finish early at 4 p.m., even though the tutor suggested using the last 30 minutes as practice time. Like Damian, most of the group said they felt they knew exactly what they were doing and chose to leave.

The following Tuesday evening Damian was back at work. He decided to use the old hoist that night to assist residents. The next morning was very busy. Damian had three people to assist who required a hoist. Again he used the old hoist because he was more familiar with it. On Thursday he worked with one of the nurses who had been at the unit for 30 years. She said, 'Use the old hoist – it's easier.' By Friday Damian was on duty with Elaine, a colleague who had successfully completed the new hoist training a month earlier. Elaine asked Damian, 'Why are you using the old hoist? It's going to be phased out over the next month.' Damian replied, 'The training was a waste of time, I don't know what I'm doing with the new hoist.'

➤ *Why do you think Damian's training was unsuccessful?*

➤ *What factors may have limited the benefits that Damian got from the training session?*

There are several possible reasons why Damian failed to learn during his training day, including:

- It was held on Friday afternoon.
- He did not practise enough during the session.
- He did not feel comfortable in the session.
- He was not concentrating in the session.
- He did not use the hoist immediately at work.
- He did not have a plan.
- He did not have support.
- Nobody followed up the training.
- Other people put him off.

To summarise, the conditions that are required for effective learning were absent and this undermined Damian's ability to learn effectively. You may have been on training sessions which were just as ineffective as Damian's.

Establishing the right conditions for learning

You should establish the right conditions for your own learning if you are going to gain enough from the professional development activities that you take part in. The factors that help learning are often very personal and we all have different concerns and needs. Think about your own learning preferences and needs. For example, do you prefer:

- Formal or informal learning situations?
- Teacher-led or self-directed learning?
- Classroom or work-based learning?
- A highly structured programme of learning or more personalised and individual learning packages?

Different forms of training suit different people. Try to plan for your training to be based on your learning preferences and strengths. Whatever you choose to do, you must take personal responsibility for making your own learning happen. Just going to training sessions will not make you learn. You need to play an active part in the sessions and make sense of and apply your understanding of them afterwards. Learning is an active not a passive process.

Overcoming the barriers to learning

There are many factors that can reduce your ability to learn. Acknowledging which ones affect you may be the first step in reducing their effects on your development.

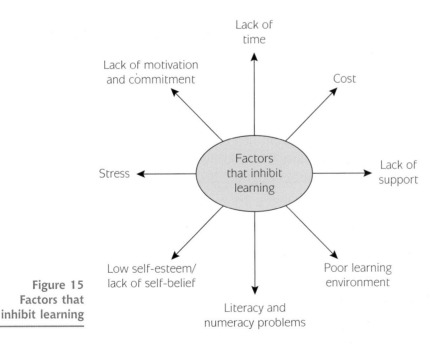

**Figure 15
Factors that
inhibit learning**

Recognising the barriers that affect your learning may not be sufficient to overcome them. You may have to make use of other, more active, strategies to achieve personal progress (see below for some suggestions).

KUS 10

Strategies for overcoming personal barriers to learning

- Many colleges and training departments offer student support services that can help people overcome personal problems that inhibit their learning.
- Workplace mentors should be able to offer support or advise you about ways of tackling personal problems that are affecting your learning.
- Tell your family and friends that you are studying. People can be very supportive if they know what you are doing.
- Ask your employer to be flexible about study time and work rotas so that you can fit your studying in. Many will be supportive and will adapt to at least some of your needs some of the time.

KUS 10

Strategies for developing your study skills

- Plan your study time effectively by allowing time for study and time for relaxation.
- Use quiet times at work and at home for study (should these ever occur!).
- Identify a place to study. Sometimes it is hard to study in the workplace or at home because there are too many distractions. Use a library or go into a quieter room away from noise if necessary.
- Additional support may be available if English is your second language or if you have a specific learning problem such as dyslexia or a physical disability.
- Read efficiently by using unit headings and the indexes of your books to guide you to the parts that you need to know about. You do not always have to read books from the beginning.
- Make brief but effective notes. Try to summarise key points as this will help you to retain information. Do not just copy from your books as you will not learn very much.
- When you have to write something, plan what you are going to write and think about why you are writing it. This will help to keep your work focused.
- Ask people to proof-read your work, and use a dictionary or the spell checker on your computer to check your spelling.
- Keep an open mind and be receptive to new ideas and sources of information. Radio and television programmes about your area of care can often be helpful.

- Keep to deadlines wherever possible. These can be motivating and will also help you to contain your learning into specific periods of your time. Try not to let studying take over your life.

- If you are struggling with your learning or are going to miss a deadline, talk to your tutor, supervisor or assessor. The sooner you tell someone about it the more likely it is that they will be able to help you.

Using new skills and knowledge in practice

Developing and using new knowledge is exciting. It can make care work more interesting as it encourages people to think and question and not just accept that things are done a certain way. This is not always easy as working in new ways and applying new skills may take more time in the short term. Sometimes it is easier to revert to old ways to get things done, but this is not necessarily advisable even when you are short of time.

Always ensure that you use any newly developed skills or knowledge in an appropriate way. This means that you should not practise beyond your level of competence and should ensure that there is appropriate monitoring and supervision of your practice. New knowledge and skills should only be used for the benefit of the individuals you care for and to make your practice more efficient and effective. You should not try out new techniques on individuals requiring care unless you are being monitored by a supervisor who can take responsibility for what you do. The individual requiring care must also give their full, informed consent.

Do's and don'ts for using new skills and knowledge in practice

- Do look for more efficient ways of working.
- Don't look for short cuts because they usually do not work.
- Do ask questions.
- Don't be afraid to challenge people.
- Do look up information in books, at the library, on the internet and in journals.
- Don't accept bad practice.
- Do give yourself opportunities for learning.
- Don't think that attending talks or lectures is just for one group of staff – learning is for everyone.
- Do allow yourself time to develop.
- Don't think that everyone learns in the same way and at the same rate.
- Do review your progress and use your development plan.
- Don't give up if you do not achieve the first time.

Dealing with resistance and opposition

Your mentor may be a colleague who remains in the background, to be contacted and consulted when needed. They should offer encouragement but allow you to get on with your job so that you can grow in confidence. However, colleagues and other people in the workplace can sometimes hinder your development. It is important that you are aware of this and challenge it appropriately.

Ignore what those tutors tell you, they do not know what it is like in the real world. I will show you a couple of shortcuts that mean you can get all your work done in half the time so you can put your feet up for a couple of hours!

You may meet challenges while completing your NVQ

Some people feel threatened by changes and, if they see you studying and working in new ways, they may feel vulnerable. Some people may also be unaware that they are using outdated ways of working, whereas others may be worried that they are doing things wrong but are unsure what to do. Some of these people may react by being very negative towards you and your ideas. They may resent you bringing your new up-to-date ideas into the workplace.

To overcome resistance and opposition to changes in your practice you will need support from colleagues, managers and the individuals you care for. The positive relationships that you have with others will help with your personal development. Let people know what you are doing and ask for their advice. Supervision and support are essential when you are using new knowledge, and having the opportunity to practise and build confidence should not be underestimated. A few ways of dealing with this kind of hostility and resistance are suggested below.

How to challenge hostility and resistance

- Be constructive by coming up with positive, useful suggestions and by saying how something could be better rather than saying, 'You are doing it wrong'.
- Stick to your high standards of practice.
- Try to influence others by being a role model or setting a good example.
- Explain why you are doing something in a certain way.
- Discuss issues at team meetings.
- Present your ideas and comments in a way that supports your colleagues and does not undermine them.
- Promote the benefits for everyone.
- Respect and listen to other care workers.

Reviewing personal development plans

As you are studying and building up skills and knowledge you should monitor your development and progress. Your personal development plan will help you to monitor your progress. It should contain information on your current skills, abilities and achievements and should also set out your development goals or targets. Reviewing these goals or targets is a good way of checking whether you have acquired new skills and further knowledge.

Figure 17
Reviewing
your personal
development
plan

It is important to remember that a personal development plan is just that – a plan. In other words, it is about things that you would like to happen, but it is also flexible. You should see it as a tool to help you achieve your development goals and to give you direction and guidance. Look at it regularly and use it as a central part of your ongoing development as a care worker. Whenever necessary, arrange to discuss and update your plan so that it always reflects your needs, achievements and goals. You can ask yourself a number of review questions to assess your progress.

Review questions

- Are you making progress towards achieving your goals?
- Are the methods that you have identified to achieve your goals working?
- Have you got the skills and knowledge you need and are you starting to use them in the workplace?

Remember that if your work or personal circumstances change it may not be possible for you to meet all of the goals in your personal development plan within the original timescale. Some or all of your goals may need to be changed or rescheduled to reflect your new situation. Therefore, it is essential to review your personal development plan and to check your own progress at regular intervals. Do not wait for your six-monthly appraisal or annual performance review meeting as it may be too late to change anything then.

Maintaining your skills and knowledge

KUS 3, 6

As care settings are constantly changing, it is necessary for care workers to continually learn and develop. This is why learning at work is often called continuing professional development or CPD.

Mandatory study or training (sometimes also called essential or compulsory training) covers subjects or issues that are common in many caring roles. Although your employer is responsible for providing mandatory training opportunities, it is your responsibility as a care worker to attend and learn from them. If that training is not completed on a regular (usually annual) basis a care worker may be deemed not safe to do their job. Learning of any sort is an opportunity to think about things, even when it relates to subjects that you feel you know about. Changes and developments happen all the time and there are always improvements in technology or further research that may indicate a better way of doing something.

As you go through your NVQ you will be continually developing your practice as a care worker. Your progression through the award and completion of the units should provide you with opportunities to demonstrate that you can evaluate your work and use your new knowledge and skills in practice. As changes occur in your workplace, you will need to review and re-evaluate your work and your knowledge so that you can adapt to these.

Identifying what you know and what you need to know, clarifying what is going well and what requires further development are essential parts of this process. It is important to be always open to new ideas. If you discover a conflict of opinions or new ways of doing something, try to find out more and, with appropriate supervision and mentoring, look for ways to use this to develop your practice and the quality of care that you provide.

Developing your care practice safely

KUS 1, 2

The purpose of developing new skills and knowledge is to become a better care worker.

However, new skills and knowledge are only useful when you are able to apply or use them in practice. Practice is very important for effective learning. Research shows that people learn only 20% of what they are told, but they retain 80% of what they learn through practice. Think about how you learnt to drive, swim or cook. You will probably agree that your **skills** were not learnt through theory lessons.

One of the dilemmas that you may face as a care worker who is developing their knowledge and skills is whether (and when) to say that you are learning. This can be off-putting for some individuals receiving care and your colleagues may suspect a lack of competence. However, it is important to alert people to situations where you are learning new skills and to get supervision for procedures that you need to practise. There may be situations when it is not safe, or even legal, to apply your new knowledge or skills in the workplace and you should never practise beyond your level of competence.

Figure 18
Practice makes
perfect

Saying that you are practising or need supervision is not the same thing as saying that you do not know what you are doing. As a learner, you might be slower than a more experienced member of staff. However, you might also be more thorough because you are doing everything carefully. When you do something new or use a procedure for the first time, a risk assessment should be conducted beforehand to ensure that both you and the individual are safe. Remember that in many work situations you cannot practise by yourself until you are assessed as competent. For example, you must always be supervised when using new equipment and whilst you are building up the skills needed to use it safely and effectively. Before you try out any skills that you have learnt on a training course or which a colleague has shown you, always check with your supervisor or manager to see if direct supervision is required.

Mentoring, supervision and coaching in the workplace

KUS 12

To make practising and building new skills as effective as possible, your employer should provide adequate supervision and, ideally, work-based coaching and mentoring. You can then be given feedback about what you are doing well and which aspects still need improving. You should find out what supervision, support and mentoring systems are available in your care organisation and you should use them to obtain support and guidance as you develop.

Remember that it was probably through these supervision and support systems that you initially identified your strengths and weaknesses (see page 77). You should continue to make use of these systems as you learn and start developing skills and knowledge in practice. Remember also that learning does not have to be formal. It can be achieved through working with your mentor as you discuss and share ideas and obtain feedback on what you are doing.

Key points – using new and improved skills in practice

- The aim of professional development is to gain new skills and knowledge so that you can improve your current level of performance.
- Producing and working through a personal development plan with a supervisor or mentor is the most effective way of achieving progress.
- A personal development plan involves an assessment of strengths and weaknesses, the setting of goals or objectives for improvement, and a learning process through which you can make changes and improvements to your practice.
- It is important to ensure that you are supported by others and that you use the kinds of training and learning activity that best suit your preferred learning style and development needs.
- New skills and knowledge should be used in a safe and supported way when you introduce them into your care practice.
- Personal development plans should be monitored and reviewed regularly to ensure that you are making progress and are continually working to achieve higher standards of care practice.

Unit
HSC23 Are you ready for assessment?
Develop your knowledge and practice

This unit is all about how to think carefully about your work practice and ensure your knowledge and understanding. It is about how you seek appropriate help and opportunities to develop your skills and understanding, and then how you use these new skills and knowledge in your work.

It is helpful to look at the content of this unit at the beginning of your assessment for the NVQ. The initial assessment planning with your assessor is an ideal opportunity for you to consider and review your skills in each of the units you will be taking as part of the qualification. Looking at the Scope, performance criteria and knowledge in each of the NVQ units will prompt you to think carefully about your skills, as will feedback from your assessor. Your progress through the NVQ assessment itself, evaluating your skills in each unit and how you use any additional training should provide plenty of evidence for this unit.

Your assessment will be carried out mainly through observation by your assessor and should provide most of the evidence for the elements in this unit. This could include your assessor observing your discussions with colleagues, individuals and your manager. Observation will also be a key way of assessing how you are using your new skills and knowledge in real work activities covered in the other units.

Direct observation by your assessor

Your assessor will need to plan to see you carry out the performance criteria (PCs) in each of the elements in this unit.

Preparing to be observed

You must make sure that your workplace and any individuals and key people involved in your work agree to you being assessed. Explicit, informed consent must be obtained before you carry out any assessment activity that involves individuals or which involves access to confidential information.

Before your assessments you should read carefully the performance criteria for each element in the unit. Try to cover as much as you can *during your observations*. Remember that you and your assessor can also plan for additional sources of evidence if full coverage of all performance criteria is not possible.

▶

Other types of evidence

You may need to present other forms of evidence in order to:

- Cover criteria not observed by your assessor.
- Show that you have the required knowledge, understanding and skills to claim competence in this area of practice.
- Ensure that your approach to developing your knowledge and work practice is consistent.

Your assessor may also need to ask you questions to confirm your knowledge and understanding of this unit.

Check your knowledge

1   Identify at least three different sources of information that you could use to evaluate your current knowledge and skills in care work.

2   Describe the important role that self-awareness plays when you evaluate your current knowledge and skills for care work.

3   Describe the purpose of an appraisal.

4   Identify and describe what you would need to do to put together a personal development plan.

5   Explain how you could monitor the progress you are making towards achieving personal development goals.

6   Explain what continuing professional development (CPD) involves and give reasons why it is important for care workers to use CPD opportunities when they are available.

Ensure your actions support the care, protection and well-being of individuals

*This unit focuses on ways of valuing, respecting and treating individuals and other people equally and with dignity. The unit also considers how and why care workers should challenge and respond to **unfair discrimination** and work to protect individuals from actual or likely danger, harm and abuse. You need to know how to minimise the likelihood of individuals being maltreated, neglected or abused. You should also understand that a range of **legislation** exists to protect individuals from such situations. This should be put into practice through the policies and procedures of your care organisation.*

This unit links with all other NVQ units because individuals should have their legal and human rights respected in all aspects of their lives. You will have to show your assessor that you are aware, and respectful, of the rights of individuals throughout your study and in all observations of your care practice.

This unit contains three elements:

⌒ *HSC24a Relate to and support individuals in a way they choose*

⌒ *HSC24b Treat individuals with respect and dignity*

⌒ *HSC24c Assist in the protection of individuals*

⌒ Introduction

The people you provide care for are the most important people in care settings. Their needs for care, protection and support should be the **paramount** concern of care workers and others who work in a care organisation.

In your care practice you should aim to put individuals' needs first. Sometimes care workers do this for moral reasons. The idea of caring suggests that we should be concerned for others and pay careful attention to their needs. Our actions as care workers should be driven by a desire to do what is best for individuals, not by what is in our own best interests. There are no circumstances in which it is acceptable to harm or endanger the well-being of an individual.

This positive view of care practice is reflected in and supported by:

- The value base of care.
- The legal framework of care practice.
- Organisational policies and procedures.
- Professional codes of practice.

Values in care

The value base of care is an important and widely used concept in the fields of health and social care.

The term 'care value base' is used to describe a set of **values** and principles that are thought to be relevant and common to health and social-care work. The value base of care is now widely used as an **ethical** guide to care practice within health and social-care workplaces.

Figure 1
Examples of values that provide the value base for care work

The term 'care value base' may not be familiar to some registered, qualified care workers. Registered nurses, occupational therapists and physiotherapists, for example, are familiar with care values but may see their own professional **codes of practice** as the source of these values. Despite this, care workers generally tend to be committed to basing their practice on a very similar value base.

Why we need a value base in care

You are working in a **multicultural** society and may come into contact with lots of different individuals with various care needs and problems. In your everyday work you need to be able to recognise individual needs and differences in those you provide care for, whilst also treating each person equally and fairly. How can you achieve this? By applying care values consistently.

The value base of care provides clear guidance on how to achieve best practice. Its use protects individuals from poor-quality care, neglect and mistreatment and gives care workers positive guidance on how to achieve high standards of practice.

KUS 4, 8, 9

The value base of care is founded on the two core principles that every individual:

- Should be respected and treated as worthy and important in their own right.
- Deserves to receive fair and correct treatment in society.

Figure 2
Care workers
come into
contact with
ethnically/
socially
diverse people

These fundamental principles can be put into practice by:

- Promoting equality in care practice.
- Respecting differences.
- Supporting individuals' rights.
- Promoting choice and **empowerment**.
- Maintaining confidentiality and privacy.
- Promoting **anti-discriminatory practice**.

In addition, care values find their way into practice through:

- *Laws* that grant and protect the rights of individuals including the Sex Discrimination Act 1975 and 1986 and the Race Relations Act 1976 and 2000 and the Data Protection Act 1984 and 1998, for example.
- *Codes of practice* that set standards and offer guidance to care workers.
- The *policies and procedures* of care organisations that identify how care workers are expected to deal with specific issues, such as health and safety, complaints or equal opportunities.

KUS 1, 7, 8, 9, 10

Care workers put the value base into practice by using effective communication and through the supportive care relationships that they develop with individuals.

The legal framework of care practice

All care workers have a responsibility to work within a legal framework. This means, for example, that care workers have a legal obligation to respect individuals' rights and treat all individuals fairly and equally. The law relating to equality and care practice comes from a number of sources. These include the:

- Human Rights Act 1998.
- Race Relations Act 1976 and 2000.

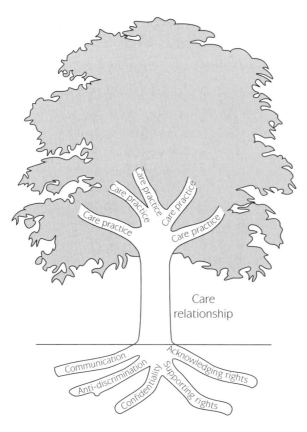

Care practice
Care practice
Care practice
Care practice
Care practice

Care relationship

Communication
Anti-discrimination
Confidentiality
Supporting rights
Acknowledging rights

Figure 3
Communication and care values are the roots of good care relationships

- Sex Discrimination Act 1975 and 1986.
- Disability Discrimination Act 1995.

The interests of the individuals you provide care for are also protected by the legal rights that they have under the:

- Data Protection Act 1998.
- Care Standards Act 2000/Codes of Practice.
- Protection of Vulnerable Adults 2004 (POVA 2004).

KUS 1, 2, 3, 7, 8, 9

KUS 3, 4, 21

As well as treating individuals fairly and equally, you have a responsibility to protect them from unfair discrimination, neglect and abuse. To do this you must be aware of the laws that have been written to protect members of vulnerable groups. You also must be aware of your own attitudes to **diversity** and difference.

Providing positive care

Positive care practice is based on, and always occurs through, the relationships that you develop with the individuals you provide care for. To some extent these relationships rely on care workers having appropriate personal qualities. The ability to be kind, understanding, sensitive and compassionate towards others plays a part in this. However, by themselves these personal qualities are not enough. As well as being caring, effective care workers also need:

- A range of communication and interpersonal skills (see unit HSC21).

- A person-centred approach to individuals that is based on the use of **empathy** and respect for each person.
- A commitment to care values.
- An anti-discriminatory approach to practice.

KUS 2, 3, 4, 9, 12, 14

Positive care practice requires a combination of appropriate personal qualities and an understanding of how the care needs of all individuals can be met in ways that are respectful, supportive and focused on individual health and well-being.

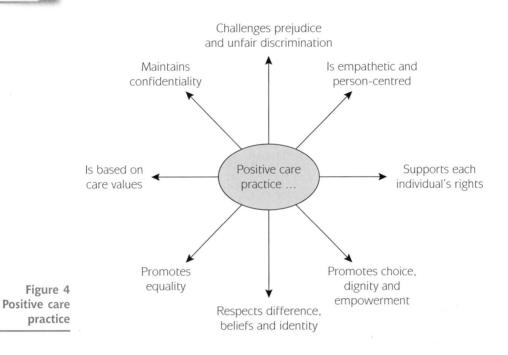

Figure 4 Positive care practice

Challenges prejudice and unfair discrimination

Maintains confidentiality

Is empathetic and person-centred

Is based on care values

Positive care practice …

Supports each individual's rights

Promotes equality

Promotes choice, dignity and empowerment

Respects difference, beliefs and identity

Element HSC24a

Relate to and support individuals in a way they choose

People who need care often feel vulnerable and relatively powerless in relation to the care workers who work with them. The experience of a significant illness, disease or condition can be disabling for anyone. However, regardless of the health and/or social-care needs that an individual has, you should always accept that they retain the right to make their own choices and decisions. In this section of the unit we will explore how you can relate to and support individuals in ways that empower them to make their own choices and decisions.

Treating people as individuals

Each of the people you work with is an individual in their own right. Sometimes this may be forgotten, especially if you or your colleagues find yourselves concentrating on task-orientated care. For example, there may be lots of baths to do and apparently non-stop meals, linen and medication to give out. However, there is always a person involved in each of these situations.

The particular needs, wishes and preferences of each individual should come first when you are planning, preparing and actually providing care for them. This is more demanding and time-consuming than treating everyone the same because they are all old or they have all got dementia, for example. This type of 'conveyor-belt care' may be efficient, time-saving and cost effective but it is also impersonal, dehumanising and undermines individuals' rights. It puts the task of getting the job done before the needs of the individual who should be the main focus of your attention.

KUS 2, 3, 12

Putting people's individual needs, wishes and preferences first can be difficult when you have a demanding workload and a busy timetable. Despite this, you should work with your colleagues and supervisors to identify ways of delivering care effectively whilst also ensuring that each person is treated and respected as an individual.

Finding out about individuals

Behind every hospital or social services number, every diagnosis, and every client, patient and service-user label there is an individual. This is a unique person who has particular characteristics, needs, wishes and preferences. It is this person that you need to build a relationship with and provide care for.

In some ways, obtaining information about the individuals in your care setting is not difficult. Most people will have a range of medical records and other official notes that contain lots of information about them. If you read these records you may find out about the person's personal and medical history, for example. You may also read about their past operations, previous treatments and current problems. But what does this tell you about the person's individual needs, wishes and preferences? You cannot get the views of the individual from notes written by someone else. You may not get details about the person's everyday life that are important to them. To do this you must develop an effective relationship and use your communication skills to get to know the person *as a person*. For example, if you think about individuals you currently provide care for, do you know:

- Whether they prefer tea or coffee (or something else) to drink?
- What sort of clothes they like to wear?
- What their favourite food is?
- What personal care they can provide for themselves and what they need help with?
- How they want specific aspects of their care provided?
- What their favourite hobbies and leisure activities are?
- What they do not like to do and what might annoy them?

KUS 2, 3, 11, 12

Asking questions about the individual's past life and experiences is important. It helps the individual to tell their story and have others recognise them as a person who is a lot more than their current situation, diagnosis or care needs.

Promoting and supporting choice

Adults who need or are receiving care should continue to feel in control of their lives. Individuals need to be encouraged to make their own choices. They should be enabled to make decisions on the basis of their own wishes and preferences. You can promote and support choice by:

- Finding out what each individual's likes and dislikes are.

- Developing a unique relationship with each of the people you provide care for.

- Adapting your communication style to ensure each individual can communicate as effectively as possible.

- Encouraging and supporting each individual to do what they can for themselves. This is known as providing active support.

- Offering individuals a choice of activities and the choice as to whether and how they participate in them.

- Giving people different options on both large- and small-scale decisions that affect them.

KUS 2, 3, 4, 11, 12

Individuals may not always be able to make major lifestyle or treatment choices independently. However, every person should be given the chance to make the choices and decisions that they are able to make. To support individuals in doing this, you should be aware of their particular wishes and abilities. If you have developed an effective relationship with the people you are caring for, they will feel more confident about making their wishes and preferences known. If a person is unable to make their needs, wishes or preferences known, you should do what is in their best interests not what is quickest or easiest for you.

Putting choice into practice

'Giving individuals choices' is a nice, well-meaning phrase that few care workers would dispute. The difficult part is finding ways of putting this into practice every day. It is worth reflecting on your own current practice and the way that your care setting deals with issues of individual choice:

- How much choice do individuals currently have in your care setting?

- Could they be given more choice or supported to make more of current opportunities to make their own decisions?

- What do you currently do to offer individuals choice and to support them in making their own decisions?

- How could you improve the way that you promote and support individual choices in the future?

It is worth thinking about the everyday aspects of individuals' lives in your care setting and your role in this. For example, eating, personal hygiene, leisure activity and sleeping routines all provide lots of chances to identify and promote individuals' particular wishes and preferences.

Practical Example

Working with an individual to promote choice

Kelly arrived at Mr Kwame Mafuso's house to bathe him. She had never met Mr Mafuso before and was replacing her colleague Deirdre, who was on holiday. Mr Mafuso was in bed when Kelly arrived and let herself in. He was not expecting to see someone different. Kelly thought that Mr Mafuso was a bit grumpy, and later she said that he did not speak to her politely.

Kelly and Mr Mafuso soon disagreed about whether he would have a bath. Kelly had already run the bath, had chosen some clothes for him and collected some towels and toiletries together. Then she told Mr Mafuso that he needed to have a bath. Mr Mafuso said something that Kelly did not understand. She noticed that he looked a bit annoyed and he refused to let her help him out of bed. Kelly asked Mr Mafuso to co-operate, telling him, 'I'm just doing my job.' Mr Mafuso told her to leave his house. Kelly left and she reported the problem to her supervisor.

➤ *Identify the care values that Kelly should have used in her interaction with Mr Mafuso.*

➤ *To what extent has Kelly offered Mr Mafuso a choice in the way his care is provided?*

➤ *Suggest how Kelly could have promoted and supported choice in this situation.*

Promoting and supporting potential

KUS 2, 3, 4, 8, 11, 14

Each person that you provide care for has the right to expect more than simply being kept clean, comfortable and well fed. Do your best to support them in using their skills, interests and abilities to give them a fulfilling life. Part of your role is to

Figure 5
Involvement in recreational activity allows people to use the skills and abilities that they have

encourage and enable individuals to use leisure and recreation activities, their existing abilities and skills and any educational opportunities that may be available to them. Being old, unwell or disabled does not stop a person having a varied and interesting life. Boring routines, restricted opportunities, isolation and a lack of support are the real things that hold back potential and reduce the quality of individuals' lives. Each person has the right to expect that care workers will look for ways to promote and support their potential and to maximise their quality of life. There are limits to what can be achieved within any particular care setting, but do your best to make people's lives interesting and worth living.

KUS 5, 6, 8

> ### Identifying individual interests and potential
> - What strengths and abilities does the person you provide care for have?
> - Does the person have a particular interest, or did they have one in the past?
> - What activities bring them pleasure?
> - Do they experience any problems taking part in their favourite activities? Are there ways of overcoming these problems?
> - What new activities could be introduced to match the person's interests?

Experiencing and resolving conflict

KUS 4, 5, 12, 20

Providing choice and enabling individuals to make their own decisions is generally a good thing and is seen as a positive approach to practice. However, there may be situations where individuals' wishes and preferences cannot be met. A conflict may arise in this situation. For example, you may be instructed to carry out some care that the person does not wish to have. An example of this would be someone not wanting a bath, or not wanting to get out of bed at a particular time, or a person with diabetes wanting to have the same food as everyone else.

KUS 1, 2, 3, 8

As we have already said, adults have the right to choice but certain choices may result in risks to themselves or others. Some risk-taking by individuals is acceptable and is supported by laws such as the Human Rights Act 1998 and professional codes of practice. However, it is also important to manage this type of behaviour to ensure that other people are not at risk and that minor risk-taking does not become more serious. For example, although refusing to bathe may be only very minor risk-taking, if it happens often, constantly refusing to wash may cause skin problems and may also make the individual socially unacceptable to others. In such circumstances the conflict of views or wishes needs to be dealt with sensitively and fairly.

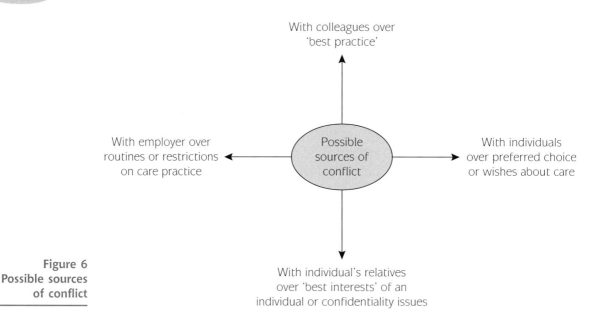

Figure 6
Possible sources
of conflict

Dealing with individual-related conflict

KUS 1, 3,
4, 6, 20

As a care worker you have to find a balance between promoting individual choice for each person and providing planned care for them. When an individual makes a choice or has a preference that does not fit in with their care plan, you are likely to experience tension or problems. There may also be a conflict with your organisation's policies and procedures on how to provide care for them. In these circumstances, it is essential that you try to resolve any conflict rather than simply overruling the individual because you think you know best.

The relationship that you have with an individual is your main tool for resolving conflicts. Mutual respect, being able to communicate well with the people you provide care for and negotiating the different ways of achieving your different goals are important parts of this kind of problem solving.

If you have developed a good relationship with the person you provide care for and can use it appropriately, you may be able to resolve conflicts with minimum fuss whilst also ensuring that you continue to meet the needs and wishes of the individual. When you cannot agree on a solution you should ask for support from someone more senior in order to help resolve the conflict. For example, this would be essential if someone with a medical condition refused to continue treatment or refused a special diet.

Conflicts with colleagues

KUS 20

Sometimes you may have a conflict with colleagues. This may be due to a disagreement over how to care for an individual or how you are delivering the care. Again you should discuss this with a senior member of staff. If this is the person you are in conflict with then you should inform them that you will be seeking further advice. You should request a meeting with a manager to try to resolve the dispute.

Reporting observations and changes

Care workers spend a lot of time with the people they provide care for. If you work shifts you may become familiar with how different people behave during the night and evening as well as during the daytime. This should give you a good idea about the state of each individual's health and well-being. In fact, observation of the person's conditions, behaviour and moods is one of the skills that you should develop. The aim of observation is to notice changes that affect an individual's care needs. For example, amongst other things, you might observe:

- How good an individual's appetite and fluid intake are.
- How well an individual manages to do the things they like to do for themselves.
- What mood the person is in and whether they are experiencing any pain or distress.
- Whether the individual has any marks on their skin or other physical changes.
- Any changes in the person's usual behaviour.
- How often an individual goes to the toilet.
- Whether an individual is incontinent.

Your observations should be reported, either verbally or in writing in an appropriate way. This issue is covered in more detail in unit HSC21 (see page 29) and in HSC25 (see page 159). However, you should be familiar with the observation and reporting policies and procedures of your particular care setting. Usually this will involve reporting and making notes about significant changes and issues that affect the individual's care needs or planned care. Your observations should be reported in a concise and clear way so that senior staff, or the particular person responsible for an individual's care, can update and adjust care plans and treatment records.

Key points – relating to and supporting individuals

- Care workers have an important responsibility to support and respect the rights and dignity of every individual.
- Treating each person as an individual is a key value in care practice.
- To support and promote individuality you need to get to know your 'clients' as individuals. You should provide them with choices and should try to meet each person's individual needs in the way that they prefer.
- Where conflict occurs over the way that care is provided, you should try to resolve the difficulties through respectful negotiation. Where this is not possible, you should seek the guidance and support of senior colleagues in order to achieve a solution.

Treat individuals with respect and dignity

Element
HSC24b

KUS 1, 4,
5, 7

This element is about how you behave towards the people you are caring for and your colleagues. You will be expected to treat all of the people you care for and your colleagues with dignity and respect. During your assessments you will need to show that you are aware of the legislation and organisational policies that affect your practice in this element. In order to treat everyone with dignity and respect you will need to be aware of why we take **diversity** and difference into account when valuing people as individuals.

Valuing people as individuals

Providing individualised care is a goal that all care workers should try to achieve. This involves identifying individual needs and adapting the way that you provide care to meet the particular needs of a person. This can only be achieved when the people you care for are genuinely valued as individuals.

There are many situations where 'client', 'patient' and 'service user' labels, medical diagnoses ('hip fracture', 'confusion', 'renal failure') and the jargon of a care setting ('EMI', 'chronic', 'diabetic') mean that we forget that we are caring for individuals. Valuing people as individuals means that you do not **stereotype** or engage in **labelling** them.

Figure 7
Don't label
people

KUS II, 12

If you are going to avoid labelling and stereotyping, take time to get to know the people you provide care for. You need to:

- Find out about each individual's beliefs and values.
- Talk to them about their preferences and wishes regarding diet, personal care, clothing and other aspects of their everyday lives that are important to them.
- Accept and show respect for diversity and difference.
- Find out about their life so that you can understand them as a person.
- Find out how they prefer to be addressed. For example, do they prefer Mr, Ms, Miss, Mrs, their first name or some other form of address?

Respecting individuals' dignity and privacy

KUS 2, 3,
6, 7, 16

Care settings can be difficult and impersonal places in which to live. People who require care are often at a vulnerable point in their lives because of illness, disease or impairment. So an individual may not be able to meet their own needs independently and may rely on care workers to support them. It is essential in such situations that you respect each individual's dignity and privacy.

Figure 8
It is important that you remember to respect individuals' privacy in a busy care setting

The issue of dignity and privacy crops up frequently in everyday care work, for example when an individual needs assistance with personal tasks such as washing, dressing, eating and using the toilet. A person's **self-esteem** may be damaged if they are unable to carry out these personal tasks independently. They may think they are a burden on others, helpless or somehow incapable. When providing support and help in response to an individual's needs you should show respect and protect the individual's **dignity**. You must try to understand the individual's feelings, provide emotional and practical support and respond to the individual's wishes and preferences as much as possible. It is disrespectful and abusive to openly draw attention to the individual's problems or to criticise or complain about any difficulties that you may have in meeting their particular needs.

Individuals should always have privacy when personal care is being provided. When they are being dressed, undressed, taken to the toilet or being helped to wash, individuals should be out of sight of other people. You need to take simple precautions like closing doors, keeping curtains drawn and not leaving individuals partially undressed in situations where other people may walk in or see them. Also, you should respect an individual's right to privacy in their room. Knock before you enter and check that it is all right to come in. That is much more respectful than simply throwing the door open, carrying out tasks without asking or sitting on a person's bed or chair without asking permission. Showing respect for each person's dignity and privacy is an important way of demonstrating that you value them as an individual. It also shows that you acknowledge their rights and want to treat each person fairly and equally whatever their needs, problems or personal difficulties.

Respecting individuals' diversity, culture and personal values

Care workers have to be open-minded and adaptable enough to meet the health, developmental and welfare needs of all potential individuals. This is a challenge because people who use care services come from a UK population that has social and cultural differences. For example, services have to meet the needs of people of different ages, genders and sexual orientation, people who have differing ethnic backgrounds, and people with a broad range of abilities, disabilities, illnesses and impairments.

Also, the people you provide care for may have a wide range of spiritual and religious beliefs and personal values that are very important to them. These may affect the way that they want care services to be provided for them. People who have an active faith may have particular worship, dietary and personal-care needs. People who have no specific faith or who reject the idea of religion have the right not to participate in worship activities. This should be respected even where it is inconvenient to make alternative arrangements for them. Therefore, it is important to find out what a person's **culture** and religion mean to them and to find out which festivals they celebrate and which customs they keep.

Ultimately, care workers have to be positive about social and cultural diversity in order to provide care in a fair and equal way to individuals from all backgrounds. Lack of awareness of social, religious or cultural difference can lead to insensitive care. Deliberately ignoring a person's particular needs because of prejudice or a lack of respect for diversity and difference is unacceptable and **discriminatory**.

Challenging prejudice and unfair discrimination

Care organisations should encourage equality of access and the fair and equal treatment of all individuals. These issues are usually covered in the equal opportunities policy and the admission and other procedures that are associated with this. Despite this, members of some social and cultural groups regularly complain that they are treated less fairly or that they have been unfairly discriminated against. In the past these complaints have been made against care organisations and individual care workers.

The complaints made against care organisations and individual care workers about **prejudice** and unfair discrimination reflect broader problems in British society. Some sections of the British population are still struggling to achieve equal rights and equal treatment. For example, members of black and minority ethnic groups, women, disabled people, lesbian women and gay men, older people and members of Muslim, Jewish and other non-Christian communities are the focus of prejudice and unfair discrimination in many parts of their lives. These groups may experience:

- *Direct discrimination* when they are deliberately and unfairly treated in a less favourable way compared with other people. The motive or intention behind such treatment is not relevant, though it is probably related to prejudice.

- *Indirect discrimination* where a condition or requirement means that some social groups are disadvantaged because they are less able to satisfy that condition.

Table 1 Prejudice

Focus of prejudice	Type of prejudice	Example of unfair discrimination
Sex and gender	Sexism	Paying a woman less than a man for doing the same job or similar work.
Race or ethnicity	Racism	Refusing to assess or work with an individual because of prejudices about their ethnic group.
Sexual orientation	Homophobia	Preventing gay men or lesbian women from gaining positions of responsibility and authority because 'they cannot be trusted'.
Disability	Disablism	Failing to provide toilet facilities and work conditions that are accessible to disabled people.
Age	Ageism	Having a policy of only recruiting 'young people' where age is irrelevant to a person's ability to perform a job.
Religious beliefs	Anti-semitism, sectarianism, Islamophobia	Denying a person the opportunity to worship, express or practise their faith and denigrating the value of their beliefs.

Refusing to admit a black woman with disabilities to a residential home simply because she was black and 'may not fit in too well' is an example of direct discrimination and would be unlawful. Requiring potential applicants for a care worker vacancy to 'have very good spoken English' is a condition or requirement that disadvantages some social groups (and gives others an advantage) and is an example of indirect discrimination. Unfair discrimination may be due to individual prejudice and the discriminatory activities of individual people. However, institutions, including care organisations, have also been accused of operating in ways that discriminate unfairly.

KUS 1, 4,
7, 9, 11

Institutional discrimination is usually associated with indirect forms of discrimination. This can occur, for example, where the policies or procedures of a care organisation disadvantage a particular social group whose members are less able to follow them. Because care organisations are generally keen to promote open and equal access for everyone in their local communities, they tend to take a positive approach towards identifying and tackling situations that may lead to institutional discrimination.

Anti-discriminatory care practice

In law, all users of care services have the right to fair and equal treatment. The general laws of the UK make various forms of unfair discrimination unlawful. However, anti-discrimination laws cannot stop people being prejudiced. They are a **deterrent** and provide a legal way of punishing people who act on their prejudices.

Care workers can promote equality and reduce the impact of prejudice affecting people in care settings by adopting an anti-discriminatory approach to care practice.

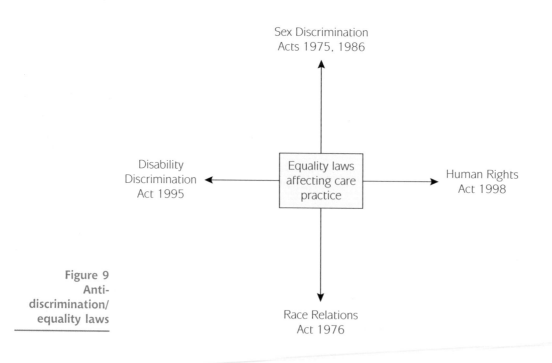

Figure 9
Anti-
discrimination/
equality laws

Anti-discriminatory practice aims to challenge all forms of prejudice and unfair discrimination. It offers care practitioners an effective and powerful way of applying equal-opportunities ideas in everyday work situations. This means you should develop ways of working that:

- Recognise the needs of people from different backgrounds including those who come from minority religious and cultural backgrounds.
- Challenge forms of stereotyping and prejudice that affect individuals' lives, including racism, sexism, homophobia and disablism.
- Actively challenge any unfair discrimination that people experience.

Anti-discriminatory care practice is achieved:

KUS 8, 9, 11, 12

- Through developing a personal awareness of how your own and other people's prejudices reveal themselves.
- By adopting a non-discriminatory approach to language (for example using non-sexist, non-racist and non-disablist words and phrases).
- By being committed to the care value base.
- By working within the legal, ethical and policy guidelines set by legislation, professional bodies and employers.

Acknowledging and reflecting on prejudices

You cannot challenge prejudice and use anti-discriminatory practice until you are aware of your own prejudices (see the box on page 128). Recognising that you may have values and beliefs that are prejudiced requires a great deal of honesty and personal reflection. It does not necessarily mean that you are admitting to being a bad person. Instead it should be seen as a positive step. Knowing your own beliefs and values and understanding how they affect your relationships with others puts you in a better position to work constructively with people who are different to you.

Understanding the roots of prejudice

KUS 6, 11

Everybody grows up with the feelings, attitudes and values that they learn as children. These feelings, attitudes and values were taught and passed on by parents, friends, brothers/sisters and teachers – in fact by anyone who had a strong influence on us during childhood. Typically people are not aware that they are developing particular attitudes and values. The process is **subconscious** as we accept what other people think and tell us as being our own views too. Without being aware of it, we do this to ensure that we are accepted by our family or our friends. We copy what they do and accept their feelings and attitudes as our own.

So we may all have some deeply ingrained attitudes, thoughts and feelings that we are not aware of. We may only become aware of them when a situation provokes an unconscious reaction that we may not even understand. This could be something as simple as feeling dislike for a particular individual or discomfort in the presence of a particular group of people. Whilst we may realise that this is irrational, and even unacceptable, being rational about it may not make the negative feelings go away.

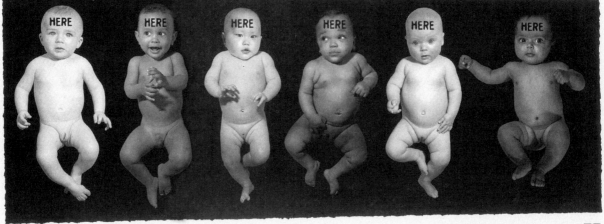

THERE ARE LOTS OF PLACES IN BRITAIN WHERE RACISM DOESN'T EXIST.

COMMISSION FOR RACIAL EQUALITY

Figure 10 The Commission for Racial Equality advertise to raise awareness

Acknowledging your own prejudice involves becoming aware of these feelings, attitudes and values so that you can control and hopefully modify them. Always make sure that you do not allow any of your prejudices to influence the way you treat the individuals for whom you provide care.

Responding to unfair discrimination in care

Care practitioners should not ignore prejudice or unfair discrimination when it occurs. Doing so could be seen as supporting the unequal and unacceptable treatment of an individual or group of people. Challenging prejudice and unfair discrimination is a part of the job of every care practitioner. You should not leave this to more senior colleagues or managers as harm and distress may already have been caused by the time they become involved.

Anti-discriminatory practice – what can you do?

- Be self-aware, question your own assumptions and be prepared to change your ideas and views about people.
- Continue developing yourself and reflecting on your ideas about equality.
- Adopt the view that people are different but of equal value regardless of their physical, mental or cultural characteristics.
- Do not judge people.
- Accept other people's physical, social and cultural differences as a positive and interesting feature of care work rather than as a problem.

- Read and become familiar with the policies and procedures of the care organisations in which you work. Ask questions about, and seek advice on, ways of putting into practice the equality and anti-discriminatory policies and procedures of the organisation.

Treating everyone the same is not necessarily a good approach to tackling unfair discrimination. This may result in you being blind to important aspects of difference and diversity. It is better to acknowledge people's differences and accept that they should be equally valued. In this way each individual's cultural, religious and identity needs are more clearly respected and can be used as a guide to providing appropriate and sensitive care.

Discrimination

Neil Sharma, aged 27, lives in a supported bungalow for people with learning disabilities. Neil is normally a very sociable, friendly and talkative person who enjoys the company of others and has good relationships with care staff. Janet, his main support worker for the last three years, recently left to begin a new job working in a day centre. Neil's dad Jim thought very highly of Janet and was quite upset about her leaving but seemed to gradually accept it. However, during recent visits to see Neil, Jim has been quite hostile to Josh the new support worker who was appointed to replace Janet. Neil has established a good relationship with Josh and does not seem to share his dad's concerns.

On a recent visit Jim shouted abuse at Josh for letting Neil hug him. Jim then told another care worker that he wanted to make a complaint because 'Josh is gay and keeps trying to touch Neil.' On his most recent visit to see Neil, Jim made an obscene gesture and directed homophobic comments towards Josh.

➤ *Identify the prejudice that is being expressed in this situation.*

➤ *How do you think Josh should respond to the hostility and abuse from Jim?*

➤ *Suggest ways in which Josh's colleagues and his manager could provide support for him in this situation.*

➤ *How could you respond in an anti-discriminatory way if you were present when Jim made homophobic comments to Josh?*

Using legal, ethical and policy guidelines

KUS 1, 8, 9

The laws that promote equal rights and equality of opportunity principles are included in a number of different types of document that can be found in care settings, such as:

- Government charters that identify entitlement to services and define national standards of care that individuals can expect to receive.
- Codes of practice produced by bodies such as the Commission for Racial Equality, the Equal Opportunities Commission, the General Social Care Council and the Nursing and Midwifery Council.
- Organisational policies produced by individual care organisations and which apply to all of their employees.

Each of these documents places responsibilities on care workers and the managers of care organisations. Failing to fulfil them can lead to care practitioners and care organisations facing a variety of punishments. Applying best practice may be demanding, but it is an important way of delivering positive care.

Acknowledging problems and limitations

You may find there are times when your feelings and attitudes prevent you from providing care in a fair and equal way. Self-awareness and perhaps the difficulties that you experience in particular individual relationships should alert you to this. Alternatively, colleagues or the person's relatives may provide feedback that suggests you need to reflect on why you struggle to care for particular individuals.

If such problems occur, you should acknowledge them and seek appropriate support and guidance. This may involve getting advice from colleagues, modifying your approach slightly or having a series of supervision sessions with your manager or supervisor where you can reflect on and discuss the issue and ways of dealing with it. Do not hide such problems or blame individuals for being difficult or unlikeable.

You must also be aware of how colleagues and individuals behave towards others and be prepared to report any action or behaviour that involves unfair discrimination. This might involve making a complaint about prejudice or unfair discrimination. Remember that you also have a right to be valued and respected. Being a care worker does not mean that you **forfeit** your own legal rights to equal opportunity or fair and equal treatment. This should have been made clear to you at the start of your employment when you were given a copy of your organisation's equal opportunities policy. Therefore, if you find you are the victim of unfair discrimination or abuse, you have a right to make a complaint and should do so.

Encouraging feedback from individuals

KUS 11, 12, 15, 16, 18, 19, 20

Every person to whom you are delivering care has the right to expect you to behave in a way that shows that you value and respect them as individuals. Remember that they have the same rights as you. Therefore, you should be able to tell individuals how to offer comments on their care. For example, they should be given the chance to comment on the extent to which they are satisfied or dissatisfied with the way that their care is being delivered. Your care organisation should have developed a feedback procedure and a complaints policy to enable this to happen. Ensure that you are aware of these and know how to use them. Your supervisor or manager should be able to provide you with information about this.

Table 2 Positive care practice

Positive care practice involves:	Example
Treating individuals with dignity and respect	This means that each individual's choices and wishes should be reflected in the way you work with them. Within your everyday work there will be routines that you will be expected to follow. These may conflict with the wishes of the people you care for but you must put their needs, wishes and preferences first wherever possible.
Ensuring individuals have privacy in all areas of their lives	The simple act of knocking on a door before entering shows that you are aware of and are respecting the individual's right to privacy.
Enabling individuals to express their beliefs and practise their religion	Remember that not all adults want to go to church on Sunday. Some may want to pray two or three times a day whilst others may not want to participate in any kind of religious worship at all.
Respecting individuals' cultural values and preferences	Some cultural beliefs may be very different to those you hold. For example, some cultures do not like baths as this means they are sitting in their own dirt; therefore they prefer showers as this washes the dirt away.
Challenging prejudice and unfair discrimination	It would be unfair discrimination to refuse to acknowledge the rights that individuals have because they do not comply with what you consider normal.

Key points – treating individuals with respect and dignity

- Care workers have a responsibility to respect each individual's dignity and privacy.
- Always show respect for the culture, beliefs and personal values of individuals.
- You should challenge prejudice and unfair discrimination by using anti-discriminatory care practice.

Assist in the protection of individuals

This element focuses on the ways you can help to protect individuals from risk, harm and abuse. To contribute to this you will need to be aware of:

- Different types of danger, harm and abuse that individuals can be subjected to.
- Factors that can contribute to the occurrence of abuse.
- The signs and symptoms of abuse and neglect.
- Ways of responding to and reporting abuse situations.

The problems of neglect and abuse

KUS 8, 9, 10, 12, 21

Some people need to use care services because they have been, or are currently being, abused, neglected or exploited. Care workers tend to be very concerned to offer care and protection to those in this position. However, sometimes a care worker becomes the person responsible for neglect and abuse when they misuse the power and influence that they have in relation to a vulnerable individual. The neglect or abuse of an individual is never acceptable. Care workers should at least notice when individuals are at risk from, or are actually experiencing, neglect or abuse and respond appropriately to ensure they are protected.

Factors that contribute to abuse

An insight into the risk factors that make abuse and neglect more likely may help you to prevent it from occurring in the first place or notice when it is occurring.

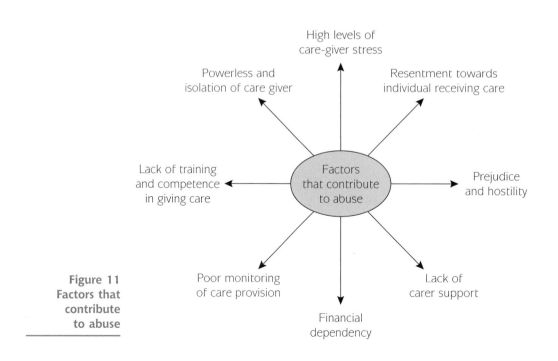

Figure 11 Factors that contribute to abuse

High levels of care-giver stress

Powerless and isolation of care giver

Resentment towards individual receiving care

Lack of training and competence in giving care

Factors that contribute to abuse

Prejudice and hostility

Poor monitoring of care provision

Lack of carer support

Financial dependency

Factors that are known to contribute to neglect and abuse situations include:

- Care-giver stress resulting from feelings of powerlessness and isolation.
- Feelings of resentment and hostility towards the individual.
- Deeply held prejudices towards members of particular social groups.
- Financial dependency on the individual.
- Unrestricted and unmonitored access to the individual's finances.
- Lack of care training and poor levels of practical competence.
- Absence of effective monitoring and supervision of a carer or care worker.

Remember also that people who need care are not always grateful or pleasant to be with. Sometimes individuals can appear deliberately ungrateful or difficult. They may not be, but when under pressure, you may lose sight of the different reasons why individuals behave or respond in the ways that they do. Anger and retaliation are inappropriate emotional responses even when the individual is actually being ungrateful, difficult, dominating or abusive towards the person caring for them.

Types of abuse

Understanding the signs and symptoms of abuse may help you to recognise and respond to warning signals or to prevent further abuse where it has already happened. Age Concern has identified several types of abuse and neglect and examples of behaviour that is associated with each (see Table 3 on page 134).

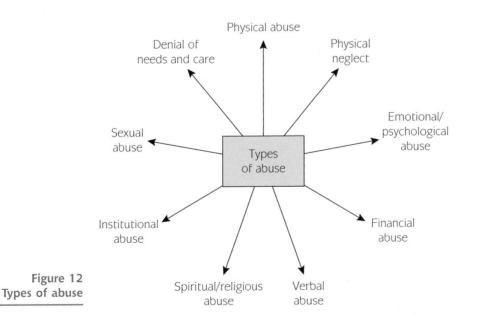

Figure 12
Types of abuse

There may be many more types of abuse depending on the kind of individuals you are caring for.

Table 3 Types of abuse and related behaviour

Type of abuse	Examples of abusive behaviour
Physical	Restraining in any way; kicking, slapping or hitting; cutting or burning; throwing things at victim; pushing or pulling; choking or smothering; force feeding; any form of unwanted physical contact.
Psychological/emotional	Mind games; putting people down; silence, ignoring the victim; treating the victim as a child; withholding affection; making the victim think he or she is stupid.
Verbal	Name calling; intimidation; being verbally threatening; shouting; using sarcasm.
Financial	Taking the victim's money; removing money from bank/post office without the individual's permission; using Power of Attorney inappropriately; shopping and not giving correct change.
Sexual	Any unwanted sexual advances; being made to watch/look at pornography without consent; rape; making jokes/comments about the victim's body.
Spiritual/religious	Degrading the victim's beliefs; withholding the means to practise; forcing adherence to a different belief system.
Neglect	Refusing to do things for the victim; isolating the victim; not allowing contact with others; keeping television/radio switched off; seating victim in a corner away from the window; keeping room door shut.
Denying the victim's needs	Not giving food and drink; not giving medication; denying need to wash or use toilet; withholding medication; overmedicating; allowing the individual to self-harm.
Institutional abuse	Treating one individual differently to all the others; not allowing individual's choices; withholding fluids to prevent incontinence; preventing individual from following religious practices; not allowing individual to vote in local/general elections; all/any of those abuses stated above.

Identifying neglect and abuse

KUS 13, 15, 17, 20, 21

Some types of abuse are easier to notice than others. For example, the signs of physical abuse can often be seen in the form of cuts, bruises and other injuries. Although the evidence of physical abuse is easily seen, emotional and verbal abuse and the denial of an individual's needs may be more difficult to recognise.

The signs and symptoms of physical abuse include:

- Unexplained bruising, especially bruising on areas of the body that are unlikely to bruise through naturally occurring accidents. For example, bruising on the inside of the thigh or on an individual's underarm would be suspicious.

- Any sign of burns or scalding should be a cause for concern.
- Regular bruising in the same place, such as fingertip bruising on a person's skin, may indicate abuse that is caused from time to time by rough handling.
- Unexplained falls resulting in injuries such as bruising on the individual's knees and hands, or breaks in their skin, or conflicting explanations about how the injuries occurred.
- Guarding reactions, such as when an individual unconsciously holds up their hands to protect themselves when approached or touched.
- Unexplained and unconscious signs of fear, similar to guarding, but usually only when a particular person is near, or when a particular procedure (washing or dressing for example) is being carried out.

Figure 13
Institutional
abuse denies
service
users their
individuality

The signs and symptoms of emotional, psychological and verbal abuse include:

- Self-induced isolation, particularly when the person is normally more outgoing and sociable towards others.
- Emotional withdrawal, especially when the person seems emotionally hurt, fearful or watchful.
- Lowering of mood, especially when this is pronounced or prolonged and unusual for a normally cheerful and outgoing person.
- Changes in sleep patterns, such as the onset of nightmares, difficulty going to sleep or broken sleep.
- Lowering of self-esteem, with the person stating or indicating that they are useless or worthless, or being harshly self-critical in a similar way.

- Loss of confidence and increases in anxiety-based behaviour. The individual may be weepy and distressed at times as well as apprehensive or overly anxious to please.
- Self-harming behaviour, such as cutting, self-neglect, attempted overdose, refusing to eat and drink or refusing prescribed medication.

The signs and symptoms of financial abuse include:

- Not having money to pay for everyday things as in the past.
- Constantly worrying about bills being paid on time or losing their place in the nursing/residential home.
- A lack of clothes that fit or are suitable for the time of year, being unable to buy new ones when weight is lost or gained.
- Unpaid bills lying around the house.
- Missing money, chequebooks or other possessions.
- Unmonitored access to the individual's cash, chequebook or bank accounts by relatives or carers.
- No food in the house (in cases of **domiciliary care**).

The signs and symptoms of sexual abuse include:

- Fear of physical contact, such as when accessing toilet or bathing facilities.
- Unexplained crying and withdrawal from social contact.
- Physical trauma such as scratches, bite marks, bruising or bleeding in the **perineal area**.
- Sexualised language used unexpectedly and inappropriately.
- Vaginal infections.
- Torn clothing, especially underwear and night clothes.

Evidence of spiritual or religious abuse is difficult to identify. Abusive actions may include:

KUS 15, 16

- Criticising or belittling an individual's religious or spiritual beliefs.
- Being actively hostile towards members of particular religious groups or faiths.
- Denying an individual the opportunity to worship or express their faith (for example, by displaying pictures or icons associated with their faith) or making them take part in services of another faith.
- Failing to support or respond to an individual's requests to see a faith leader.
- Overriding or ignoring an individual's request for particular types of food (**halal** or **kosher**, for example) or for a same-sex care worker to provide personal care.

Whilst some of these actions may be intentional, others may occur because of a lack of awareness of a person's spiritual or religious needs. The effects on an individual could include:

- Being openly distressed about what people say to them, about the denial of their needs or about the way they are treated.

- Secret performance of their own spiritual or religious rituals.
- Expressing worries and anxieties about their spiritual well-being or about what will happen to them when they die.

Like spiritual and religious abuse, it is sometimes difficult to notice that an individual is experiencing neglect. Neglect may be easier to identify in an individual's own home, but it can and does happen in residential care. Some of the signs and symptoms include:

KUS 13, 15, 17, 20, 21

- Incontinence, in an individual who is normally continent, because they cannot access toilet facilities.
- Poor physical condition due to unwashed, dirty skin, uncombed, matted and dirty hair, excessively long fingernails and toenails.
- Lack of stimulation and isolation of an individual in their room.
- The individual is relieved or overly pleased to see you and seems to feel safer while you are there.
- Noticeable loss of weight, possibly because food and drink is being withheld.
- Excessive drowsiness or confusion due to being sedated or over-medicated.
- Return of illness or disease symptoms due to not being given prescribed medication.
- Obvious evidence of self-harm (cutting, refusing food, pulling own hair out, not taking medication, self-neglect) that has not been noted or responded to by carers.

You should note that some forms of self-harm and self-neglect are not deliberate. For example, an individual might not take their medication because they are confused or have short-term memory loss as a result of other conditions. Deliberate self-harm can also be a way of expressing mental-health problems. If you come

KUS 12

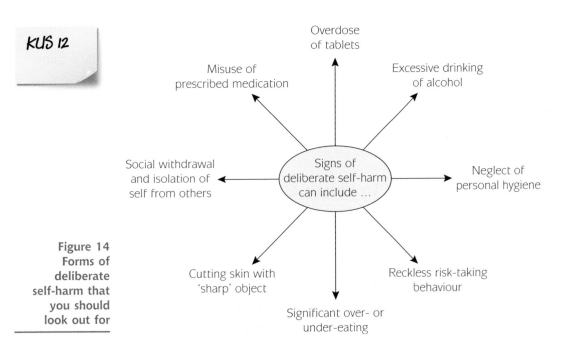

Figure 14 Forms of deliberate self-harm that you should look out for

across any of these symptoms then you should observe the individuals closely for signs of self-harm.

It is often very difficult to identify evidence of non-physical forms of abuse and neglect. Your knowledge and understanding of an individual's usual behaviour, habits and ways of responding to people and situations is often the important factor in identifying these forms of abuse. Changes in an individual's behaviour, mood or way of responding to you and other people during meal times, everyday interactions or when providing personal care may make you suspect that something distressing has happened or is happening to the person. It is important that you make effective use of your observation skills and that you respond sensitively and appropriately to any concerns or suspicions that you have.

You should be alert for any sign or symptom that is out of the ordinary for the people you provide care for. However, you should also remember that there are circumstances where unexpected marks, unusual behaviour and unexplained changes in an individual's circumstances or appearance may not be evidence of abuse or neglect. What you note may have a very different and straightforward explanation. The important thing is to note and report the unexpected, unusual or unexplained. However, do not assume that the things you are suspicious about are definitely the consequence of abuse. You should never directly accuse anyone of being neglectful or abusive unless you are an eyewitness and can verify what you have seen. Your responsibility, and the duty you have towards the people you provide care for, is to act upon what you notice in an appropriate way.

False allegations of abuse

These can sometimes be made because of:

- A personality clash between an individual and a care worker.
- Prejudice by an individual against particular carers.
- Confusion and disorientation where people report what they think happened rather than what actually happened.
- An unknown history of abuse in an individual's background that may surface when they are being helped with intimate personal care.

Responding to abuse concerns

Individuals who experience abuse or neglect in a care situation are likely to be frightened and to feel very vulnerable. If the abuse or neglect is being carried out by one of their relatives, by another care worker or by someone else closely involved in their life, they may also feel powerless and reluctant to draw attention to it. However, they are more likely to do so if they have developed a trusting relationship with you. Being reliable, honest and genuinely interested in the individuals you provide care for and always treating them with dignity and respect will provide the basis for a trusting relationship. Where this exists an individual is likely to feel more comfortable about revealing their concerns and feelings about potential and actual abuse.

When you suspect that the person for whom you are providing care may be at risk of neglect or abuse:

- Ask the individual if anything is worrying them.
- Offer to ask a more senior person, a manager or a doctor, to come and talk to them.
- If there is some obvious physical injury to an individual, such as a cut or bruise, ask the person how it happened.

The individual may insist that nothing is wrong or may ask you to keep the situation to yourself. You should never promise that you will keep a secret in these circumstances. The person may tell you about an abusive incident or ongoing situation and you may be legally obliged to reveal the information they give you. In this situation, tell the individual that the information will have to be shared with your manager, that other members of staff may need to be alerted too. Reassure them that telling you about the situation is an important first step in dealing with it.

Dealing with evidence of abuse

KUS 2, 15, 17, 18, 19, 20

A person who has experienced abuse may not wish to talk about it. They may feel ashamed, useless, or that it is their fault and that they are no longer in control of their life. Others may tell you that something has happened to them but they might ask you not to tell anyone. It is important to note that a care worker should never promise confidentiality beyond the level of their authority.

Where there are more-obvious signs of abuse, such as bruising, or where an individual has told you that they are being abused:

- Reassure the person that you will try to help them to deal with the situation.
- If your workplace policy allows, ask some questions to enable you to document the facts.
- If your workplace policy does not permit this, report the situation immediately to a senior colleague or supervisor.

When asking questions remember that you are gathering information that will be used to report back to your manager and which may form part of legal action. You should ask simple questions clearly and you should do so in a way that will not distress the individual further. The information that you need is:

- How did this happen?
- When did it happen?
- Who did it?

You should avoid asking the person why it happened to them. A person who has suffered abuse may feel that they are partly to blame. This is not likely to be true and it will not help their recovery if they feel responsible.

Reporting incidents of abuse

KUS 1, 9

Report any alleged or suspected abuse to your supervisor or a senior manager as soon as possible. Under no circumstances should you discuss your concerns with any alleged or suspected abuser. Follow the policy and procedures of your care organisation. They may direct you to document your observations and any allegation in particular records or on a specific type of incident form. Remember to keep notes on what was said, writing down times, dates and who you informed.

Figure 15
It is important to report any concerns about abuse to a supervisor or manager as soon as you are able to

KUS 10, 16, 18

If you cannot report this to your supervisor or line manager because you feel unable to do so for personal reasons or because your supervisor or line manager is the person being accused of the abuse, then you must report to someone else in authority. For example, you could report to a more senior manager, the owner of the nursing home, domiciliary care company or agency that employs you, or your Local Authority Social Services department. You could make an anonymous call if for some reason you did not wish to leave your name. Your report should still be investigated.

Dealing with an abuse allegation

You must:

- Report any signs or suspicions of danger/harm/abuse at once.
- Document what you have seen or been told, making sure that you sign and date all documentation and keep a copy for yourself in a secure place.
- Do not take information about an individual or an abuse incident from your workplace unless you are in the individual's own home.

What happens when an abuse report is made?

How abuse and neglect allegations are dealt with depends on organisational policies and procedures. Usually, the manager responsible for the care setting where the incident is alleged to have occurred will investigate after receiving your report. If the accusation is found to be correct, the manager is likely to:

- Call a doctor to examine the individual and document any physical or **psychological** signs of abuse.
- Report the allegation to Social Services.
- Report the allegation to the police.

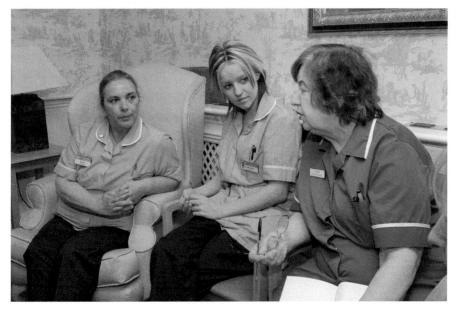

Figure 16
A senior colleague or manager should co-ordinate the response to any allegations of abuse or neglect

If the individual is being cared for at home and the suspected abuser is a family member, the Local Authority Social Services department may call a case conference. The aim of this will be to investigate the cause of the abuse and try to resolve the situation. It may result in the incident being reported to the police or the victim being moved to a place of safety.

If the suspected abuser is an employee of a care home, then the manager of the home will deal with the situation under the policies and procedures. This may result in disciplinary action against the employee and possible dismissal. It may also result in the employee being listed on the Protection of Vulnerable Adults (POVA) register and police action being taken against them.

Practical Example

Abuse

Mr Bill Eastham, aged 82, is a resident in The Brook residential and nursing home. He is confused at times and has short-term memory loss. However, Bill's long-term memory is still very good, but what he remembers can trouble him. This is because Bill was a prisoner of war for most of the Second World War and has started to have nightmares about this.

Bill's 16-year-old grandson, Michael, visits him once or twice a week. All the staff like Michael and think he is very dedicated to his grandfather. However, today, Jenna, a care student on placement, noticed that when Michael arrived to visit his grandfather he sneaked up behind Bill and whispered something in his ear. Bill became very distressed and started calling out. This made Michael laugh. Then Michael stood in front of his grandfather, so that Bill could see him, and Bill settled down and became his usual self. That night he had prisoner-of-war nightmares again.

Before he left, Jenna asked Michael what he had whispered to his grandfather. Michael looked a bit suspicious of her and seemed a little guilty. However, after persisting, Michael said, 'It's just fun, nothing really. I say, "The Germans are coming," and he gets a bit excited, that's all.'

➤ *Is Michael abusing his grandfather? If so, what type of abuse is this? If not, suggest reasons why this behaviour is not abusive.*

➤ *What would you do next if Jenna told you about the incident and Michael's explanation?*

➤ *What do you think should happen next in response to this situation?*

Key points – protecting individuals

- People who need care and support are often vulnerable to abuse and exploitation by others.
- A variety of factors contribute to the abuse of individuals in care situations. These are generally due to an imbalance in power between the carer and the person who is being cared for.
- Individuals may suffer from a number of different types of abuse or exploitation. These include, for example, physical, sexual, verbal and emotional abuse.
- Be aware of and watchful for the signs and symptoms of abuse.
- Always follow the policies and procedures of your care organisation when you need to respond to concerns about abuse or exploitation.
- Concerns or allegations of alleged or suspected abuse should be reported to a supervisor or senior manager as soon as possible.

Are you ready for assessment?

Ensure your own actions support the care, protection and well-being of individuals

This unit is all about how you regard and value people equally and with respect and dignity. It is about encouraging individuals to express their preferences, respecting their choices and ensuring they are protected from danger, harm and abuse.

Most of the evidence you need to cover the performance criteria and knowledge specification in this unit can be gathered during your assessment in other units from your qualification, especially the optional units and also HSC21. You should consider this when planning these other units with your assessor.

Your assessment will be carried out mainly through observation by your assessor and should provide most of the evidence for the elements in this unit.

It may be that opportunities for observation by your assessor in the element relating to protection of individuals from harm and abuse are less obvious, and therefore you will need to consider the definition of harm and abuse found in the Scope of the NVQ when planning your assessment. If observation by an assessor could intrude on the privacy of individuals then some performance criteria may require alternative sources of evidence of your work practice such as expert witness testimony.

Direct observation by your assessor

Your assessor will need to plan to see you carry out the performance criteria (PCs) in each of the elements in this unit.

The performance criteria that may be difficult to meet through observation are:

- **HSC24a PCs 6, 7**
- **HSC24b PCs 6, 7**
- **HSC24c PC 6**

usually because the activities do not occur routinely.

Preparing to be observed

You must make sure that your workplace and any individuals and key people involved in your work agree to you being assessed. Explicit, informed consent must be obtained before you carry out any assessment activity that involves individuals or which involves access to confidential information related to their care.

Before your assessments you should read carefully the performance criteria for each element in the unit. Try to cover as much as you can *during your observations*. Remember that you and your assessor can also plan for additional sources of evidence if full coverage of all performance criteria is not possible.

▶

Other types of evidence

You may need to present other forms of evidence in order to:

- Cover criteria not observed by your assessor.
- Show that you have the required knowledge, understanding and skills to claim competence in this area of practice.
- Ensure that your work practice is consistent.

Your assessor may also need to ask you questions to confirm your knowledge and understanding of this unit.

Check your knowledge

1 Identify two different forms of prejudice that can lead to unfair discrimination.

2 Describe examples of care values that are used in health and social-care work.

3 Explain how care organisations ensure that care values are put into practice.

4 Describe ways in which care workers can promote and support choice for individuals receiving care.

5 Explain how a care worker can demonstrate respect for the individuals they work with.

6 Identify different types of abuse that a care worker should look out for.

7 Describe examples of the signs and symptoms of physical abuse.

Carry out and provide feedback on specific plan of care activities

This unit covers the role and responsibilities of care workers in delivering planned care for individuals. We will look at how individual care plans are developed, delivered and evaluated by care workers. The unit also looks at how care workers contribute to the monitoring and revision of planned care so that the changing needs of an individual can continue to be met.

This unit has three elements:

- *HSC25a Carry out specific plan of care activities*
- *HSC25b Provide feedback on specific plan of care activities*
- *HSC25c Contribute to revisions of specific plan of care activities*

While you are working through this unit, you will find it useful to look at the other units and cross-reference them as there are many links between them.

Introduction

KUS 2

Individualised care is a key feature of good practice throughout the health and social-care field. This type of care is based on the thorough assessment of each individual's care needs and the selection and delivery of care interventions specifically to meet those needs. Providing individualised care involves a very different approach to practice than that involved in task-focused care work. For example, a task-focused approach may involve making sure that every individual is washed, dressed and taken to the toilet before breakfast. However, a care worker using an individualised care approach would find out about each individual's particular needs, strengths and abilities and would then provide help and support for those individuals who want and need it. Care is targeted to meet particular individual needs rather than provided in an impersonal, more general way.

Individualised care can only be provided after a full assessment of an individual's care needs has been carried out. The information obtained from a needs assessment is then used to produce an individual care plan. This should identify an individual's particular care needs, set some goals or objectives that care workers are aiming to achieve by providing care and also identify the type of care required and the way it will be provided.

Ideally individual care plans should be **holistic**. That is, they should consider the needs of the whole person who is being assessed and cared for rather than concentrating on specific medical, psychological or social problems that the person has.

Care planning processes

KUS 3, 4

The assessment and care planning process begins when an individual first comes into contact with a care service. In some care organisations care workers will be very involved in all aspects of the assessment and care planning process. In other care organisations, registered, qualified or specialist care professionals carry out some or all of the assessment process and produce care plans that are then carried out by care workers. Find out what your organisation's assessment and care planning policies and procedures say about roles and responsibilities.

Although everyone has different and particular care needs, the process for assessing those needs and for ensuring that the plan of care continues to meet them is the same (see Figure 1).

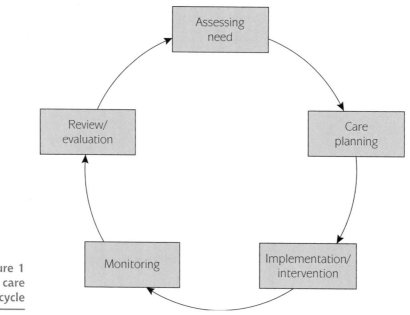

Figure 1
The care
planning cycle

Figure 1 shows what is known as the care planning cycle. The series of stages involved in the care planning cycle occur one after the other, though some parts overlap. The result of any care planning cycle should be an individualised plan of care activity that aims to meet an individual's particular needs. If you look closely at the care planning cycle you should be able to identify the four main areas of assessment, planning, implementation and evaluation.

KUS 9

Any changes in an individual's needs should be documented in their care plan notes. These should also be discussed with other care team members and, where appropriate, a new assessment should be carried out and new care goals produced. It is not usually necessary to change a care plan on a daily basis. Sometimes

Table 1 The main stages that care plans go through

Stage	What happens?
1. Assessment	This is a process of assessing an individual's abilities and needs and should cover all aspects of human functioning. For example, assessment should cover the individual's ability to mobilise, access toilet facilities, wash and dress, communicate and care for themselves.
2. Planning	A plan of care is written using the information gained from the assessment. This plan details the activities and instructions that care workers need to implement in order to ensure that the individual's particular needs are met. The plan is likely to define the level and frequency of care provision and should set goals or targets against which the care delivery can be evaluated at specified points in time.
3. Implementation	This is the stage when care is actually provided by carrying out the activities and instructions contained in the care plan.
4. Evaluation	This is the process of checking whether or not the care plan is meeting the needs of the individual. This part of the process is governed by the needs of the individual. The effectiveness of the plan should be monitored continually and commented on in the individual's records each day. A more formal review is carried out at stages when care plan goals or targets should have been achieved. A plan of care should be revised and updated to ensure the individual is cared for in ways that comply with their wishes and ensure their health and safety.

changes in an individual's needs and general condition will take months (or even longer) to occur and may be relatively minor. Despite this, there should always be an ongoing process of monitoring and evaluation to ensure that a care plan remains appropriate to an individual's needs.

Reasons for care planning

There are many positive reasons for developing and using care plans in everyday care practice. Figure 2 (overleaf) outlines several of these.

KUS 5, 6

Planned care is more likely to be individualised, targeted at an individual's **priority needs** and provided in a more consistent and efficient way than unplanned care. All care team members can look at care plans for information. The shared approach and guidance that they contain ensures that the different care workers are all working towards the same carefully selected and individualised goals. The monitoring and evaluation phases of a planned-care approach also ensure that care interventions are reviewed and are only either changed or continued if that would benefit the particular individual. This should help all care workers to provide high-quality care consistently whilst also recognising each individual's needs and preferences.

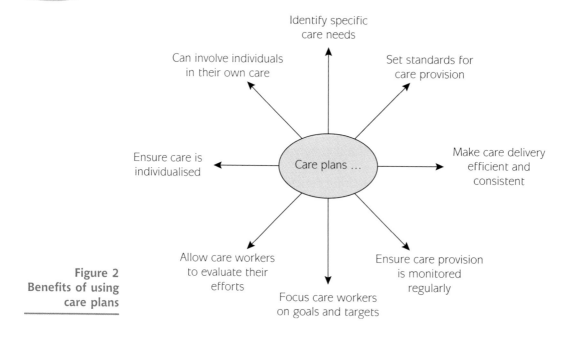

**Figure 2
Benefits of using
care plans**

Sources of information

A range of different individuals may provide information about an individual's background, needs, strengths and abilities and usual level of functioning during the assessment stage of planning care. These individuals may include:

- The family and friends of the individual.
- Other care practitioners already involved with the individual.
- Specialist care practitioners working in your care organisation who become involved with the individual when they are admitted to your care setting.

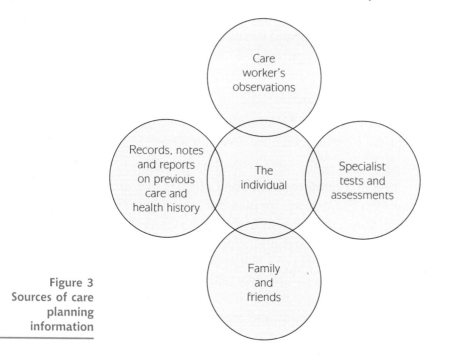

**Figure 3
Sources of care
planning
information**

It is useful to involve a variety of key people in the assessment phase of planning care as it helps to ensure that a more holistic approach is taken. It also ensures that the expertise and experience of a range of people who already have a relationship with the individual play a part in developing planned care. People who know and understand the individual already are likely to be sensitive to their needs and preferences. They may help you to gain a clearer understanding of the kind of care that will and will not help a particular individual.

KUS 1, 2

The group of people who have detailed knowledge and experience of an individual's needs and background may, at some point, include you if you have spent some time delivering care for them. You should be able to contribute to reviews and specialist assessments of an individual's needs because you will have spent a great deal of time with them. This should give you a high level of **insight**, experience and knowledge that those reviewing the plan of care can use to ensure the individual's particular wishes and needs are met.

Element HSC25a

Carry out specific plan of care activities

This element assesses your competence in carrying out specific plan of care activities. You will need to be aware of legal and organisation requirements when delivering a package of care (see units HSC22 and HSC24). You should also practise in a way that promotes equality and respects diversity and individuals' rights and dignity (see units HSC21, HSC22 and HSC24).

KUS 1, 2, 3, 4

You should have a clear understanding of any organisational policies and procedures that relate directly to how you provide care for particular individuals (such as those who are MRSA positive) as well as those policies that affect all individuals (such as general infection control issues). These policies and procedures should provide general guidance on your role and responsibilities as a care worker. They should indicate who you should request additional support from and who you should report your observations and concerns to.

Roles and responsibilities for planned care

KUS 1, 2, 3, 4

As already stated, you should have a good idea about the general requirements of your role as a care worker before you take on any responsibility for providing care directly for specific individuals. In reality, care practice requires care workers to function with others as part of a team. This means that you will also need to understand what your role and responsibilities are in relation to those of your fellow team members. You need to understand what aspects of care you are responsible for and who has responsibility for aspects of care that are beyond your level of competence and area of responsibility.

One way of clarifying your responsibilities within the care team is to consider the part that you are expected to play at each stage of the care planning cycle. Table 2 overleaf outlines a number of questions that you should reflect on and work out

**Figure 4
Care planning**

Table 2 Contributing to the care plan cycle

Stage	What role and responsibilities do you have?
Assessment	• Are you expected to carry out formal assessments of individuals' care needs when they are first admitted? • Are you expected to support and assist others who carry out formal assessments of individuals' care needs when they are first admitted? • How might you be able to contribute information to a formal assessment of an individual's need for care?
Planning	• Are you expected to write part or all of an individual's care plan? • Are you expected to work with other team members to produce written care plans for individuals? • How might you be able to make a contribution to the planning of individual care?
Implementation	• How are you expected to make use of individual care plans in your everyday work with individuals? • Are you expected to take responsibility for implementing specific plan of care activities for an individual? • How can you access and make use of related information that outlines planned care activity? • How are you expected to monitor and report on the implementation of planned care for individuals?
Evaluation	• Are you expected to take responsibility for evaluating the care plans of specific individuals with whom you work? • Are you expected to work with other team members in the evaluation of individuals' care plans? • How can you contribute your views and observations to the review and evaluation of individuals' care plans?

KUS 4, 6, 7

responses to. The answers that you provide are likely to depend on factors such as local practices in your care setting, the policies and procedures of your care organisation and your level of knowledge and experience.

As already mentioned, your role and responsibilities with regard to care planning will depend on a number of factors. You may not be as directly involved in and responsible for the assessment, planning and evaluation of individual care plans as your more experienced and registered colleagues. Despite this, all care workers will have a full and important role to play in carrying out specific care plans for particular individuals. The first stage of putting a care plan in force involves gaining access to any relevant information, records, risk assessments and guidance that apply to it.

Accessing information, records and risk assessments

The care organisation that you work for should have an individualised care planning system. This should ensure that each individual has a personal, written care plan that guides the way care is provided for them. The plan should be continually monitored and regularly evaluated and updated. Each individual's care plan and any other relevant information should be kept in a care plan file that is stored in a secure but accessible place. In your role as a care worker you must know how to access and use each individual's care plan and any records or risk assessments that go with it. Accessing care plans is generally a matter of knowing where documents are kept and what the procedures are for obtaining them. It is your responsibility to find this out and to base your care practice around the use of an individual's care plan. Remember that the information contained in an individual's care plan is confidential.

Always consult an individual's care plan before you provide care for them, even if you think that you know an individual well and understand their package of care. Check whether any changes have been made to the plan of care activities and also to update yourself on any recent feedback or comments that have been made by other care workers.

Understanding care plans and risk assessments

The way in which care planning and risk assessment information is recorded and presented will depend on the format adopted in your care setting. Large care organisations, such as NHS Trust hospitals, typically use a standard set of care planning, risk assessment and note-making forms so that the approach across all of their care areas is the same. However, the documentation you use may be unique to your workplace. In either case, it is vital that you understand how the documentation system works so that you recognise the significance of the information that it contains.

KUS 3, 6, 7, 9

Regardless of its format, care planning documentation typically contains information about:

- An individual's particular care needs or problems.

- The reasons or rationale for providing care.
- The goals or objectives that care interventions are designed to achieve.
- The particular care interventions that should be provided in order to achieve the goals/objectives.
- The timescale or date(s) for achieving the goals or for carrying out a review to evaluate the effect of the care that has been provided up to this point.
- Evaluation sheets documenting periodic reviews of progress and changes to the individual's care plan.

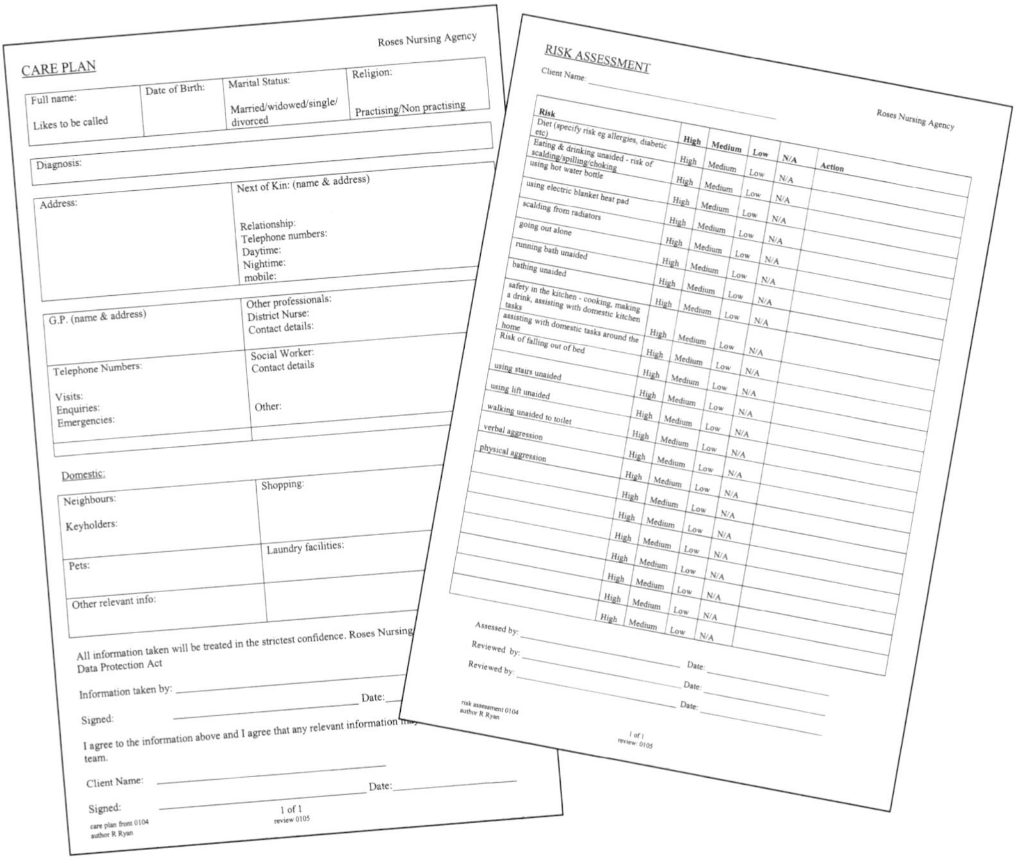

Figure 5
Examples of assessment and care planning documentation

Assessment information is usually kept in a separate part of an individual's care plan file and is typically contained on separate documentation from the care plan itself. Ideally you should read any assessment documents relating to an individual before you first provide care for them. These should help you to understand the reasons for the care that is planned. Assessment reports should also give you some insight into the individual's particular background and recent situation.

Individuals' care plans may refer to other sources of information that you will also need to read and understand. Risk assessments relating to aspects of clinical practice are one form of additional information that you should always take into account when accessing and using an individual's care plan. An example of a specific type of risk assessment used in care is the Waterlow Score (see Figure 6).

This looks at the individual's risk of developing a pressure sore. The risk assessment is divided into different areas. These areas cover all aspects of the individual's life and assess the risk of their skin breaking down. The risk assessment produces a numerical score that indicates whether the individual has a low, high or very high risk of developing pressure sores.

Guidelines
1. Waterlow score update according to patient requirement (minimum weekly)

Patient's Name:

Unit No.

Ward:

10+ AT RISK   **15+ HIGH RISK**   **20+ VERY HIGH RISK**

DATE	Month –															
TIME																
WEIGHT	Average	0														
	Above average	1														
	Obese	2														
	Below average	3														
CONTINENCE	complete/catheter	0														
	Occasional incont.	1														
	Catheter/faeces incont.	2														
	Double incont.	3														
SKIN TYPE	Healthy	0														
	Tissue paper	1														
	Dry	1														
	Odematous	1														
	Clammy	1														
	Discoloured	2														
	Broken spot	3														
MOBILITY	Fully mobile	0														
	Restless/fidgety	1														
	Apathetic	2														
	Restricted	3														
	Inert/traction	5														
	Chairbound	5														
SEX/AGE	Male	1														
	Female	2														
	14–49	1														
	50–64	2														
	65–74	3														
	75–80	4														
	>81	5														
APPETITE	Average	0														
	Poor	1														
	N.G. tube	2														
	Anorexia	3														
TISSUE MALNUTRITION	Terminal cachexia	8														
	Cardiac failure	5														
	Peripheral vascular dis.	5														
	Anaemia	2														
	Smoking	2														
NEURO	Diabetes, CVA M.S. paraplegia	4/6														
SURGERY	Orthopaedic below waist	5														
	spinal. >2 hrs on the table*	5														
MEDICATION	Anti-inflammatory Drugs	4														
TOTAL																
NURSE INITIALS																

**Figure 6
Example of
Waterlow risk
assessment tool**

*up to 48 hrs post-operative

Audit date:

If any risk assessments are used to plan care for individuals, they should be documented in the plan of care and you, as the person delivering the care, should be aware of them.

Using a care plan in practice

When you have been assigned a particular individual to support, you should first check their care plan to ensure that you can deliver the care in a way that meets the wishes of the individual. There should be clear, concise instructions within the care plan that tell you how to provide the care that the person needs. You should also be aware of any special aids or equipment that are required to enable the individual to maintain their level of independence. You should know how to use this equipment safely and must check that it is safe and in good working order before you use it (see unit HSC22, page 42).

Before you attempt to provide care for an individual, you have a responsibility to discuss anything in the care plan that you do not understand with the senior member of staff responsible for that person's care. If you are concerned about your ability to provide care in the required way or at the required standard, you should make this clear to the person in charge. Do not attempt to muddle through as this may place the individual and yourself at risk of injury.

As your knowledge and experience of care work increases you will become skilled at reading individuals' care plans. You will learn to automatically ask questions and look for key pieces of information that will help you to deliver sensitive and effective care for each individual. Some of the information you will need to know in order to carry out your duties will include the following.

Communication

KUS 1, 6, 7

- How does this individual communicate?
- Has the individual's ability to communicate been assessed?
- Do they use a hearing aid?
- Does the individual have a speech or language problem?
- What aids or types of extra support are available to enable communication?

Mobility

- Can the individual walk?
- Do they need a walking aid?
- Can they stand to get dressed?
- What level of help will you be expected to give?
- What level of assistance will the individual allow you to give them?
- Do you need to ask for help with moving and handling?
- What equipment is available to help with moving and handling this individual?
- Has a manual-handling risk assessment been carried out on this individual?

Figure 7
Assisting
individuals with
meeting their
basic needs is an
important part
of care practice

Personal hygiene

- Which aspects of personal hygiene does the individual manage indepen-dently?
- What are the individual's preferences for washing and bathing?
- Does the individual prefer to use soap, creams or gels?
- Can the individual get in and out of the bath unaided?
- Has a pressure sore risk assessment been carried out?
- What is the current condition of the individual's skin?
- What is the condition of their mouth?
- Are there any religious or cultural needs and wishes that must be met? (For example, never being totally unclothed, wanting a carer of the same sex to provide personal care.)
- What type of clothing do they like to wear?

Eating and drinking

- Does the individual have any special dietary requirements?
- Do they use any aids to help with eating and drinking?
- Does the individual have their own teeth or do they have dentures?
- Do they need support to eat or drink?
- What food and drink do they like and dislike?
- Are there any religious or cultural needs to be taken into consideration?

Accessing toilet facilities

- Has the individual had a continence assessment carried out?

- Do they have continence needs?
- Is the continence equipment available and appropriate?
- Can the individual walk to the toilet?
- Do they need any kind of help to access toilet facilities?
- How often does the individual need to use toilet facilities?

Ability to stay safe

- Has any risk assessment been carried out on the individual's ability to maintain their own safety?
- What risks (from themselves and others), if any, have been identified?
- Is the individual at risk from falls, wandering off the premises, confusion, being abused/abusive or from self-harm, for example?

Religious and cultural needs

- Does the individual have any specific dietary, worship or personal-care requirements related to their religious or cultural needs?
- Does the individual have any particular beliefs or values that you will need to take into account when working with them?
- Are you able to deliver care in a way that meets the individual's religious and cultural needs?

Practical Example

Specific care requirements

Barbara has been asked to care for Mrs Khan. English is not Mrs Khan's first language though she can understand some spoken English. Barbara cannot speak or understand Urdu, Mrs Khan's preferred language. Barbara has never met Mrs Khan and did not read her plan of care today because a more senior member of staff told her directly that she and a colleague should help Mrs Khan to have a bath and wash her hair. When Barbara and Kevin, a trainee care worker, went into Mrs Khan's room with towels and a wheelchair to take her to the bathroom, Mrs Khan became distressed and started speaking rapidly in Urdu. It was clear that she would not let Barbara or Kevin near her.

➤ *What do you think the problem is?*

➤ *What should Barbara have done before going into Mrs Khan's room?*

➤ *How could Barbara ensure that she has all of the information she needs to provide care for Mrs Khan in a safe, sensitive and effective way in future?*

Involving individuals in planned care

Earlier in the unit we said that care work is a team-based activity and that a range of people may contribute positively to the care planning process because they have different but equally valuable sources of information and expertise to offer. The key person missing from this discussion was the individual. It is vital to recognise that the individual should always be at the centre of care work. This is very much the case when planning and delivering care for individuals. Therefore, it is good care practice to involve an individual in the care planning cycle as early as possible.

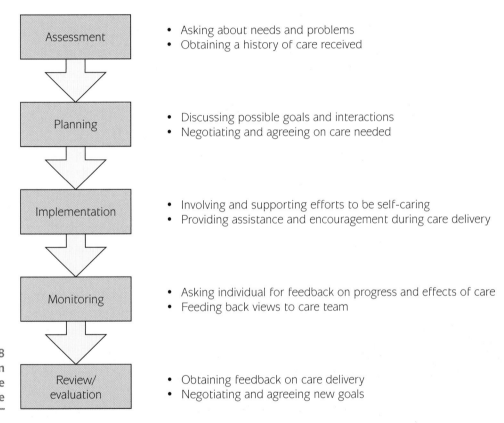

Care plan process

Involve the individual by ...

Assessment
- Asking about needs and problems
- Obtaining a history of care received

Planning
- Discussing possible goals and interactions
- Negotiating and agreeing on care needed

Implementation
- Involving and supporting efforts to be self-caring
- Providing assistance and encouragement during care delivery

Monitoring
- Asking individual for feedback on progress and effects of care
- Feeding back views to care team

Review/evaluation
- Obtaining feedback on care delivery
- Negotiating and agreeing new goals

Figure 8
Involving an individual in the care plan cycle

The assessment stage provides the first opportunity to involve an individual in planned care. Ask the individual for information about their background, needs and preferences as this may provide a lot of useful information that can be used to plan their care. It also allows them to indicate their wishes and preferences and provides the ideal opportunity to negotiate about and gain their consent for the delivery of specific forms of care.

Wherever possible you should discuss a *proposed* care plan with the individual. This discussion should be seen as an opportunity to describe and explain the care needs that have been identified, to negotiate some goals and to agree on care interventions. Discussing proposed care interventions is an important way of gaining consent and of preparing individuals for forms of care that may be intrusive or personal. It is also an opportunity to motivate and encourage individuals to maintain and make use of their existing self-care skills and abilities. This is known as using an active support approach.

KUS 2, 6

Involving individuals at this stage of the care planning cycle is likely to produce a care plan that is realistic and meaningful to the person. They should also be more inclined to co-operate with it.

If the individual has not been involved in the care planning process, you may experience some problems when you try to provide them with care. Even if they have, when you are actually caring for the individual it is important to discuss with them what you need to do and explain why. Ideally you should gain the individual's permission and agreement for everything that you do for them. Something as simple as washing someone's face, for example, could cause distress if it is not done as the individual likes it to be done or if it happens unexpectedly. An individual who prefers to use creams rather than soap and water, for example, may object strongly if they are not consulted about how you provide personal care, like washing and bathing. This kind of preference should be noted and included in an individual's care plan.

KUS 4, 8

The last stage of the care plan cycle is evaluation and review. Care workers can involve individuals in reviewing their care plans by asking them to provide feedback on what they feel has helped and how their care needs may have changed since the care plan was started. The individual's views and observations should be taken into account when reviewing and evaluating the effectiveness of a care plan and when planning further care to meet their changing needs.

HSC24, KUS 1

Involving individuals in the care planning cycle will increase the likelihood that you will be able to create and deliver a plan of care that reflects the priorities and wishes of each individual. It is not good practice to develop a care plan without consulting or gaining the consent of an individual. Individuals are much less likely to co-operate with such care plans and may feel that care is being imposed on them in ways that they do not like or agree with.

KUS 6, 7

Using support and guidance

As we have seen, individuals may be able to provide you with useful information and guidance on how best to deliver care for them. However, sometimes they are unable to actively participate in the planning, delivery or evaluation of their care because of the nature of their illness, degenerative disease or disabilities. In situations like this you may want or need to use other sources of support or guidance to confirm your understanding of specific plan of care activities.

Senior colleagues, specialist care practitioners and the relatives and friends of an individual may all offer useful support and guidance on that person's care needs or preferences. They may be able to explain detailed aspects of their care plan to you. Whenever you have difficulty understanding an aspect of an individual's care plan you should ask a senior colleague to explain it. This might occur when somebody has a particularly complex care package or when they require specialist care interventions because they have unusual care needs. If you do not understand the meaning of some of the terms used in an individual's care plan, you should always say so and ask for them to be clarified. Do not assume that you will be the only person who does not know! Acknowledging your limitations and seeking opportunities to learn is part of being a safe practitioner. Covering up and bluffing your way through situations you do not understand is likely to lead to mistakes and poor standards of care. It is not consistent with being or becoming a competent care practitioner.

KUS 1, 2, 6, 7

Sometimes an individual's family and friends can help in the care planning process. People who have an existing relationship with an individual may, for example, be able to provide information that is useful at the assessment stage of care planning. However, you should also remember that there are confidentiality issues involved. The involvement of family members and other key people must always be discussed with the individual receiving care. If the individual refuses this input, or does not want their business discussed with others, always respect their wishes, preferences and privacy.

Observation of planned care

KUS 9

Observing and reporting the effects of planned care on an individual is an important part of your care role. Try to take a holistic approach to your observations (that is, observe the individual as a whole). This means noting how care activities affect the person physically, intellectually, emotionally and socially. You should identify and note both the positive and the negative effects of care on the person and should report all changes. Sometimes apparently minor changes can be more significant than you first realise.

It is often tempting to simply observe and note whether a care intervention, such as pressure area care, is having a positive effect on the problem that it is designed to deal with (in this case the pressure sore). However, using a more holistic approach you should also observe how the person is affected emotionally by the care – especially if they are distressed by it or are becoming depressed – and whether it affects their usual pattern of social activity or causes them to behave differently (such as withdrawing or becoming isolated). It is also important to look out for situations where the care is having no effect or is making the individual's condition or situation worse. Reporting these observations could be vital in preventing further suffering and deterioration in an individual's condition.

> ### Key points – carrying out care plan activities
> - A personal-care plan should be produced for each individual that you look after.
> - Care plans identify each individual's care needs and the care services or interventions that they require.

- You should regularly consult and be familiar with each individual's care plan so that you can provide care effectively.

- Care plans should provide sufficient information on what kinds of care an individual requires and how it should be provided.

- Wherever possible individuals should be involved in planning their own care. This is likely to lead to a more appropriate and effective care plan.

Element HSC25b
Provide feedback on specific plan of care activities

This element focuses on your role in observing and providing **feedback** on specific plan of care activities. During your normal working routine you will be expected to observe each of the individuals you work with. You should also know how to report any changes in the individual's needs and preferences that are relevant to their planned care. Your observation and feedback skills should help to ensure that each individual's plan of care continues to meet their actual needs.

Feedback on care

KUS 5, 9

Feedback is simply information about something that has been done. It is an information-giving process. Whilst you may spend some of your time working independently with individuals, care work is largely based around teamwork. You may be allocated individuals to look after each day, and you may even be responsible for monitoring some individuals' care plans, but you will share the general responsibility for delivering and monitoring care with your colleagues.

The professionals who make up your care team, and who need to be included in feedback reports, will vary depending on the type of care setting in which you work. In a medical or health-care setting, for example, your team may consist of qualified nursing staff, senior care workers, physiotherapists, occupational therapists, speech therapists and other specialist medical and health-care staff. In a social or residential care setting, a team may consist of social-care support workers, social workers, therapy workers and even education staff. Some or all of these team members may have contributed to the plan of care that you help to deliver and they may deliver some aspects of it themselves.

The main sources of information that you need to use in your feedback include:

- Your own observations.

- The individual's observations and comments.

- The observations of other key people who know and are involved in the individual's care.

Your own observations will be made whilst carrying out and monitoring the effect of the plan of care that you will be helping to deliver for the individual. This is discussed in more detail in the section on monitoring and reporting changes below.

However, individuals and the key people involved in their life may require some encouragement and support in order to offer their own views and observations on the care that they receive. Individuals and their relatives may be reluctant or unwilling to comment on care services unless they are encouraged or asked to do so. This may be because they do not wish to upset or criticise individual care workers or because they do not feel it is up to them to comment. However, you should try to find ways of encouraging individuals and key people to comment on any changes in their condition (positive or otherwise) and to say whether the specific plan of care activities that you are carrying out is meeting their particular needs and preferences.

Monitoring and reporting changes

Because you are working as part of a team, it is essential that information about each individual and the care that you have provided for them is accurately relayed to your colleagues. This ensures that everyone involved in a care team is kept up to date on developments and progress affecting each individual and can maintain continuity of care.

Figure 10
A handover
meeting

What you need to feed back will always depend on the significance of what you observe. In simple terms, you are expected to look out for any changes in the individual's condition and to note how they respond to the care that is provided for them. This means observing for both the positive and negative effects of care. Noting changes, both expected and unexpected, and the extent to which the care being provided is effective requires some judgement and a clear understanding of the plan of care itself. Care workers typically use a small notepad to jot down their observations throughout their working day. This can then be referred to when making more formal feedback entries in an individual's care record or when contributing verbally in a handover or report meeting at the end of a shift.

What you should observe and report

In general, the areas that you should observe are those that relate to the individual's activities of daily living. Assessing change involves asking questions and making observations. For example:

- Has the individual's ability to communicate with you improved or deteriorated in any way? This may change because of something simple like the need for a new hearing-aid battery, or it could have a more serious cause such as losing the ability to speak because of a cerebral bleed or stroke.

- Are there any changes in the individual's ability to self care or maintain their normal level of independence?

- Is the individual complaining of feeling unwell or functioning less well than is usual for them?

- What is the condition of the individual's skin? Are there any marks, tears or bruises not seen or recorded before? If they have been documented, are they improving or getting worse?

- What is the individual's appetite like? Are they having any problems eating, drinking or swallowing? Have their food preferences changed in any way?

- Is the individual in any pain or showing any signs of distress?

- Has the individual been able to sleep well?

- Does the individual's ability to **mobilise** continue to reflect the assessment in the plan of care? Has anything happened that has affected their mobility or ability to wash and dress?

- Is the individual happy with the plan of care and the way you are delivering it? Are there any areas that need reassessment to ensure that the activities are agreed with the individual?

**Figure 11
Individuals'
needs may
change**

The frequency of reporting and recording observations about individuals and their care varies between care settings and generally depends on local policies. In some care settings care workers write something in an individual's notes at the end of every shift. In other settings observations are recorded less frequently and only when they refer to significant changes in an individual's situation or response to care.

KUS 1, 2,
7, 8

Responding to individuals' needs

KUS 4, 9

You should always take the thoughts and views of individuals seriously when they comment on the appropriateness and effectiveness of the care you are providing. Some individuals may be confident and able to comment on their care independently and without prompting. Where this happens, you should accept their comments and feed back the individual's views accurately. This can be difficult if the individual's view on the impact and appropriateness of their care is different to your own. However, you should always remember that individuals, and to some extent the key people involved in their care, have rights. They should be given choices and opportunities to express their wishes and preferences about the way they would like their care to be delivered. You can achieve this informally through conversations about progress and how the person feels about their care or through more formal care plan reviews which the individual can attend.

Some individuals may not be able or willing to comment on their care without some support from you and your colleagues. This could simply involve encouragement to make suggestions on how care plans could be improved, but it may also involve you asking some questions about whether they think anything about their care or care plan could be changed or improved.

Evaluating planned care activities

The purpose of evaluating and reviewing an individual's care plan is to assess and comment on its impact and effectiveness. This means that you are trying to work out the extent to which care plan goals have been achieved and whether (and to what extent) changes have occurred in the individual's condition or situation.

Change can sometimes occur very slowly, especially if you work with older people, individuals with chronic health problems, or people with significant learning or physical disabilities or degenerative disorders. However, this does not mean that change does not happen or that the health and well-being of these individuals should not be monitored and their plans of care reviewed and evaluated regularly. It is always important to maintain an active and real interest in every individual's health and well-being and in the quality and impact of the care that you provide for them.

Finding out what is considered normal in terms of each individual's physical and mental state and their usual level of functioning can help you to identify even very small degrees of change. It can also help you to judge whether a particular individual is functioning in their usual way. An example of this would be to note how often an individual opens their bowels. Normal for one person may be daily, whereas normal for another may be every three days. Close observation and timely reporting of this could lead to investigation and appropriate intervention for constipation if an individual's normal pattern of bowel movements stops. On the other hand, being aware that this is not a once-daily event for another individual could also ensure that care staff do not become alarmed or suggest care interventions that are unnecessary for that person.

KUS 5, 9

As stated above, even if there are no daily changes, the plan of care should still be reviewed regularly. The frequency of review and evaluation should be documented in the care plan so that the care plan goals or objectives continue to address the individual's real needs and are updated in response to changes that occur.

Reporting on planned care delivery

KUS 3, 4

As mentioned above, it is your responsibility to monitor individuals for changes in their needs and to feed back to colleagues the effects that planned care delivery are having. Reporting can be via verbal feedback or by more formal written reporting. Verbal feedback generally involves telling senior colleagues about changes, developments or problems relating to an individual's needs. Or it may take place in handover and report meetings where an individual's care can be discussed with the whole team. Written reporting generally involves making notes in an individual's records about the effectiveness of care and the individual's responses to it. The procedures and format for doing this vary because care organisations have their own particular reporting systems and practices. Find out what the policies and procedures are in your care organisation and local care setting for making formal written reports on individual care.

Checking a plan of care

Delia has just returned to work after a two-week holiday. This morning she has been asked to care for Jon Summer, a young man with Down's Syndrome. As Delia has known Jon for several months she does not look at his plan of care. When Delia greets Jon it is obvious he is not happy about something. He allows Delia to help him to get washed and dressed, but is much less talkative than normal.

Using her previously good relationship with Jon, Delia manages to get a basic conversation going about how he is feeling. Eventually Jon tells her that he is not happy with the way some other staff are treating him in the evening when they want him to go to bed. Jon tells Delia that he thinks he is being bullied by the staff and wants to complain. Delia says that she will help him to do this. However, when Delia checks Jon's plan of care she realises that this has changed. Ten days ago he agreed that he would go to bed by 10.30 p.m. so that he could get up to go to college each morning.

➤ *Explain why Delia should have checked Jon's plan of care before she started to work with him.*

➤ *Where should Delia have looked to find information about the conflict Jon described to her?*

➤ *Which aspects of this scenario do you think Delia should feed back on when she reports on Jon and his care at the end of the shift?*

Key points – providing feedback on care

- Care workers have a vital role in observing and reporting on the effectiveness of care and any changes in an individual's condition.
- Observations should be reported verbally and in writing where they are relevant to the person's care plan.
- Feedback on care provision may be provided by the individual, their relatives, care workers and other care practitioners involved with the individual.
- Individuals should be encouraged and supported to comment and provide feedback on the care that is provided for them.
- Each individual's care plan should be reviewed and evaluated on a regular basis to ensure that it remains up to date and is appropriate to the individual's needs.

Element
HSC25c

Contribute to revisions of specific plan of care activities

So far in this unit we have looked mainly at the first three stages of the care planning cycle. The part that you play in the assessment, planning and the implementation of plans of care for individuals will depend on your level of experience and the local practices in your care setting. In this final part of the unit we will consider the role that you could play in contributing to the revision of individuals' care plans. Again, the extent to which you have a role in this, and the type of review meetings that are held, will depend on the nature of your care setting and the approach to review and evaluation that is taken locally.

Contributing to team planning

As already noted, you are likely to be a member of a team of care professionals delivering planned care for individuals. The nature of planned care tends to vary according to the type of care setting and the nature of an individual's care needs. For example, planned care could involve:

- A multi-agency care package delivered by a number of care workers such as social workers, nursing staff, home-care workers and a physiotherapist who work independently of each other but **collaborate** in delivering a complex package of care.
- A single agency but **multidisciplinary** care programme delivered by medical, nursing and social-care staff from the same agency. They also deliver parts of a

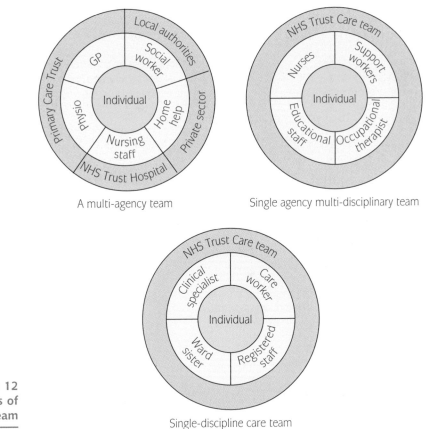

A multi-agency team

Single agency multi-disciplinary team

Single-discipline care team

**Figure 12
Types of
care team**

care programme and work independently but collaborate together in the assessment, planning and evaluation stages.

- A single-discipline care plan in which a team of care workers work together to deliver a range of care activities for an individual in a particular care setting, such as a residential or nursing home or the individual's own home.

Improving care plans with others

KUS 1, 2, 3, 9

Whilst a number of care workers would be involved in contributing to the assessment, planning and delivery of care in each of the situations described above, the evaluation and review of an individual's planned care is likely to be carried out by a smaller group. Depending on the policies and practices in your local care setting, you may be asked to participate in a team review of an individual's plan of care. You should be given enough warning of any meeting to allow you to prepare and report back accurately. You may be asked to attend one or more of these review meetings. These include:

- Place-of-work reviews.
- Multidisciplinary team meetings.
- Case conferences.

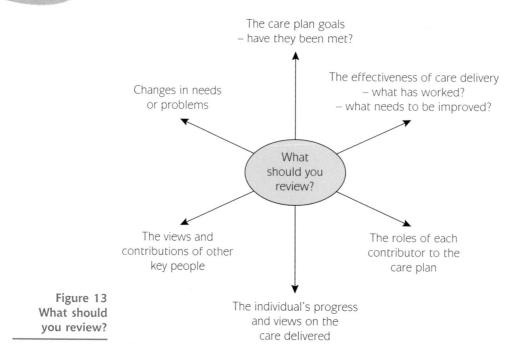

The care plan goals
– have they been met?

The effectiveness of care delivery
– what has worked?
– what needs to be improved?

Changes in needs
or problems

What
should you
review?

The views and
contributions of other
key people

The roles of each
contributor to the
care plan

The individual's progress
and views on the
care delivered

**Figure 13
What should
you review?**

Place-of-work reviews

This is the type of care plan review that would be carried out in your workplace by a care team reviewing the plan of care activities that they provide for an individual. Typically, the person responsible for the individual's care plan (perhaps you) leads the meeting and invites comments from other team members. The individual and key people involved in their care may or may not be present at a place-of-work review. This tends to depend on local practice and individuals' own preferences. It is good practice, however, to involve individuals in reviews of their planned care.

KUS 4, 7

The purpose of a place-of-work review is to give the whole care team and the individual a chance to consider whether the care currently being provided is meeting the individual's current needs. Your contribution should be constructive and aimed at sharing observations and making suggestions for improvement.

Multidisciplinary team meetings

Multidisciplinary team meetings are similar to place-of-work reviews except that a broader range of care professionals, drawn from the multidisciplinary team contributing to an individual's care, will be present. This might include, for example, medical, social work, occupational therapy, community nursing and home-care staff. If you are asked to attend a multidisciplinary team meeting you will probably do so as a representative of the care team in which you normally work. As such, you will be expected to provide feedback on the particular areas of care that you and your colleagues deliver. The other people attending the meeting will also give feedback on their specialist areas of care practice.

The purpose of multidisciplinary team meetings is to share information and co-ordinate the involvement of a number of care disciplines. It gives members of a care team who may not otherwise meet or work together directly, an opportunity to find out what other team members are doing. They can share views and feedback in order to create a new, co-ordinated approach to an individual's plan of care. The person who is the individual's key worker will usually lead a multidisciplinary team meeting. Your role will be to represent and report the views of your colleagues and the individual for whom you care.

KUS 9

Case conferences

A case conference is a different type of evaluation and review meeting. One of the differences is that a case conference is usually led by a social worker who assesses the individual's general care needs. Frequently the focus of a case conference is on a decision that will have a significant impact on an individual's life – such as future placement in a residential care setting, rehousing or retaining the current care arrangements within the individual's own home. As case conferences usually involve major issues, the individual, members of their family and any other key people involved in their care are usually invited to attend. You may be invited as a key person if, for example, you play a significant part in providing an individual with home care or support in a residential care setting. You may be asked to contribute to the discussions. For example, you could be asked to comment on:

- How well the individual's plan of care reflects the person's current needs and wishes.
- How easy the plan of care is to implement. (For example, does the individual use the equipment supplied by the occupational therapist? If not, why not?)
- Areas of the plan of care that you think are now inappropriate for the person.
- Any changes you have seen in the individual's physical and mental health.
- Whether (and what) additional input is required from other care workers to make the plan of care easier to deliver or more effective.

Whatever type of team meeting you find yourself attending in the future, it is important that you understand your role in it and are able to explain this to the other participants. As with all areas of care practice, you should ensure that you contribute as best you can but also accept and stay within the limits of your competence and area of responsibility.

KUS 1, 3

If you are attending a multidisciplinary review meeting or case conference for the first time, it would be helpful to discuss this with your manager or a senior colleague. It is best to know well before the meeting what will be expected of you, what information you will need to give, and what areas of the individual's plan of care are under review. This will enable you to contribute in a more effective and professional way than if you turn up unprepared and ill-informed.

Adapting and negotiating new care plans

KUS 6

In review meetings suggestions are usually made about ways of adapting care plans to meet the changing or new needs of an individual. You may be asked for your suggestions and you may have points to make. It is important to remember that any suggestions to alter an individual's plan of care are just *proposals* until they have been fully discussed and agreed with the individual. You should not change existing care plans or write a new one without first involving the individual and giving them a chance to express their views, preferences and wishes.

You may also find that your opinion on altering a plan of care differs from that of others involved in the discussion. If there is a difference of opinion between yourself and others taking part in the review, you should explain the reasoning behind your thinking and you should be prepared to listen to, and where appropriate accept, the opinions of the others attending the review.

Communicating care plan changes

KUS 9

If you are representing your workplace or care team at a case conference or multidisciplinary team meeting to review planned care for an individual, you should ensure that you understand any changes that are proposed and the reasons for them being made. Both of these matters will need to be communicated clearly to your colleagues and to the individual and other key people who may not have attended the meeting. If you do not fully understand any of the proposed changes you should always say so at the time and ask for further explanation.

If you are responsible for a plan of care that is developed and delivered by your colleagues within your workplace, you should ensure that any changes that are proposed and agreed following a place-of-work review are communicated to all of your colleagues. This is necessary to ensure **continuity** of care and to maintain high standards of teamwork and effectiveness. Ensure that the individuals you are caring for understand the reasons why changes to their plan of care are proposed, and that the key people involved in supporting them also have a chance to comment before the changes are agreed and implemented.

Reviewing a plan of care

Russell has been asked to work with Mr Spring this morning. This is Russell's first morning back at work after a week's holiday. During Russell's time away the rest of the care team reviewed Mr Spring's care plan. Mr Spring made it clear at the review meeting that he no longer wanted to use the equipment that the occupational therapist supplied to help maintain his independence. The items of equipment that have been supplied are a tool that looks like a long shoehorn to help Mr Spring put on his socks and shoes and a long pole with a grab on the end to allow him to pick things up without bending over. Mr Spring said that he finds it difficult to use these pieces of equipment and feels embarrassed and insulted that he has been given them. After discussing the problem with him, it became clear at the meeting that Mr Spring did not know why he had been given the equipment.

> What information should be available to Russell this morning when he reviews Mr Spring's plan of care?

> How could Russell find out more about the changes to Mr Spring's plan of care?

> Why is it important to take account of Mr Spring's views and preferences when reviewing his care?

Key points – contributing to the revision of care plans

- You may be required to contribute to a team-based review and revision of individuals' care plans.

- Review meetings focus on evaluating the effectiveness of care plans and on identifying new goals or objectives.

- Changes to care plans should be negotiated with the individual they affect and should be communicated clearly to all care workers involved in providing care for the person.

Unit
HSC25 Are you ready for assessment?

Carry out and provide feedback on specific plan of care activities

This unit is all about your involvement in supporting service users with particular aspects of their care plan. Because this unit also covers feedback and revisions to care plans it is closely linked to unit HSC21 which covers communication and completion of records.

As this unit relates to specific plan of care activities it is likely that most of the evidence you need to cover the performance criteria and knowledge specification can be gathered during your assessment in the other optional units in your qualification. You should consider this when planning with your assessor.

Your assessment will mainly be carried out through observation by your assessor and should provide most of the evidence for the elements in this unit.

As this unit is about activities specified in the care plan, there will be ample opportunities for observation by your assessor. However, if such observation might intrude on the privacy of individuals, then you can plan with your assessor to use the testimony of an expert witness instead of observation.

▶

Direct observation

Your assessor or an expert witness will need to see you carry out the performance criteria (PCs) in each of the elements in this unit.

The performance criteria that may be difficult to meet through observation or expert witness testimony are:

- **HSC25b PC 4**
- **HSC25c PC 3**

usually because they might not always occur.

Preparing to be observed

You must make sure that your workplace and any individuals and key people involved in your work agree to you being assessed. Explicit, informed consent must be obtained before you carry out any assessment activity that involves individuals or which involves access to confidential information related to their care.

Before your assessments you should read carefully the performance criteria for each element in the unit. Try to cover as much as

you can *during your observations* but remember that you and your assessor can also plan for additional sources of evidence should full coverage of all performance criteria not be possible or to help ensure that your performance is consistent and that you can apply the knowledge specification in your work practice.

Other types of evidence

You may need to present other forms of evidence in order to:

- Cover criteria not observed by your assessor or by an expert witness.
- Show that you have the required knowledge, understanding and skills to claim competence in this area of practice.
- Ensure that your work practice is consistent.

Your assessor may also need to ask you questions to confirm your knowledge and understanding of this unit.

Check your knowledge

1   Describe what happens during each of the main stages of the care planning cycle.

2   Identify the benefits of planning care for individuals.

3   What kind of additional information should you read and understand before you implement planned care?

4   Describe ways of involving individuals in the care planning cycle.

5   How do observation and feedback contribute to the care planning process?

6   What should you do if the person you are caring for does not agree with what you are doing for them?

7   What should you do if you are asked by an individual's relative to change something in their plan of care?

8   How might you be involved in reviewing a plan of care and what aspects of care or the care plan might you be asked to comment on?

Support individuals in their daily living

*P*eople's daily lives are often busy and full of activities that they take for granted. That is, until something happens which prevents the person from meeting their daily living needs. This could be the onset of illness, an injury or the increasingly disabling effects of disease or impairment. It is also likely that as people grow older they will become less able to carry out the tasks of independent daily living that are taken for granted.

This unit focuses on the role that care workers can play in:

⌣ Helping individuals to identify their need for support in daily living tasks.

⌣ Providing daily living assistance.

⌣ Helping individuals to access additional forms of support.

This unit has close links with units HSC21 (on communication), HSC22 (on health and safety) and HSC24 (on supporting the care and protection of others). This unit contains three elements:

⌣ **HSC27a** Agree with individuals the support they require for their daily living

⌣ **HSC27b** Assist individuals in activities to promote their well-being

⌣ **HSC27c** Help individuals access other support to promote their well-being

⌣ Human needs

KUS 5, 10

To be healthy and feel good about life a person must be able to meet his or her basic needs. Basic needs are the things that all human beings require in order to survive and develop. For example, human beings have a basic physical need for food and drink, shelter and warmth. There are many reasons why a person may not be able to meet their basic needs at different points in their life. For example, a life-threatening injury, too much stress, or not having enough money for food, warm clothing or shelter can all lead to health and personal problems.

As well as having basic physical needs, people also have **intellectual**, social and emotional needs.

- *Intellectual needs* relate to the human need to learn, understand and explore in order to develop and live a fulfilling life.

- *Social needs* relate to the human need for relationships and contact with other people.

● *Emotional needs* relate to the human need for love and affection, trust, and emotional bonds with family, friends and other people.

A person's needs remain unmet when they are unable to obtain the things they require for survival, good health or development. Then the person will probably experience some kind of health, social or emotional problem or difficulties in their development. These problems may be related to their physical or mental health, their ability to learn skills or simply their ability to cope with everyday life.

Maslow's hierarchy of human needs

Abraham Maslow, an American psychologist, developed a theory of human needs that links a person's needs to their behaviour. Maslow suggested that people prioritise meeting their needs so that more basic needs have to be met before higher-level needs can be satisfied. As a result, he suggested that we should see human needs as a **hierarchy** or pyramid (see Figure 1).

According to Maslow our behaviour is strongly directed by the desire we have to meet and satisfy our various needs. Care workers can make use of Maslow's hierarchy of needs when they are trying to understand an individual's behaviour

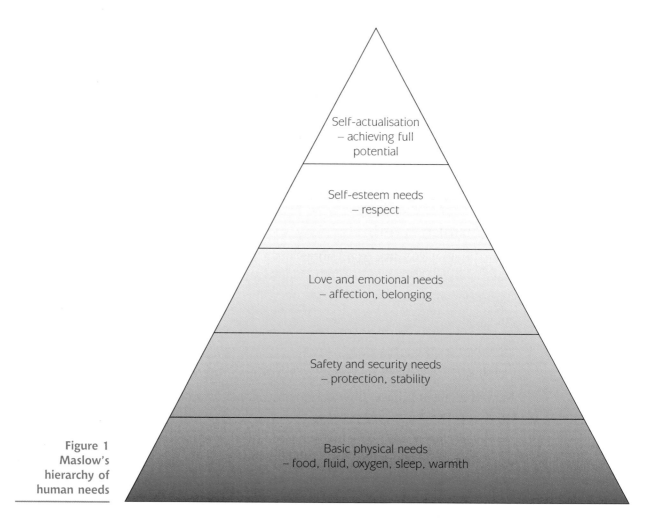

Figure 1
Maslow's
hierarchy of
human needs

and when prioritising their care interventions. When a person is experiencing problems meeting their basic physical needs or their safety and security needs, they are likely to require some kind of care or support because they will be at risk of developing physical health problems or experiencing injury or harm. Likewise, if a person has unmet love and emotional needs or has very low self-esteem they may experience psychological and emotional problems, have difficulty forming or maintaining supportive relationships with others and become socially isolated and depressed.

When you are considering the support that individuals may require in their daily lives, Maslow's hierarchy of needs, as well as the simpler PIES (physical, intellectual, emotional and social needs) approach, can be useful in helping you to think about the range of human needs that an individual has. It is important to consider all of the individual's needs, from the most basic to the more complex, when thinking about a person's functioning and support requirements.

Activities of daily living

People meet their human needs through the activities that they engage in as part of their everyday life. Care workers often refer to these as a person's **activities of daily living**. The idea of activities of daily living is well known and widely used in care work. It is a central part of the Activities of Daily Living (ADL) model of nursing that was developed by Roper, Logan and Tierney in 1996.

The ADL model of nursing identifies 12 key activities of daily life that have a direct influence on a person's health and well-being. These are

- Maintaining a safe environment.
- Communication.
- Breathing.
- Eating and drinking.
- Elimination.
- Personal cleansing and dressing.
- Controlling body temperature.
- Mobilising.
- Working and playing.
- Expressing sexuality.
- Sleeping.
- Death and dying.

The activities of daily living approach is a useful guide for care workers who have to assess and respond to individuals' needs. It also links well to Abraham Maslow's ideas about a hierarchy of needs because it reinforces the point that if a person's human needs are neglected or unmet the person's health and well-being will be affected.

It might seem rather strange to include death and dying in a list of activities of daily living, particularly if you are working with young people who are all physically fit. However, if you work in a hospice, in elderly care or in the acute hospital sector the death of individuals is a feature of daily life that has to be dealt with, even though this can be very difficult at times. The ADL model of care highlights the fact that our thoughts, wishes and concerns about death and dying do sometimes play a part in our own life and the lives of the individuals we care for.

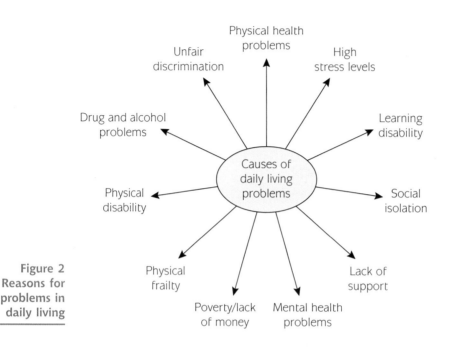

Figure 2 Reasons for problems in daily living

It is important to recognise that at different stages of our lives we have different priorities, but there are many basic activities of daily living that affect us all. If a person is prevented from doing any of the activities of living that they depend on to meet their needs the outcome could be anything from inconvenience, discomfort and boredom to significant ill-health, extreme pain or personal humiliation. In order to provide appropriate care and support for individuals you should develop a good understanding of human needs and the way they are met through activities of daily living.

Agree with individuals the support they require for their daily living

This unit is about ways of providing support for individuals who are unable to meet their daily living needs independently. We will consider what your role might be in providing an individual with the types of daily living support that they need. We will explore how you can find out and agree this with the individuals you provide care for, and we will consider what the goals of providing support might be.

Working in partnership

How would you describe your role as a care worker to someone you have just met? What words would you use? Would you describe your role as *working with* people or *doing things for* people? There used to be a general expectation that care workers did things for individuals. Now the emphasis has changed and you are expected to work in partnership with individuals.

Part of your role as a care worker involves providing people with enough support to enable them to get on with their daily life. The relationship that you develop with an individual and the approach that you take to providing support for them should be based on the idea of partnership. Partnership is all about working together in a relatively equal and collaborative way. Within the care partnerships that you develop you should enable and support individuals to make as many decisions as possible and to do as much as they can for themselves. An individual's problems may be made worse by a care worker who provides too much care and support even though this may be given with the best intentions.

Care workers are sometimes tempted to do too much for individuals because they are trying to compensate for skills and abilities that people have lost. Maybe they do not like to see individuals struggle, take risks and sometimes fail in their efforts to be self-caring. However, encouraging and supporting individuals to be involved in their own care and to take as much control as possible is a crucial way of helping them to maintain their skills and their self-esteem.

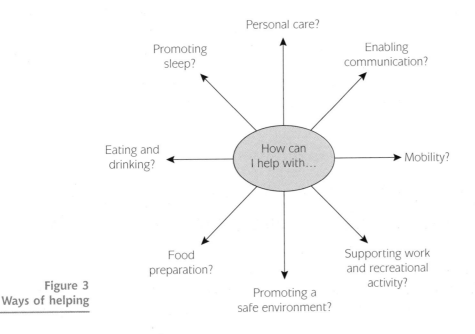

Figure 3
Ways of helping

Forms of daily living support

The daily living support that you offer to individuals will vary according to your workplace, your skills and the individual's needs. It could involve:

- Helping an individual to manage a chronic condition – this may involve ensuring people have adequate medication and that they have access to adapted mobility, cooking or personal-care equipment that they require.
- Enabling people to manage an acute condition – this may involve supporting them to use the toilet or bathing people during an illness or following surgery in a hospital setting.
- Supporting people to live independently at home – this may involve supporting a person with learning disabilities to go shopping, carry out household tasks, perform personal care, use transport, or so that they can live independently.
- Assisting carers in an individual's own home by providing extra help with personal care, mobility or social activities for the person.
- Providing rehabilitation support through a programme of physio-therapy or occupational therapy that aims to develop or improve a person's self-care, mobility or practical skills.
- Providing total care in all aspects of daily life for an individual living in a nursing home, hospice or hospital who is unable to care for themselves because of a terminal illness or a degenerative or disabling condition.

Establishing your role

KUS 2, 3, 7

The role that you play in supporting an individual in meeting their daily living needs should be negotiated and agreed with the person or with the people responsible for their care. You need to be clear about:

- What you are expected to do for the individual.
- The limits or boundaries to your involvement.
- What the individual is expected or wishes to do for themselves.

The detail of this will vary with each individual because everyone has different needs and abilities. Each individual's care plan should provide clear guidance on their particular needs and the levels of care and support that they need. However, you should also discuss the above points with the individual and other people involved in their care so that everyone understands what is expected.

As a general rule, care workers should provide active support when working in partnership with individuals. This means encouraging people to be as independent and self-managing as possible. If an individual is able to wash and bathe without help, you should not normally become involved in this aspect of their daily living. However, some individuals may not be able to manage their own personal care independently. So it is best to approach your work and each individual's needs with an open mind. Remember that the person you are caring for is an individual who has their own ideas, preferences and priorities regarding their care needs.

You should aim to have a working relationship that is based upon mutual respect. Developing a 'more support/less support' mentality can help you to find the right balance in your relationship and approach to individuals. This means providing more support when the person requests and needs it but being prepared to reduce your input and provide less support when the individual feels able or is capable of meeting their daily living needs more independently.

There may be situations where you feel that an individual requires more or less support than their care plan suggests. Or an individual may disagree with the level of care or the approach to support that has been proposed or negotiated for them. In such instances you should try to:

- Clarify with the individual what the problem or cause of conflict is.
- Carry out a risk assessment to work out whether the individual's request or any proposed change is safe to implement.
- Negotiate a new approach or solution to the problem. This should be acceptable to both the individual and yourself and it should not alter your agreed role or make excessive new demands on you.
- Inform your supervisor or line manager of the problems that have arisen and, where relevant, document the issue in the individual's records including any discussions that you have had.

It would not be appropriate for you to alter an individual's daily living routines suddenly or to make major changes to their care without getting their agreement. Talk to your line manager and all of the other people concerned with their care before you suggest or make changes to the type of care or the way that support is provided.

Getting to know individuals

In order to establish an effective partnership with them, you need to get to know as individuals each of the people you provide care for. You will have to work hard at that and it will be an ongoing process. When you meet an individual for the first time, you may have to base your knowledge of their likes and dislikes on the information that you can obtain from their records, any verbal reports that you are given and on what they are able to tell you in a relatively brief first conversation. As you work with an individual you will learn more from what they say, what you observe and how they respond to you and the other people around them in the care setting. So you should get to know them better as a person. Then you will be in a position to provide them with more appropriate, individualised support. Ideally you should be trying to provide **holistic care** to each individual.

Understanding the situation

As already mentioned, it is always necessary to find out from each individual the type and level of support that they require from you in order to carry out particular aspects of daily living. It is also important that you support people to live their lives as they choose rather than impose a lifestyle on them that has more to do with your own values, priorities and preferences. This can only be achieved if you really do work in partnership with each individual.

Use your communication skills and the relationship that you develop with each individual to find out about their daily living situation and their needs and preferences. This requires some sensitivity as people may feel this is intrusive and personal. They may be defensive and reluctant to admit to any difficulty. However, some individuals may be happy to discuss problems, difficulties and personal issues with you. The aim of these kinds of conversation should be to identify the types and level of support and assistance that an individual requires to meet their own particular needs. You should not impose your own views or ideas about an individual's needs, even where the person appears to ignore or dispute an apparent need for support.

Enabling communication

Effective communication is a basic part of every care worker's skills. Good communication skills will help you to obtain the information that you need about how best to support the individuals you provide care for on a daily basis. Simply asking people what they want and what they need is the most direct way of obtaining information. However, the way that you ask a question and the individual's ability to understand and respond to it can be very important. You should use open and closed questions appropriately and provide the individual

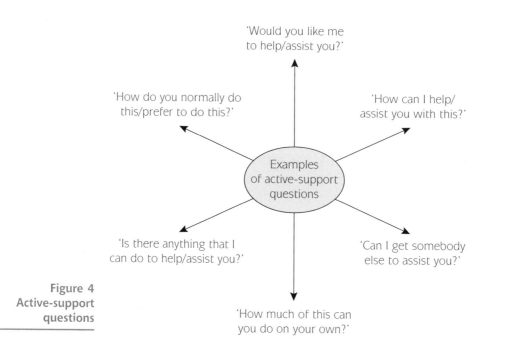

'Would you like me to help/assist you?'

'How do you normally do this/prefer to do this?'

'How can I help/assist you with this?'

Examples of active-support questions

'Is there anything that I can do to help/assist you?'

'Can I get somebody else to assist you?'

'How much of this can you do on your own?'

Figure 4
Active-support questions

with any communication support that they require in order to obtain relevant and appropriate information.

The use of open and closed questions is discussed in some detail on page 22 of unit HSC21. We will only review it briefly here. Open questions are used when you want to encourage the person to give a full or detailed answer. For example, 'What do you think about going to the day centre once a week?' and, 'How are things going?' are both open questions that provide the individual with an opportunity to give their views. Closed questions produce answers that are much more limited and less informative. For example, 'Do you want to go to the day centre?' and 'Are you all right?' are both likely to produce very brief answers. You will need to use a variety of different open and closed questions when you are talking to individuals about their daily lives, what they are able to do for themselves and what they would like you to help them with.

Remember, try to avoid using leading questions when you are seeking information from individuals. These are questions that lead the person towards the answer you want to hear. For example, 'You are happy about going to the day centre, aren't you?' and, 'You look much better, that's good, isn't it?' are both leading questions as the individual would be in little doubt about the expected answer. Also, avoid asking multiple questions whenever possible. A multiple question is an apparently simple question that becomes more complicated because the speaker adds or links a number of other questions to it before the listener has had a chance to answer. This makes it very difficult for the individual to answer, especially if they are confused or have hearing or concentration problems.

Communicating with key people involved in an individual's care

An individual's family, friends and other key people may play an important part in helping to meet their daily living needs. Consequently it is important to make contact and communicate with them regularly. Working with them to support a person can benefit both the individual and the other people involved with them. For example, effective communication can ensure that the individual's family and friends do not feel resentful or guilty about the involvement of additional care services. It can also be vital for ensuring that care and support services are delivered in a way that is co-ordinated and effective.

Motivating people to become involved in their own care

KUS 8, 10

So far we have discussed the idea of involving individuals in their own care in a way that assumes they will want, and be able, to meet their own daily living needs. However, in reality individuals do not always want to live independently or use the skills and abilities that they have. This is not the same as saying that some people are lazy. On the contrary, a variety of factors can prevent people developing their independence and self-care skills. Some of these are referred to in the practical example below.

Barriers that may prevent people developing independence and self-care skills

Rania works as a home help. She has recently visited two individuals to provide support for their daily living needs.

The first visit was to Susan, aged 70. Susan has recently had a stroke that has left her with reduced mobility, problems swallowing and slurred speech. Rania has been told to help Susan to get up, washed and dressed so that she is ready to go to the day centre at 9.30 a.m. Susan lives with her husband John. He is very supportive and wants to do as much as possible to help Susan. In fact, John feels that he should be able to support Susan on his own, but a social worker has advised him to accept additional home help.

When Rania arrived she found Susan sitting up in bed looking rather unhappy. John looked tired and was irritable. Rania also noticed that there was uneaten toast on Susan's lap and the house was quite cold.

Rania's second visit was to Rob, aged 23. Rob was involved in a motorbike accident six months ago that left him severely physically disabled. Rob is now unable to walk, has no movement in his left arm and only limited use of his right arm. He currently lives at home with his mother and his girlfriend.

Rania has been asked to assist Rob with washing and dressing. However, when she arrived he was already up and dressed. Rob's mother says she helped him and has also tidied his room and got him to sit in the living room. Rania also observed Rob's mum straightening his clothes and combing his hair whilst she explained that 'everything has been done'.

Rob seemed low in spirits during Rania's visit. However, after chatting to him for a while she found out that Rob had studied mechanical engineering at university and had not worked in a formal job since he finished his course and then had his accident. She also found out that Rob's girlfriend goes out to work very early and is often back late. His mother stays in the house with him most of the time and discourages him from going out 'in case something else happens'.

Think about each individual and answer the following questions:

➤ *What aspects of each individual's daily living needs are being met?*

➤ *What aspects of each individual's daily living needs are not being met?*

➤ *How could you find out what Susan and Rob want in terms of help and support?*

➤ *How could you involve their families and friends?*

➤ *What action could you take to improve the situation for all individuals mentioned in the case studies?*

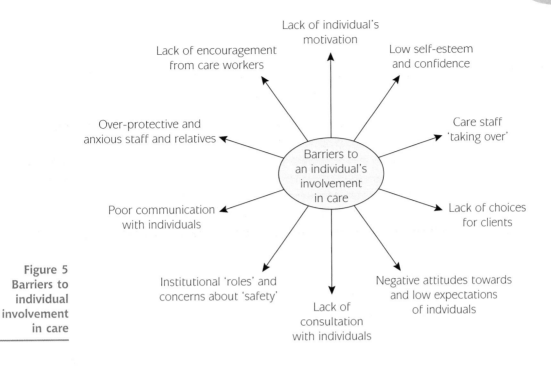

Figure 5
Barriers to
individual
involvement
in care

Key points – involving people in their own care

- Assess and reassess what individuals can do for themselves as things inevitably change.
- Write realistic care plans, review them regularly and involve the individual in the care planning process as much as you can.
- Get to know the individual as a person and try to build trust and a good working relationship so that you communicate effectively and can share decision making.
- Involve the individual and other key people in as much of the care and support activity as possible and always encourage individuals to try to do things for themselves.
- Break daily living activities into a series of smaller and more manageable and achievable tasks. If an activity seems too difficult the individual may not feel capable of tackling it.
- Share information appropriately with individuals and educate the key people involved in their care about their condition.

Using additional support

There may be times when you are unable to provide the care and support that an individual requests or needs. This may be because the support is of a specialist nature and requires skills that you do not have. For example, if you have not been trained to use hoists or other mobility aids you should not attempt to provide care and support that depend on those pieces of equipment. Alternatively, an individual who has mental health or challenging behavioural needs may require support from a care worker who has had specific training in these areas of care practice. Whatever the situation, you should:

- Recognise and acknowledge that extra support is required.
- Accept that providing this support goes beyond your level of competence and skill.
- Report the situation to your supervisor or line manager.
- Seek additional help from colleagues or other professionals who have the skills and experience that are required to provide appropriate support.

KUS 1, 2

Key points – ways of agreeing support

In order to agree the level of support required by an individual you will need to:

- Work in partnership with the individual.
- Resist the temptation to impose your own views on the individual.
- Be non-judgemental and objective in your approach to the individual and their situation.
- Get to know the individual. This can take time so do not jump to conclusions too quickly.
- Communicate and listen to the individual, finding out about their likes and dislikes.
- Talk with the individual about their needs and their wishes and preferences for the types and level of support they require.
- Observe the individual and note their strengths, abilities and skills as well as the areas where they have problems or experience difficulties.
- Observe the environment in which the individual lives, noting any aspects that affect or act as barriers to them meeting their daily living needs.
- Communicate with others involved in the individual's care such as their family and friends, your colleagues during handover or reporting, and your manager.

Assist individuals in activities to promote their well-being

This element focuses on the way that you provide assistance to individuals who need support with their daily living activities. We will consider how you should identify and provide support through your role as a care worker.

Understanding well-being

Providing individuals with support and assistance to meet their daily living needs is a major part of your role as a care worker. As we have already seen, a variety of skills and a broad range of knowledge and understanding are required before you can do this competently and effectively. However, before we explore the ways you can approach this core part of your care role, we need to reflect on the basic reasons for providing care.

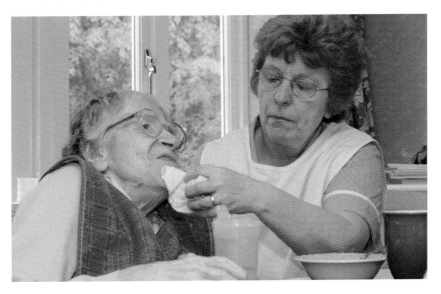

Figure 6
Helping with basic needs is a skilled part of care practice

The basic aim of health and social-care work is to protect and promote the health and well-being of people who are experiencing physical, social or mental-health problems or who are vulnerable because of disability or infirmity. Care work therefore involves more than providing medically based treatment or nursing care for specific illnesses or social problems. Through working with individuals in an individualised, holistic way, you should be trying to assist them to meet their daily living needs whilst also promoting their well-being.

What is health?

According to the World Health Organization (WHO), health can be defined as 'a state of complete physical, social and mental well-being and not merely the absence of disease or infirmity'.

The World Health Organization's reference to well-being in its famous and widely used definition of health (see above) is significant. It is also a challenging definition for health and social-care workers because it sets the standard of health very high by using the word 'complete'. So you may already be concerned that some individuals will never achieve health in these terms because they have long-term problems or degenerative conditions that cannot be improved or cured. However, there is no need to be too **pessimistic** as it is the individual's own definition and standards of well-being (rather than the WHO) that you should be most concerned with.

The people you work with and provide care for will have their own ideas about what is normal and acceptable as far as their well-being is concerned. Individuals can still live happy, fulfilling and independent lives despite having a chronic condition or disease or long-term social or mental-health problems. A person can have a positive sense of well-being even though they are very unwell, have learning disabilities, a mental-health problem or a physical disability. As a care worker you should focus on supporting the individual to achieve and maintain their sense of well-being by assisting them to make the most of their quality of life.

Daily living, needs and well-being

You need to be able to make connections between an individual's activities of daily living, their care needs and their well-being in order to appreciate how you can best work with them. Figure 7 illustrates these connections.

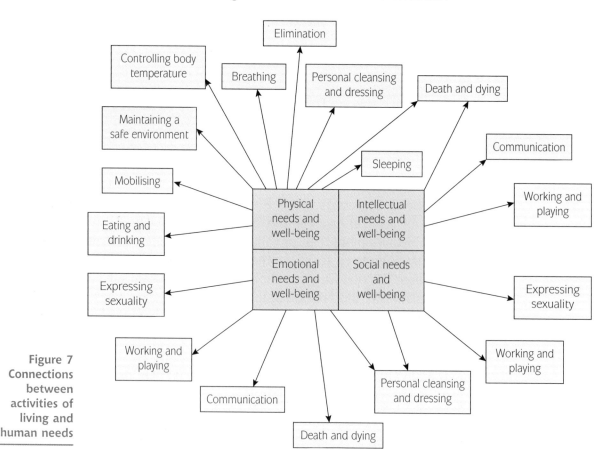

Figure 7 Connections between activities of living and human needs

Figure 7 begins by showing that each individual has human needs. These can be understood generally as physical, intellectual, emotional or social needs (see page 173) or by using a framework like Maslow's hierarchy of needs (see page 174). An individual will meet their human needs by carrying out activities of daily living to the best of their ability. We have used the ADL model of care (see page 175) to identify the kinds of activities that individuals undertake in order to meet their needs in everyday life. A person who is self-caring and can successfully meet their needs in the way that they wish is likely to have a positive sense of well-being. However, some people have difficulties in meeting their needs because they cannot carry out their activities of daily living independently or in the way that they want. So their health and sense of well-being may suffer. This is where you, as a care worker, can help.

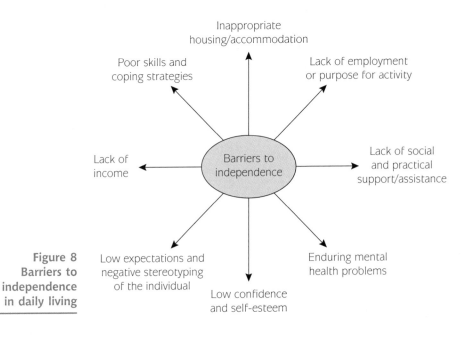

Figure 8
Barriers to
independence
in daily living

An individual may have difficulty in carrying out one or more of their activities of daily living for a variety of reasons (see Figure 8). That individual's problems or areas of difficulty will be specific to them. Part of your care and support task is to identify those activities with which you can offer the individual help. If the individual is already known to care services, you may be able to obtain and use their assessment records and care plan to identify the activities they need help with. Always access information regarding an individual following organisational guidelines. Ideally they will already have discussed and agreed their support needs with the care workers who carried out their assessment.

Agreeing and clarifying support and assistance

It is useful to have some information about an individual's care needs as it will provide you with an indication of the type of help you might be required to offer. However, it is always good practice to discuss an individual's support needs and

Thinking about an individual's well-being needs

- What physical, intellectual, emotional and social needs does this individual have?
- What physical activities does the individual want to be involved in?
- What physical assistance, if any, does the individual want?
- How would the individual prefer you to provide them with physical assistance?
- What intellectual and social activities does the individual wish to take part in?
- How can you support or assist the individual in meeting their intellectual and social needs?
- What kind of emotional support does the individual want to receive?
- How can you provide the kind of emotional support that the individual wishes to receive?

preferences with them directly as well. If you are the first person to do this you may have to complete assessment and care planning documentation as part of the care planning process. If not, you should clarify and agree how the individual would like you to assist them. Remember that you are aiming to achieve a partnership where you collaborate with the individual by providing the type and level of support that they say is necessary and helpful. In terms of the ADL model of care, an individual may require support and assistance relating to one or more of the 12 different activity areas.

Figure 9
There are many ways to help a service user to be as independent as possible

Most people do not like to be told when and how they should carry out their activities of daily living. Being told what to do and how to do something reinforces a person's sense of not being in control and of lacking an independent living ability or skill. Therefore, it is usually better and more respectful to work with an individual to agree how they would like you to assist them. This may take some time, but it is worth putting effort into engaging the individual in their care as this will improve co-operation and the quality of the service that you are able to offer them. Effective use of your listening and responding skills and paying close attention to the individual's rights and communication needs will all play a part in this process. You will also need to consider any risk assessments relating to an individual's functioning, skills or behaviour as well as the policies, procedures and **protocols** that your employer has set out that are relevant to the kind of care and support that the individual needs.

Assisting in daily living activity

KUS 2, 10, 11

The provision of support and assistance and the promotion of well-being will occur in different ways in different care settings. For example, an individual who has a mild learning disability and who is living in a group home without live-in carers will have different support needs and priorities compared to a frail, older person receiving care in a nursing home. If you are working in a residential care unit for older people, mobility and socialising might be important activities of daily living that you could assist individuals with. If you are working in a supported housing setting, you may instead focus on reinforcing residents' health and safety and their security in the home. Alternatively, if you are working with people with learning disabilities or helping disabled people to live independent lives, you may be teaching them life skills relating to:

- Shopping for and cooking food.
- Keeping their home or room clean.
- Catching a bus.
- Getting to work, college or a day centre on time.
- Social skills.
- Sexual health and contraception.

In other situations none of this may be possible or appropriate and your role may be to prepare food for an individual and assist them with eating and drinking and all aspects of personal care. However, you can still promote well-being through the way you work, interact and communicate with the individual. Whatever an individual's support and assistance needs, your aim should always be to provide care in a way that respects the person's dignity and rights and accommodates their wishes and preferences.

Providing support

The quality of an individual's life can often be dramatically improved by providing what seems to be very basic assistance, such as helping them with their mobility

Figure 10
Providing help
at home can
prolong a
person's
independent
living skills

around the home. Always look for ways of maximising an individual's involvement in daily living activities to promote self-care and maintain the use of existing skills. This will promote better well-being for the person because it will improve their level of independence and functioning and boost their sense of personal competence and self-esteem.

Promoting well-being

Ramon is employed as a home help. John, aged 83, is one of the individuals he helps to care for. John smokes, lives alone and pays very little attention to his diet. He says he enjoys watching TV, betting on the horses, smoking and walking his dog. Ramon has identified a number of areas of John's activities of daily living where he thinks he may be able to provide assistance and promote John's well-being.

Table 1 Activities that promote well-being

Activity	How it promotes well-being	What could Ramon do?
Choosing food	Provides a balanced diet	Discuss food, write shopping lists together, go shopping together
Walking	This is excellent exercise	Encourage John to walk his dog – time home visits to fit in with this
Social interaction	Improves relationships and use of social skills	Spend time talking, show interest in John's life and in his pet
Cleaning	Ensures a clean and safe environment	Clean living areas as agreed, reinforce with John the need to keep the kitchen and bathroom clean. Check storage of food

➤ *Identify the activities of daily living that Ramon is trying to help John with.*

➤ *Describe how Ramon could assess improvements in John's well-being.*

➤ *Explain why it is important for Ramon to encourage John to carry out these activities rather than Ramon taking responsibility for them.*

Some activities of daily living naturally lend themselves to involving other people in an individual's care, such as socialising and maintaining a safe environment. Others, such as **elimination**, washing and dressing, are private functions which people are sensitive about. Individuals may therefore experience psychological stress and problems when they need support and assistance with these very personal activities. Care workers can also find it difficult to provide intimate, personal care and support for individuals. There are no easy solutions to such situations. The key is to be aware of an individual's sensitivities and to provide the support and assistance that a person needs in a respectful, dignified and compassionate manner.

Working safely and managing risk

KUS 3, 4, 9

Health and safety and risk management are important features of care work that you need to be aware of. These topics have been covered in some detail in unit HSC22. In this section we will briefly review and focus attention on how these issues are relevant when assisting individuals with their activities of daily living.

The risks posed by common hazards, such as hot water, electricity and potentially dangerous equipment, that are found in domestic homes and care settings can frequently be reduced by following simple health and safety precautions. These are likely to be detailed in the health and safety policies and procedures produced by your employer. Whilst many of the activities of living that you will help individuals with are quite straightforward, you will need to apply your understanding of health and safety and infection control principles to protect yourself and the individuals you provide care for from harm.

Figure 11
Hygiene
equipment and
food-handling
procedures
should be used
to minimise the
risk of food
poisoning
occurring in a
care setting

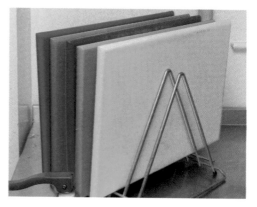

Table 2 Hazards and responses

Activity of living	Example of possible hazards	Health and safety response
Eating and drinking – food storage, preparation and cooking	Food poisoning	Correct food hygiene and storage
Personal cleansing and dressing	Scalds; trip and slip hazards	Checking water temperatures; managing the care environment, using support equipment appropriately
Mobilising	Falls; pressure sores	Using correct moving and handling techniques, providing individual with adapted equipment and mobility aids; monitoring and assisting immobile individuals to change position in bed or on chairs

The best way of protecting your own and the individual's health and safety is to carry out a risk assessment before you begin any particular task or activity (see unit HSC22 for more on this issue). Making safety checks and applying basic health and safety knowledge will reduce the risks that you face. If you are unhappy about a health and safety issue or feel that a situation is unsafe, you should report this to your supervisor and record your concerns in writing where necessary. You should not provide support or assistance in circumstances where there is a risk of harm or injury to yourself or the individual for whom you are caring.

Many activities of daily life inevitably involve a certain amount of risk, danger and difficulty for all of us, including the individuals you provide care for. When you are responsible for delivering care to other people you will naturally be concerned about the possible dangers and risks that they face in everyday life. This is appropriate because one of your key roles is to protect the individuals you work with. However, over-protection and reluctance to allow individuals to take part in activities because there *could* be danger is not always a good thing. In fact, until quite recently many people who lived in residential homes often had very restricted lives because the risks of allowing people to take part in outside activities were often considered too great. Now it is recognised that in order to develop their independent living skills and achieve a sense of fulfilment in their lives, people should be allowed to make choices and take part in activities that you may consider risky. For example, one individual may want to go out walking on their own, another individual may want to have an intimate, personal relationship with someone, whilst another may wish to shop for and cook their own food. There are hazards associated with each of these activities. However, if the level of risk is identified through an appropriate risk assessment, it is discussed with the individual and any necessary protective measures and support arrangements are put in place, the individual should be able to engage in activities that carry a manageable risk.

Observing and reporting on change

Care workers tend to spend a great deal of time with the individuals they look after. This regular, direct and prolonged contact provides many opportunities to observe changes in how an individual is functioning and coping with their various activities of living. If you think of your work as following the general care planning cycle (see Figure 12 overleaf), part of your role when implementing care is to monitor the effects of the support and assistance you are providing. You should make regular verbal reports of your observations to other members of your care team. You should note in an individual's records any significant changes and developments in their capabilities. This will provide important background information for the individual's **key worker** and others who will be involved in reviewing and evaluating their care plan.

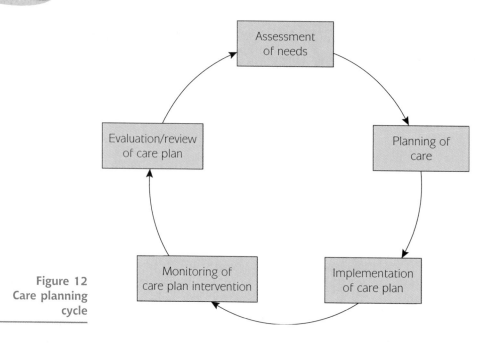

**Figure 12
Care planning
cycle**

Key points – ways of promoting well-being

- Find out what the individual thinks about their well-being and quality of life.
- Observe and obtain information about the individual's ability to carry out their activities of daily living.
- Clarify and agree with the individual the type of support and level of assistance that they require.
- Focus support and assistance on maximising self-care and independence and avoid taking over or imposing care on the individual.
- Provide support and assistance in a collaborative way that promotes and respects the individual's dignity, rights and self-esteem.
- Work in ways that maximise health and safety considerations and which minimise hazards and manage risk appropriately.
- Observe and report back on changes and developments in the individual's ability to manage their activities of living and on the types of support and levels of assistance that you need to provide for them.

Help individuals access other support to promote their well-being

This element focuses on your role in identifying other support needs of individuals and the part that you can play in helping them to access and use additional support systems effectively.

Sharing support

As we have already seen, care workers tend to work with others in care teams. The team approach to care provision ensures that individuals can receive a wide range of care and support services in a co-ordinated way. It also ensures that these services are provided by people with appropriate experience and specialist knowledge and skills. We have also said that you should only practise up to your own level of competence. Do not seek to provide care or take on responsibilities beyond this level. You should know the other members of the care team in which you work and you should be aware of the kind of health and social-care services that are available in your local area. This type of knowledge will enable you to put individuals in touch with other specialist care practitioners and allow you to share the provision of support with them where this is appropriate and necessary.

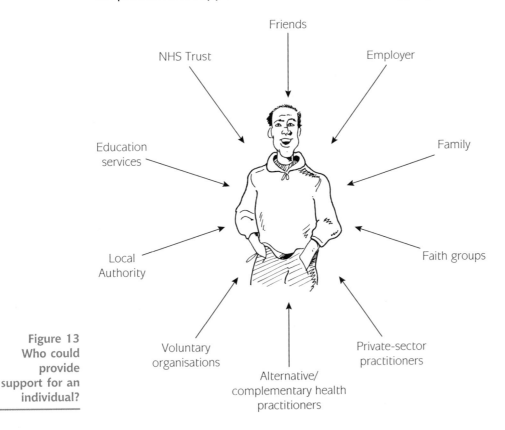

Figure 13
Who could provide support for an individual?

As Figure 13 indicates, many different specialist services and care practitioners may be available to support an individual's well-being. The range of services available to any particular individual will differ throughout the UK because some local areas have more services than others. However, even where several support services are available, individuals may not make use of them because they are unaware of their existence or experience difficulty in accessing them. Care workers like yourself can play an important role in helping individuals to overcome such barriers and get the most out of the support services that they need.

Sources of support

KUS 6

The sources of support that are available to a particular individual will depend on:

- The individual's particular care needs.
- The nature of the care setting in which the individual receives care.
- The availability of specialist practitioners and support services locally.
- Cost or eligibility factors that must be met in order to get the services.
- Your knowledge and understanding of how to access appropriate services on behalf of the individual.

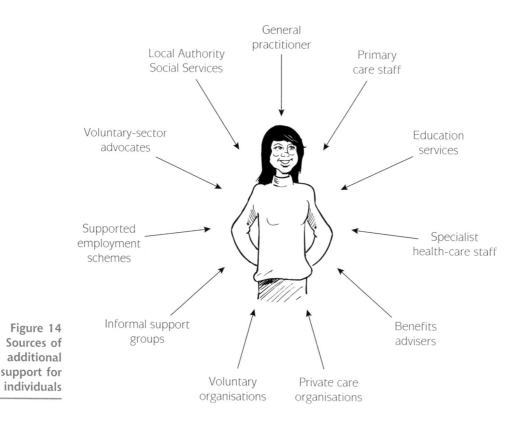

Figure 14 Sources of additional support for individuals

As well as considering additional sources of support that may be needed to deal with an individual's further problems or unmet needs, you should also consider sources of preventive care and support that may have a positive effect on their health or well-being. Individuals who have learning disabilities, mental-health problems or who are affected by old age, **social exclusion** or unfair discrimination may become socially isolated and **marginalised** in society. So they often do not

Table 3 Examples of additional support and services for individuals

Source of support	Examples of service available
General practitioners/ health centres	• Health screening (for example, cervical smears, breast screening and prostate screening). • Health checks (hearing and vision checks and referrals as well as blood cholesterol, blood sugar and blood pressure checks). • Specialist services and clinics (for diabetes, family planning, smoking cessation, counselling and immunisation programmes for example).
Specialist care and treatment services	• NHS Trusts provide a range of specialist services, including physiotherapy, occupational therapy, psychotherapy and counselling in response to medical and social-work referrals. • Private practitioners and private-sector organisations also provide specialist medical and therapy services to people who are able to pay for the services. • Private agencies provide home care and private nursing and social-care support to individuals who have a care package funded by social services or an NHS Trust or who are able to pay for their care privately.
Voluntary support groups such as: • Age Concern/Age Well/ Help the Aged • Mencap • Gateway • Multiple Sclerosis Society • Scope • MIND	• Befriending and helpline services. • Counselling and regular support-group meetings. • Social and activity groups. • Information and advice sessions and case workers. • Housing, hot meals and adapted equipment provision. • Carer support groups.
Equipment suppliers	• Local Authority Social Services and NHS Trust occupational therapy departments may be able to provide practical aids and equipment for daily living and mobility equipment. • Many aids and gadgets are now available to support people but you need to know what is required, where to get them and how much they are. Support groups or the relevant specialist practitioner would be the best source of information on such matters.
Advocacy services	• An advocate is someone who will speak on behalf of the individual and represent their wishes. This can be a formal or informal arrangement. Advocates are usually provided by voluntary-sector organisations.
Service user information	• Patient Advice and Liaison Service (PALS) officers are employed in each NHS Trust to provide information for patients, families and carers. This can involve anything from how to get to an appointment, to how to make an official complaint.

make use of basic preventive health services offered by general practitioners (GPs), dentists and opticians. This may damage their long-term health because small problems are not diagnosed or treated early and develop into much more significant and sometimes untreatable health problems later in their life. Simply knowing about the kinds of preventive health services that are available at a health centre or local GP surgery (see Table 3) could help you to get an individual back into the health system so that they can receive some additional care and support. The next step is to obtain the extra support that the individual needs.

Obtaining support

The first step in helping individuals to access other support is to identify their needs for additional support. You may do this through working closely with the individual and regularly monitoring their condition, abilities and changing care needs. If you recognise the need for additional care and support you should report this to your supervisor or line manager. A team meeting or care plan review may be the most appropriate place to do this. The individual's key worker (assuming this is not you) and the wider care team will then have an opportunity to consider how the individual's changing or additional needs can best be met. One or more of the team members may choose to take responsibility for providing the additional support or may be able to make a professional **referral** to a service or practitioner outside the care team.

Figure 15
Accessing other
support

The way that your care team deals with an individual's need for additional support will probably be covered by local policies and procedures. Find out what these policies are before you make what could be an expensive referral.

There are also situations where it may be appropriate for you to seek additional support services on behalf of an individual without having to get permission or go through a team leader, line manager or supervisor. For example, an individual or a member of their family may ask you about education or leisure services that the individual could use for social and recreational purposes. Providing information and guidance on their location, cost and appropriateness would not require a team meeting. However, it would be good practice to report back to your care team about the individual's interest in and use of any additional support services. This could affect the individual's care plan or be an important indicator of changes to their condition or situation. Also, where an individual seeks extra services from the private or voluntary sector (such as meal delivery, home help or private nursing care) you should report this to your fellow team members. Information about the use of additional services like this may help a key worker to get further funding or increased staffing to meet the individual's needs.

KUS 6

Agreeing responsibilities and your role

Part of your work role may involve directly helping an individual to access and make use of other services or sources of support. For example, if you work in a learning-disability setting you might accompany an individual to and from a day centre, provide support for them when using public transport, or you might help them when they go to college for a class. At these times you need to be clear about the nature and boundaries of your role and how it relates to that of others. You will need to:

- Liaise and communicate with the other service providers.
- Clarify what you are responsible for and are expected to do and what the other care providers are responsible for and will do.
- Work out how you will collaborate or work together where this is necessary and appropriate.
- Clarify how any problems, emergencies and conflicts that arise when you are working with others will be dealt with and resolved.

As we have mentioned, it is vital that you work within the limits of your level of competence. Do not agree to take on responsibilities beyond this when working with others. You should clarify with your supervisor or line manager how any collaboration with specialist or external care workers will work. All of your employer's policies and procedures and the general legal and ethical frameworks for safe and ethical practice will still apply and must be followed.

Monitoring, evaluating and reporting feedback

KUS 12

You have a key role in observing and monitoring individuals' well-being. Do not assume that all of the care and support that is provided for an individual will always be appropriate and effective. Sometimes adjustments will have to be made before the right type and level of support for an individual is found. Also, an individual's needs may change over time as they develop or age, or because of an improvement or deterioration in their condition.

Good observational, monitoring and communication skills are required to recognise and provide feedback about changes in the support needs of individuals. Communicating with an individual and their family and with other care workers involved in providing care and support for the individual will provide you with useful information that can be used to supplement and support your own observations. If you note significant changes in the individual's support needs, or if you have any concerns about them, you should inform your supervisor or line manager as soon as possible. Carefully document changes, both positive progress and lack of progress or deterioration, in accordance with your organisation's policies and local practices.

Evaluating support

Ivy, aged 84, lives in supported housing. She has been taking medication for her high blood pressure for a number of years. However, she is now experiencing a distressing side-effect. Ivy's blood-pressure tablets are causing her to go to the toilet frequently to pass urine. Unfortunately, because she is not always able to get to the toilet in the night, Ivy has been incontinent several times. Ivy is now very distressed by this. The warden from the housing complex has also recently called to see Ivy and noticed the stains on the carpet and the smell of urine in her flat. The warden did not have much time to talk to Ivy but did suggest that the time may have come for Ivy to consider nursing-home care. Reluctantly Ivy has started to think that she may be right.

➤ *What kind of additional support or care services does Ivy need?*

➤ *Who might be able to help in this situation?*

➤ *How might Ivy benefit from additional support to help with this problem?*

➤ *If you worked as Ivy's home-support worker, how might the additional support that you have suggested affect your own role?*

Key points – helping individuals to access other support

- Develop links with other members of your care team.
- Find out about your colleagues' work roles and the type and level of support that they can offer to individuals.
- Develop your knowledge and understanding of the range of sources of support that are available to users of care services living in your local area.
- Think about referring individuals to preventive health services as well as services that can provide additional support.

- Find out how individuals can be referred and gain access to services that offer extra support.
- Ensure that you involve your supervisor or line manager in any referral process and do not exceed the responsibilities and authority of your work role.
- Agree what your responsibilities are and what the limits of your role will be in any situations where you collaborate with other care workers or providers of support.
- Take an active role in monitoring individuals' well-being and the impact that care and support services are having.
- Provide feedback to colleagues and other care workers about the impact of support provided for individuals and on any changes that may affect the individual's future needs for support.

Unit
HSC27 Are you ready for assessment?

Support individuals in their daily living

This unit is all about your involvement in supporting individuals with aspects of their daily lives and activities that will promote their well-being. This unit is closely linked to unit HSC21 covering communication and unit HSC24 covering the principles of care and individual well-being.

As this unit relates to supporting people with daily living activities it is likely that most of the evidence you need to cover the performance criteria and knowledge specification can be gathered during your assessment in the optional units in your qualification and will also contribute to the evidence for the core units. Since there are clear links to risk assessment (HSC22) and the other core units, you should consider these when planning with your assessor.

Your assessment will mainly be carried out through observation by your assessor and should provide most of the evidence for the elements in this unit.

As this unit is about daily living activities there will be ample opportunities for observation by your assessor. However, if such observation might intrude on the privacy of individuals then you can plan with your assessor to use the testimony of an expert witness instead of observation by your assessor.

Direct observation

Your assessor or an expert witness will need to see you carry out the performance criteria (PCs) in each of the elements in this unit.

The performance criteria that may be difficult to meet through observation or expert witness testimony are:

- **HSC27a PC 4**

- HSC27b PC 6
- HSC27c PC 3

usually because they might not always occur.

Preparing to be observed

You must make sure that your workplace and any individuals and key people involved in your work agree to you being assessed. Explicit, informed consent must be obtained before you carry out any assessment activity that involves individuals or which involves access to confidential information related to their care.

Before your assessments you should read carefully the performance criteria for each element in the unit. Try to cover as much as you can *during your observations* but remember that you and your assessor can also plan for additional sources of evidence should full coverage of all performance

criteria not be possible or to help ensure that your performance is consistent and that you can apply the knowledge specification in your work practice.

Other types of evidence

You may need to present other forms of evidence in order to:

- Cover criteria not observed by your assessor or by an expert witness.
- Show that you have the required knowledge, understanding and skills to claim competence in this area of practice.
- Ensure that your work practice is consistent.

Your assessor may also need to ask you questions to confirm your knowledge and understanding of this unit.

Check your knowledge

1   Identify the different types of human needs that individuals have.

2   Describe what Maslow's hierarchy of needs consists of and explain how Maslow thought people try to satisfy their needs.

3   Identify a range of activities of daily living that individuals have to complete to satisfy their human needs.

4   Explain why care workers should seek to work in partnership with the individuals they provide care for.

5   What does providing active support involve?

6   Describe how you can clarify and establish your role when providing support for a particular individual.

7   Explain how activities of daily living are linked to an individual's well-being.

8   Describe how monitoring, observation and reporting are features of your role when providing care and support for individuals.

9   Describe how you can help individuals to access other forms of support to meet their care needs.

Support individuals to access and participate in recreational activities

*T*his unit focuses on the role that care workers play in supporting individuals to get access to and take part in recreational activities. We will consider the types of support that individuals may need to identify their recreational interests and preferences, how you can encourage and support individuals' participation in recreational activities, and the importance of reviewing the value of recreational activities for individuals.

This unit contains three elements:

⌐ **HSC210a** *Support individuals to identify their recreational interests and preferences*

⌐ **HSC210b** *Encourage and support individuals to participate in recreational activities*

⌐ **HSC210c** *Encourage and support individuals to review the value of recreational activities*

Introduction

KUS 1, 2

Recreation is any type of activity that is refreshing, relaxing and which a person wants to participate in because it brings them pleasure. This definition is very broad but it should give you an idea about the emphasis on leisure in recreational activity. Remember that people must choose and want to participate in an activity before it can be thought of as recreation for them.

Everybody needs some recreational activity in life. This is true whether a person is experiencing health, developmental or social problems or is fully able and in good health. People receiving care in hospital or a residential care setting should not be denied recreational opportunities simply because they have significant health or social-care needs. Instead, care workers who wish to provide holistic care must identify each individual's recreational needs and find ways of helping and supporting them to choose and participate in recreational activities.

Types of recreational activity

Recreational activities include any leisure or recreational pursuits that individuals wish to be involved in. There are too many possibilities to list them all, but there are different categories (see Figure 1) that can help us to think about how we could provide recreation in a care setting. As well as thinking about the types of activity that individuals might use for recreation, consider what they get out of it.

If you ask someone why they take part in an activity or pastime they will probably tell you that they do it because they enjoy it. If you ask why they enjoy this

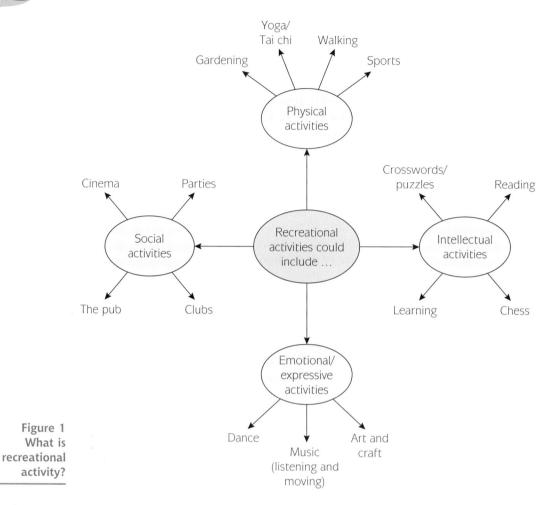

Figure 1
What is recreational activity?

particular activity and what they see as the benefits of taking part, they may give you a few more reasons. They may describe how the activity meets their needs. For example, playing cards might satisfy a person's social and intellectual needs because it gives them a chance to meet and spend time with friends and other people and is mentally stimulating. Alternatively, going to the gym or for a long walk, or doing some gardening might meet some of an individual's physical needs. Therefore, we could also categorise activities in terms of the human needs that they meet (see Table 1).

Benefits of recreational activity

KUS 9

People benefit in different ways from different types of activity:

- *Physical activity* generally benefits the body. Playing sport, taking part in gentle stretching classes and doing yoga all contribute to a person's fitness and the maintenance of their physical skills and abilities. Different physical activities provide particular physical benefits. Activities such as short walks and gentle stretching can help to maintain physical skills like mobility, whilst other activities such as using weights and exercise bikes or swimming can develop strength and stamina.

Table 1 Human needs met by activities

Type of activity	Needs that could be met	Example
Physical	Physical need for activity, exercise and the use of the body	Gardening Walking/sports Tai Chi/yoga
Intellectual	Mental need for stimulation and learning	Crosswords/puzzles Reading/studying Watching films/TV
Emotional	Emotional need to express and develop feelings	Art and craft activities Talking with friends Drama/dance/singing
Social	Social need for relationships and contact with other people	Parties/meeting friends Going out to concerts Theatre/cinema

Figure 2
Recreational
activity can take
many forms

- *Intellectual activity* generally benefits thinking, concentration and memory. Completing puzzles, reading books and studying educational courses usually require very little physical effort. However, they do require mental effort and help to develop a person's mental skills and abilities. Also, being able to complete mentally stimulating and challenging activities can help to boost and maintain a person's mood and their self-esteem.

- *Emotional activities* provide people with opportunities to express their feelings and experience the feelings of other people. Activities that are relaxing (such as yoga or Tai Chi) and those that are emotionally expressive (such as art and craft, drama and music) all provide people with an emotional outlet. Activities that have a strong emotional aspect can relieve stress, help people to experience different feelings safely, and also provide a lot of happiness and pleasure.

- *Social activity* involves the use of communication, interaction and relationship skills. Activities such as going out with or meeting friends, taking part in group pastimes like playing card games or watching television with a group of other people all have a strong social element. Social activities strengthen relationships and give people opportunities to develop and use their social skills.

It is helpful to think about the connection between activities and the different human needs that individuals have. However, you have probably noticed already that activities can meet more than one type of need. For example, going to the cinema or playing cards with a group of friends could be socially and intellectually stimulating. This is not a problem, but it does mean that you should think carefully about individuals' needs and interests when you support them to participate in any activity.

Support individuals to identify their recreational interests and preferences

Element
HSC210a

KUS 1, 2, 7

Recreational activities are the leisure pursuits that individuals wish to be involved in. In care work it is easy to make assumptions about the type of person a particular individual is because of their age, background, gender, ethnicity, disability or health problems. Making general assumptions about people in this way is called **stereotyping**. It can be unhelpful and even discriminatory. With regard to recreational activities, for example, it would be a mistake to assume that a person would be interested in bingo, ballroom dancing or going on coach trips simply because they are retired or over 65 years of age. It is vital to treat each person as an individual and to find out about their recreational interests and support needs before planning or beginning any activity programme for them.

The individuals you work with are all likely to have different backgrounds and interests. Despite their health or social problems they will have a range of previous experiences of recreation and leisure activity and possibly some ambitions to extend or develop their recreational interests. Recreational activity could play a large part or a relatively small part in an individual's life. Some people may organise their time and social life around a particular hobby or activity, such as playing bridge or bowls or watching horse racing. For others, leisure and recreation may have been very much secondary to work, travelling or studying. It is important to find out about each individual's previous recreational interests and the extent to which they played a part in that person's life. This information will help you to promote recreation and use activity appropriately and should stop you making inappropriate assumptions.

Practical Example

Helping people fulfil their desires for recreational activities

Wei Wei Chan is a 17-year-old girl who has a learning disability. She has recently begun living in a group home with four other young people. The residents of the home are supported on a daily basis by care workers and a social worker who co-ordinates their care. One care worker sleeps in the group home overnight to deal with any problems that arise. Last night Wei Wei was watching a programme about skiing and she told the care worker that she would like to learn to ski. The care worker said that she would let Wei Wei's support worker and the home manager know and ask whether they could help to arrange this for her. The care worker also pointed out that skiing is difficult to learn and that people sometimes get injured when they are learning. Wei Wei laughed and insisted that she would be all right.

➤ *How could Wei Wei's support worker respond to her reported interest in learning to ski?*

➤ *How might Wei Wei benefit from the experience of learning to ski?*

➤ *Is it discriminatory to think that a person with learning disabilities would find it difficult to learn to ski?*

Identifying recreational needs and interests

KUS 8

We discussed the assessment of an individual's care needs, activities of living and the planning of care earlier in the book (see unit HSC27). In this part of the unit we will consider ways of supporting individuals to identify their recreational interests and preferences.

In many care settings care workers use a formal, direct approach to assess recreational needs. This involves asking an individual about their recreational interests as part of a general assessment of care needs. The assessment procedure in your care setting may or may not follow this format. However, if you need to ask an individual about their recreational interests you should ensure that you communicate effectively, listen carefully and provide any communication support that the person requires (see unit HSC21, page 5).

You may have to overcome communication difficulties if the individual's physical, mental or developmental condition prevents them from communicating effectively. Some individuals, such as those who have severe learning disabilities, degenerative physical conditions or enduring mental-health problems, may not be able to provide this kind of information during an initial assessment or after their admission. You may have to use additional sources of support (such as advocates, translators or specialist care staff) in order to communicate properly. Alternatively, there may be situations where you will need to use other sources to obtain this information. Other ways of obtaining information about individuals' recreational interests include:

- Using self-assessment checklists that allow individuals who cannot give information verbally to indicate their recreational interests and preferences (see Figure 3).

- Asking key people who are normally involved in the individual's care to tell you about the person's past recreational interests and preferred activities.

- Observing the individual's behaviour and activity in the care setting to identify the kind of recreational pastimes that they enjoy or try to take part in.

| | What has been your level of interest? | | | | | | Do you currently participate in this activity? | | Would you like to pursue this in the future? | |
| | In the past 10 years | | | In the last year | | | | | | |
	Strong	Some	None	Strong	Some	None	Yes	No	Yes	No
Activity										
Gardening										
Sewing/needlework										
Playing cards										
Foreign languages										
Church activities										
Radio										
Television										
Walking										
Art and craft										
Golf										
Listening to music										

Figure 3
Activity checklist

Self-reports and interest checklists are a good way of obtaining information from the individual about their recreational needs, interests and preferences. You may be able to produce a checklist of your own which is appropriate for the type of care setting and the individuals with whom you work. If you do this remember to avoid making too many assumptions about the individual's needs or interests. Check with the individual to see whether your own observations and any information from their relatives, friends or previous carers is accurate. This is a good way of finding out if the individual's interests are the same as when they were observed or reported.

If there is no formal assessment of individuals' recreational needs in your care setting and you do not feel that a checklist is appropriate, try to use a more informal approach to identify their recreational needs, interests and preferences. An individual's previous and current interests and hobbies, as well as their ambitions and aspirations for the future, could be the focus of informal conversations. These will also help you to establish a rapport and develop your relationship with the individual. The individual will be able to talk about something other than their health or social problems. They may well feel knowledgeable and confident talking about this.

Appropriate and realistic activity

KUS 7

An individual (or their relatives) may identify a range of recreational needs and interests. You may have anticipated some of these and you and other members of your care team may feel confident supporting them. However, individuals might have unusual hobbies and recreational interests that are difficult to support or facilitate in your care setting. Maybe the activity is expensive or requires a lot of staff support, it might involve some risk or require skills and facilities that are not available in the care setting.

Rather than dismiss the unusual or unexpected, you should obtain all the information you can from the individual and then discuss this with your supervisor and colleagues. It is important to try to find appropriate and realistic ways of meeting a person's recreational interests and preferences. You may have to negotiate with the individual or their relatives. Or you may need to adapt equipment or facilities or lower the individual's expectations if their capabilities have changed or they have lost some of their skills. However, there are many examples of sporting and recreational activities that can be adapted to make them accessible to people who have lost some skills or abilities or who require support or assistance to participate. The key point is to ensure that recreational activities are appropriate to the individual's needs and abilities so that they have a realistic chance to participate and benefit from them. This means that you, or other members of your care team, will need to assess the individual's level of ability and skills.

Assessing ability

Each individual's physical, intellectual, emotional and social skills and abilities should be assessed as part of any activity-planning programme. You must obtain the individual's agreement to carry out a formal assessment of their skills and abilities, but you may also be able to use other sources of information to help with this. Information could be obtained from:

- The initial assessment carried out when the individual was admitted to the care setting.
- The individual's care plan that identifies their level of functioning and their care needs.
- Assessments of functioning and skills carried out by specialist care practitioners, such as physiotherapists, mental-health workers, social workers, education staff or occupational therapists.

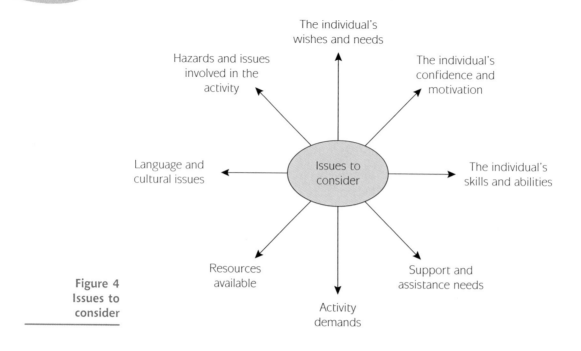

Figure 4
Issues to
consider

An individual may also be able to self-report on their abilities by answering questions that you ask them. You will need to judge an individual's various skills and abilities using these sources of information and your own recent experience of the person's activity levels. If the individual over-estimates their ability, or the reports and assessments of their functioning are out of date, you may need to think of ways to lower the individual's expectations so that they can take part in an activity in a realistic and appropriate way. An individual may also underestimate their ability to take part in recreational activity. This could happen when they have low self-esteem, low mood or where they feel frail or vulnerable because of a recent or existing health problem. In this situation part of your role would include building up the individual's confidence and motivating them to participate. Gentle encouragement and support is more appropriate here than pressurising the individual to use their abilities. Remember that the individual should always choose recreational activities freely. Nobody should be forced or nagged into taking part in anything that they do not want to do.

Using specialist assessments

KUS 5

As a care worker you will probably be just one part of a larger team of professionals providing and supporting recreational activities. For example, the care team may include:

- Nurses.
- Occupational therapists.
- Teachers or education support staff.

- Physiotherapists.

- Speech and language therapists.

- Dieticians.

The members of the care team in your local care setting may differ slightly depending on the nature of the setting, your individual group and local resources. However, care team members are usually able to offer specialist assessment and treatment skills associated with their care discipline. Occupational therapists are particularly important with regard to activity and skills assessments. Therefore, you may be able to ask an occupational therapist to carry out a specialist assessment of an individual's ability or to comment on the suitability of a particular activity for the person. You should always check an individual's records to find out whether occupational therapy assessments have been carried out. These will provide useful information to enable you to assess whether and in what capacity individuals are able to take part in recreational pursuits.

Identifying support needs

KUS 3

An individual may be able to continue to participate in their existing recreational activities despite health or social problems if they receive appropriate support. This can include:

- Using adapted equipment.

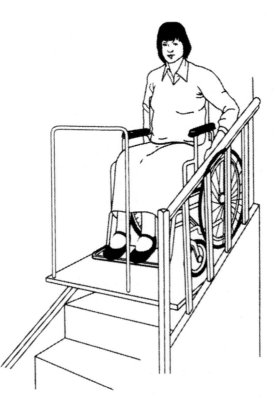

**Figure 5
Using adapted
equipment:
a stair lift**

- Obtaining assistance from a care worker in relation to transport, mobility or communication problems.

- Modifying the way they take part in a valued activity or form of recreation.

Again, an occupational therapist or experienced activity support worker may be able to suggest or provide suitable forms of support to enable this to happen. You should always discuss support needs and suggestions for providing additional support directly with the individual to ensure that what is offered and provided is suitable and acceptable to that person.

Risk assessment and activity choice

KUS 5, 10

When discussing recreational and leisure activity with individuals, always consider health and safety issues and any laws that apply. Recreational activities may carry some risk of injury or harm because they involve:

- Physical contact with others – such as judo or football.

- Some form of dangerous environment – such as scuba diving, cycling or horse riding.

- Using equipment that could be dangerous – such as in carpentry, cookery or stained-glass work.

Regardless of the type of recreational activity that the individual suggests, a risk assessment should always be carried out to evaluate the possible hazards and dangers involved. The risk assessment must consider the nature of the activity and the abilities of the individual. Wherever possible all risks should be eliminated or minimised in order for the individual to take part in the activity safely.

Managing risks in activities

KUS 4, 10

When trying to manage the risks involved in recreational activity, you should consider an individual's choice of activity in the light of various factors. Together with the individual, you should think about:

- The possible difficulties and dangers that a particular activity involves, taking into consideration the individual's abilities.

- The resources that are needed to enable the individual to take part in an activity.

- The recreational and **therapeutic** benefits of the activity to the individual.

It is not always the case that individuals should be prevented from taking part in recreational activities that carry some risk. The key issue is whether the risk can be managed and reduced to an acceptable level. This is usually a decision for the person or group of people who have managerial responsibility for a care setting or the person who holds overall responsibility for an individual's care. In your role as a care assistant, you should not take responsibility for or make decisions of this nature. You should always refer any risk issues or concerns to your supervisor or manager. Be aware of possible risks and of the agreed ways of minimising and managing them. Where a recreational activity cannot be managed safely or appears to involve an unacceptable degree of risk to an individual, you should help the individual to identify a suitable alternative. Alternatively, if the individual is unwilling to give up an apparently risky form of recreational activity, you should work with them to find ways of modifying how they take part in it in order to maximise their safety and minimise the risk of harm or injury.

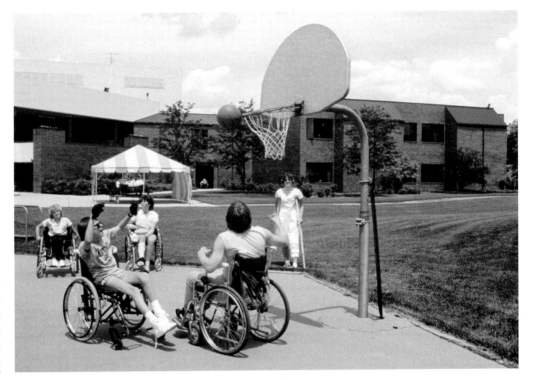

Figure 6
Nearly every recreational activity carries some risk

Key points – helping individuals to access and participate in recreational activities

- Try to get to know what each individual's recreational needs and interests are.

- Do not make stereotypical assumptions about what an individual's recreational needs and interests might be.

- Find out about and consider an individual's previous recreational interests and experiences.

- Do not let an individual's communication difficulties stop you from finding out about their recreational interests – use additional sources of support where these are available.

- Use a variety of sources of information to identify an individual's recreational needs and interests – but check information with the individual whenever possible.

- Do not assume that an individual's previous recreational interests will be the same as their current interests – find out about new interests and aspirations.

- Try to identify interests that are accessible, realistic and appropriate for the individual.

- Do not assume that an individual possesses the level of physical or intellectual ability or skill that they claim to have. Use the most recent functional assessments that are available.

- Think actively about an individual's support needs and identify with them what kind of help or assistance they would like to receive to support them with their recreational needs.

- Do not automatically assume that individuals should not participate in activities that may involve some risk.

- Think about the hazards and risks that may be involved in different forms of recreational activity and try to assess and manage the risks involved.

- Do not make decisions about risk on your own – use risk assessments and ensure that a manager or supervisor is aware of risks involved in the individual's choice of recreational activity.

Element HSC210b

Encourage and support individuals to participate in recreational activities

Supporting and enabling activity choices

KUS 2, 3, 8, 11

So far we have looked at the different types of recreational needs that individuals may have and we have considered how individuals can be supported to identify their recreational interests and preferences. This element focuses on ways of encouraging and supporting individuals to actually take part in recreational activities. This is an important 'next step' for some individuals as they may experience a gap between their interest in and wish to do an activity and their motivation and ability to actually participate.

Figure 7
Taking part in
recreational
interests

By this point, hopefully you will understand the importance of supporting individuals to identify their recreational needs, interests and preferences (see HSC210a). This approach centres more on the individual and is better than presenting an individual with your own choices of recreational activities. We have discussed various ways of obtaining information about an individual's recreational interests. The next step is to use this information to help the individual select activities that they wish to participate in. An individual's choices will depend on a number of linked factors, including:

- Their current skills and existing interests.
- The demands of different activities.
- The availability of activities.
- Language and cultural issues.
- Health, welfare and safety considerations.
- The cost of activities and the resources that are available to them.
- The level of support and assistance that an individual requires in order to participate.

An individual's choice of recreational activity may be limited by a number of these factors. For example, the individual's health, skills and interests may mean that some recreational activities are not appropriate. The level of physical skill and ability required to participate in sporting activities ranging from football and running to indoor bowls may be too demanding for individuals who are frail, physically unwell or physically disabled. However, they may be entirely appropriate and accessible for others. Moreover, individuals who experience confusion, poor concentration due to mental-health problems, or limited intellectual development due to learning disabilities may find the level of intellectual ability required for reading novels, doing crosswords or playing some computer games too demanding. Others with similar difficulties may find that they can adapt. The key point is to support individuals to choose appropriate activities that interest them and which they can access and benefit from.

Exploring and assessing recreational activities

Philip Malcolm, aged 39, has been a lifelong fan of motorcycle racing. He has always dreamt of owning a touring bike though he has never had the chance to learn to ride a motorbike.

Philip has spent most of his adult life living in psychiatric units where he has received care for enduring mental-health problems. When he becomes unwell Philip is withdrawn and thinks that other people are trying to harm him. He has said that this has caused him to think about taking his own life.

Philip is relatively well at the moment. In fact, he is about to move from hospital to a supported hostel. He has been speaking to his named nurse and social worker as part of his discharge planning programme. They have suggested that Philip should think about the kind of recreational activities he might be interested in doing when he leaves hospital. So far Philip's only interest is in learning to ride a motorbike.

➤ Do you think that Philip's desire to learn to ride a motorbike is an appropriate and reasonable use of his recreation time?

➤ Would you be concerned about Philip doing this activity? If so, explain what your concerns would be.

➤ How could Philip be supported to broaden his recreational interests to activities other than motorcycle riding?

You will need to make good use of your relationship with the individual in order to help them identify and select appropriate recreational activities. In order to find out about an individual's recreational preferences and their previous interests and experiences you will need effective communication skills. You should use open and closed questions effectively and listen actively (see unit HSC21, pages 13 and 22). You will also need a good understanding of the individual's skills and abilities, perhaps obtained from an assessment of their activities of daily living (see unit HSC27). Whilst some individuals may be very motivated and confident about participating in both new and familiar recreational activities, you might have to encourage others to either resume the recreational activities they are familiar with or try new ones. In either of these situations a sensitive and supportive approach is needed so that the individual actively engages in activity.

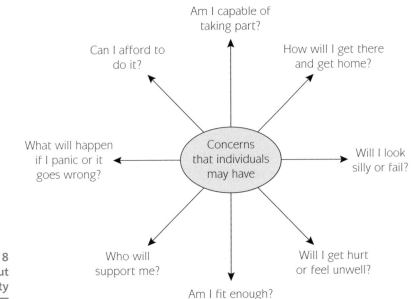

Am I capable of
taking part?

Can I afford to
do it?

How will I get there
and get home?

What will happen
if I panic or it
goes wrong?

Concerns
that individuals
may have

Will I look
silly or fail?

Who will
support me?

Will I get hurt
or feel unwell?

Am I fit enough?

Figure 8
Concerns about
activity

Availability of activities

There are lots of care settings in the UK. These include specialist medical and hospital-based settings, more informal residential and nursing-care homes, supported housing and individuals' own homes. The nature and location of an individual's care setting will affect the range of recreational activities available to them.

Individuals who are receiving care in hospitals or other specialist nursing homes may have their choice of recreational activities restricted to relatively sedentary games and pastimes that can be carried out safely within such settings. Playing cards, reading, watching television and listening to the radio or a personal stereo, or going on short walks around the hospital or home may be realistic choices. In some care settings specialist activity workers, occupational-therapy and nursing staff or volunteers may organise group activities such as parties, dances or games sessions. However, trips out to theatres, cinemas or the seaside may not be available or may be inappropriate for individuals with extensive care needs. On the other hand, individuals who have learning disabilities or mental-health problems may welcome, benefit from and have more access to recreational activities based in the local community or which involve going away on holiday whilst supported by care workers.

The nature of your local care setting, the funding that is available for recreational activity and the needs and interests that individuals have will all influence what recreational activity is available to individuals. If your care organisation employs specialist-activities workers, a programme of activities and some funding may be available to individuals. It is worth finding out about this. Consider how you and your colleagues could provide recreational opportunities for individuals in order to support this aspect of individual care.

Adapting activities to changing needs

KUS 7

An individual's skills and abilities will change over time possibly because of changes in their physical or mental health or in their social circumstances. This may affect the individual's recreational needs or their ability to participate in recreational activity. When an individual experiences a decline or significant change in their physical or mental health or in their mobility, movement or thinking skills, for example, you should consider how best you could help them to take part in recreational activity. If you know that an individual's abilities will be affected by an event such as surgery or some other form of treatment, or by a likely deterioration in their skills or abilities, you may be able to anticipate and plan for their additional support needs. For example, you might anticipate a need for additional assistance, adapted equipment or a change in the way that the individual participates in the activity. However, you might notice unexpected changes in an individual's abilities or skills and have to respond to these. Again, you could do this by adapting the recreational activity to make it more suitable for the individual or by providing more support and assistance to help them to participate. Whenever you respond to expected or unexpected changes in an individual's ability to participate in recreational activity, you should discuss with them the need for support and any proposed changes to that support. It is the individual who should make the key choices and decisions about their participation in recreational activity.

Supporting participation in activity

KUS 3, 5, 8, 11

We have touched on the need to support individuals' participation in recreational activity a number of times so far in this element. The main issue is how to enable an individual to actually take part in the recreational activities that they wish to participate in. There are a number of possibilities, including:

- Obtaining and providing adapted equipment.
- Obtaining and providing information.
- Ensuring individuals have access to buildings and particular rooms within a building.
- Arranging transport.
- Providing additional support and direct assistance.

The ways that you provide support to enable an individual to participate in their chosen recreational activities will depend on:

- The individual's needs, skills and abilities.
- The individual's wishes and preferences for support and assistance.
- The type of activities involved.
- The problems that have to be overcome.
- The resources that are available for you to use.

An individual's recreational support needs should, ideally, be documented in their care plan. This should make clear links between the person's skills, abilities and needs and the type of support or assistance that they require. For example, because of their frailty or lack of independent living skills an older person or a person with learning disabilities may require direct help to get to and participate in recreational activity. However, a more physically able older person, an individual with mental-health problems or a person with a non-disabling physical illness may only require information about where they can find particular recreational activities locally and some encouragement to take part.

Health and safety issues

KUS 4, 5

Health and safety should be a feature of your thinking whenever you are supporting an individual's participation in recreational activity. Health and safety issues may arise because of:

- The hazardous nature of the recreational activity itself. For example, what is the likelihood of the individual having an accident at the swimming baths, drinking too much alcohol at the pub or accidentally hurting themselves with wood-working equipment?

- The hazards involved in the individual going out to attend the activity. For example, can this particular individual safely make their way to and from the sports centre, bingo hall or pub?

- The individual's vulnerability to harm or injury being increased by taking part in a particular type of recreational activity. For example, is playing football a good idea soon after a serious operation? Should an individual with recent short-term memory problems go out to play bingo unaccompanied? How might an older individual's unstable angina and diabetes interfere with their ability to complete a sponsored walk for the local hospice?

The precise nature of the health and safety issues that you need to consider will depend on the individual and the recreational activity that they wish to participate

Figure 9
Some activities
may involve
health and
safety risks

in. You should apply the health and safety principles referred to in unit HSC22 and always ensure that you work within the law to protect the individual from injury or harm. Through their policies and procedures, your employer is also likely to provide guidance on health and safety issues related to recreational activity. Check and become familiar with these and always work within them. If a situation arises where you believe that the health and safety risks involved in a particular form of recreational activity are too great or are unacceptably high to you – though the individual may disagree – you should report your concerns to your supervisor or manager. Do not provide support or assistance in circumstances where you cannot justify participation or manage the health and safety risks involved.

Providing and seeking additional support

KUS 3, 10, 11

There are always limits to what you can offer individuals in terms of care and assistance and the boundaries of your role as a care worker. You may find that you cannot support or assist an individual to participate in the recreational activity that they choose because, for example:

- You cannot motivate the individual sufficiently.
- You do not have the activity skills or experience to participate alongside or to assist the individual in a particular activity.
- You do not have the specialist care skills needed to support or assist the individual to participate.
- You do not have the authority to book or pay for necessary transport, buy equipment or authorise additional support for the individual.

In any situation involving these types of issues seek additional support for the individual. Your role is still one of enabling the individual's participation in recreational activity. However, it is more appropriate and responsible to recognise your own limitations and to obtain extra support where this is clearly needed. Not doing so may increase the health and safety risks involved in the activity. It is likely to limit the extent to which the individual can benefit from participation in the recreational activity.

Key points – supporting participation in recreational activities

- When encouraging participation in recreational activity, take into account individuals' previous interests and abilities, their current skills and condition and other relevant factors, like health and safety and language issues.
- Acknowledge and be realistic about factors that may limit an individual's participation in recreational activity.
- Make good use of your communication skills and your relationship with an individual to find out about their recreational interests, experiences and preferences.

- Check the individual's records for any assessments that may provide information on their current skills or abilities that are relevant to recreational activity.
- Wherever possible adapt recreational activities to meet an individual's changing needs or abilities.
- Provide information, equipment and practical assistance where they are wanted and needed by the individual.
- Health and safety issues should always be considered and taken seriously when supporting individuals to participate in recreational activity.
- Seek extra support from your supervisor, service manager or a specialist care practitioner if you are unable to provide the support that an individual needs to participate in recreational activity.

Element HSC210c — *Encourage and support individuals to review the value of recreational activities*

Ways of reviewing activity participation

A review is an opportunity to look back on, or inspect, something. A review of an individual's activity participation is an opportunity to assess:

- The individual's level of participation in their chosen recreational activities.
- The individual's feelings and views about what they have gained from participating in these recreational activities.
- Any problems, difficulties or barriers to participation that have limited the individual's opportunities to participate in or enjoy recreational activities.
- Whether and how problems and barriers to participation can be overcome.

As well as assessing current or recent participation in recreational activity, a review will also consider future plans.

Taking part in an activity review

KUS 1, 4, 5

A review of activity participation could be carried out in a formal or informal way. A formal review would involve a meeting with the individual and perhaps other key people and professionals involved in their care. This could be part of a broader care-plan review. An informal review is more likely to be based on a conversation or series of brief meetings with the individual that occur over time. The individual's recreational activities are discussed and you would find out whether these are meeting their leisure and recreation needs. Alternatively, where an individual is unwilling or unable to talk about their participation in recreational activities, they might complete a brief questionnaire or checklist (see Figure 6) as a way of expressing their thoughts and views.

The individual's direct participation in an activity review is important because you must consider their views and needs and they are in the best position to know what these are. However, actually getting an individual to take part in an activity review may not be straightforward. For example, the individual may experience communication difficulties and require considerable support to make a contribution. Or a deterioration in an individual's mental or physical health may make direct participation much more difficult. To set up an activity review a number of issues need to be considered. You should:

- Find out how the individual will participate in a review of their recreational activities.

- Identify and provide appropriate forms of support (such as communication aids, language support, advocacy) to enable the individual to make their thoughts and views known.

- Identify who should be involved in a review of the individual's recreational activities (e.g. key people, other professionals).

- Decide how the information produced in the review will be handled. For example, will it be:

  - Reported and communicated to others through the usual care plan reporting processes?

  - Relayed to colleagues through a report or handover meeting?

  - Written down as a formal report and placed in the individual's records?

This process involves a lot of communication and management skills. Your role in it will depend on local policies and practices. In some care settings care workers may organise and run a review meeting. In other care settings a registered nurse, social worker or a person who has managerial or supervisory responsibilities would carry out this work. Whoever takes on the task of organising and running a review meeting, they will need to spend time talking with the individual, making contact with other key people and co-ordinating all of this to arrive at a practical time and date for a review meeting. Practical issues relating to where the meeting is held, who will produce and run the **agenda** and who will take notes about what is said and decided should also be considered. In addition confidentiality issues must be handled appropriately.

It is important that you find out what your local policies and procedures say about this area of practice. You need to understand your own role in any review meeting so that you can prepare and participate appropriately. If you are not directly involved in organising and co-ordinating the review, you are likely to have a role in discussing the meeting with the individual and explaining who will be there and what will happen.

Negotiating and implementing changes

KUS 8, 11

A meeting that aims to review an individual's participation in recreational activity should focus clearly on obtaining and listening to that person's views and feedback. It is appropriate to focus on both the positive and negative aspects of the individual's experience. The meeting might begin by identifying the benefits and enjoyment that the individual has gained from their recreational activity. As well as the individual's views, other care workers and key people involved in the

Figure 10
Reviewing
recreational
activity

individual's care may contribute their views and perspectives. For example, occupational-therapy, nursing, medical or education staff may comment on the extent to which the individual appears to be benefiting from participation and on how they think this is affecting the person's physical, intellectual, emotional or social needs and skills.

An individual's communication skills, levels of personal confidence and perhaps also their familiarity with review meetings will affect their ability to participate in such meetings. Some individuals may have the skills, confidence and ability to participate fully and even lead the discussions. However, other individuals may find it more difficult to participate. This might be because of communication difficulties arising from learning disability, mental-health problems or strokes. Alternatively, a person may be naturally more withdrawn or have less confidence. They may be reluctant to discuss their thoughts, experiences and interests in public. Identifying and making use of appropriate forms of support should help an individual to overcome some if not all of these problems so that they are able to make some kind of contribution to the review meeting.

In addition to identifying the ways in which an individual is benefiting from recreational activity, a review meeting is also likely to consider problems, difficulties and opportunities for extending or changing the individual's participation in recreation. For example, the individual or a care worker may report difficulties that the individual experienced gaining access to specific activities because of mobility, transport or cost. Alternatively, an individual may say that they are not enjoying or benefiting from their current recreational activities. It is also possible, and in some care settings very likely, that changes in an individual's condition will make their participation in recreational activities more difficult. In all of these circumstances, you should support and encourage the individual to identify and talk about the changes to their recreational activity that are necessary and which they would like to see. These changes could involve:

- Beginning new activities and ending or adding to current activities.

- Finding new ways of participating in activities.

- Obtaining additional support and assistance to participate in chosen recreational activities.

Review of recreational activities

Sophie James is a 65-year-old woman living in a residential home. Sophie has osteoporosis which affects her ability to walk and mobilise. She lived at home until about a year ago when her condition caused her to become housebound and isolated. Sophie enjoys other people's company and is a very keen card player. She has recently started to use an electric wheelchair to mobilise and is generally happy with the freedom of movement that this gives her. However, the bridge club that she attends near to the residential home is not accessible to wheelchair users. Sophie is frustrated by this and wishes to review her current programme of recreational activity and support in order to maintain her interests and social life.

➤ *How have changes in Sophie's condition affected her opportunity to take part in recreational activities?*

➤ *What might the participants in a review meeting focus on when reviewing the value of recreational activity for Sophie?*

➤ *How would a care worker be required to make use of their communication and relationship skills in this meeting?*

➤ *What kind of changes to Sophie's current recreational activity programme could be considered at the review meeting?*

- Seeking additional funding or equipment to enable them to take up new activities or continue participating in current activities.

The aim of the review should be to negotiate changes with the individual so that their needs and preferences are met appropriately and safely. This might also involve persuading other care professionals, managers and your colleagues to change the way that they provide support and assistance to the individual.

Providing feedback and reporting

KUS 6

The discussions that you have in the review meeting should be fully documented and relayed to other members of the care team who need to know about them. The main points raised by the individual and others in the review meeting should be noted. It is essential that any changes or points of agreement are clearly recorded and that you relay and record in writing the details of any changes in support or the allocation of any new responsibilities. This means that you should be clear about who has agreed to do what and when.

The individual and other members of the care team will expect that all of the changes and action points agreed upon in the review meeting are put into practice. If you discover that changes to the individual's recreational activity plan that were agreed are not being made, you should respond appropriately. You may need to speak directly to the person who is supposed to be making the changes. Alternatively, you may need to speak to a supervisor or manager if they are better placed to enquire about and discuss the issues involved in getting changes implemented. Avoid confronting colleagues with direct complaints about their lack of activity or failure to implement changes until you have found out about the possible reasons for the delay. It is better to remind others about the changes that were agreed and to offer support and assistance to help them put these into practice.

Key points – reviewing recreational activities

- A review of an individual's recreational activities should focus on the value or benefits of the activity for the individual, any problems or difficulties that they are experiencing and possible ways of overcoming them and developing further interest in recreation.
- Review can be carried out in formal and informal ways.
- Individuals should be as involved in the review of their recreational activity as they wish to be. Individuals should be given the chance to participate but should not be forced to do so.

- Appropriate and sufficient support and assistance should be provided for individuals who have additional communication needs.
- Changes to an individual's recreational activity should be negotiated and agreed with the individual and any other key people involved in their care.
- Care workers present at a review meeting have a responsibility to provide feedback on what was discussed and report to colleagues any changes that were agreed at the meeting.
- If agreed changes to an individual's plan of recreational activity do not occur, you should respond by taking up the issue in an appropriate way with colleagues, a supervisor or manager.

Unit HSC210 Are you ready for assessment?

Support individuals to access and participate in recreational activities

This unit is all about your involvement in supporting service users to identify, select and participate in the recreational activities that they choose. This unit is closely linked to unit HSC21 covering communication and unit HSC22 covering risk assessment and health, safety and security.

Since this unit covers the preparation leading up to the recreational activities and a review of the impact, it is likely that most of the evidence you need to cover the performance criteria and knowledge specification will be gathered over a period of time.

Your assessment will mainly be carried out through observation by your assessor and this should provide most of the evidence for the elements in this unit.

As this unit is about your role in supporting individuals in recreational activities there will be ample opportunities for observation by your assessor. However, if such observation might intrude on the privacy of individuals or take place over a long period of time then you can plan with your assessor to use the testimony of an expert witness instead of observation by your assessor or as an additional source of evidence.

▶

Direct observation

Your assessor or an expert witness will need to see you carry out the performance criteria (PCs) in each of the elements in this unit.

The performance criteria that may be difficult to meet through observation or expert witness testimony are:

- HSC210a PC 2
- HSC210b PC 4
- HSC210c PC 5

usually because they might not always occur.

Preparing to be observed

You must make sure that your workplace and any individuals and key people involved in your work agree to you being assessed. Explicit, informed consent must be obtained before you carry out any assessment activity that involves individuals or which involves access to confidential information related to their care.

Before your assessments you should read carefully the performance criteria for each element in the unit. Try to cover as much as you can *during your observations* but remember that you and your assessor can also plan for additional sources of evidence should full coverage of all performance criteria not be possible or to help ensure that your performance is consistent and that you can apply the knowledge specification in your work practice.

Other types of evidence

You may need to present other forms of evidence in order to:

- Cover criteria not observed by your assessor or by an expert witness.
- Show that you have the required knowledge, understanding and skills to claim competence in this area of practice.
- Ensure that your work practice is consistent.

Your assessor may also need to ask you questions to confirm your knowledge and understanding of this unit.

Check your knowledge

1 Identify four different types of recreational activity.

2 Describe examples of the benefits of recreational activity.

3 Identify three ways of assessing an individual's recreational needs.

4 Explain why risk assessment is important when providing and supporting recreational activities.

5 Describe three ways of supporting individuals' participation in recreational activities.

6 Identify situations where a care worker should seek additional support to enable an individual to take part in recreational activities.

7 Explain the purpose of an activity review.

Help individuals to eat and drink

*T*his unit focuses on the essential and probably very familiar task of helping individuals to eat and drink. The unit requires you to consider how you can contribute to the assessment of an individual's nutritional needs and help to assess the support that they need to eat and drink independently. You will also need to demonstrate that you are able to assist individuals to eat and drink and provide appropriate care during mealtimes. We will also consider your role in observing and reporting on individuals' dietary intake.

This unit has three elements:

⌒ *HSC214a Make preparations to support individuals to eat and drink*

⌒ *HSC214b Support individuals to get ready to eat and drink*

⌒ *HSC214c Help individuals consume food and drink*

The content of this unit is linked to the following NVQ units that you may also cover as part of your NVQ award:

⌒ *HSC21 Communicate with and complete records for individuals*

⌒ *HSC22 Support your own health and safety and that of others*

⌒ *HSC25 Carry out and provide feedback on specific plan of care activities*

⌒ *HSC27 Support individuals in their daily living*

⌒ Introduction

Eating and drinking are basic human activities that most individuals undertake independently very early in life. Adequate nutrition is essential in order to stay alive, but eating and drinking also has another purpose for most people. Eating and drinking are important social activities and frequently play an important part in social, cultural and religious celebrations (such as Christmas, Easter, Eid and Passover). So the loss of, or deterioration in, a person's ability to eat and drink independently is likely to have a major impact on them in both practical and emotional terms. This is difficult to appreciate until you cannot grab a quick snack or make a cup of tea or coffee when you feel like one, or you find that simple feeding skills are beyond your control.

Nutritional needs

In basic terms food is needed by the human body to provide the fuel or energy that we need to live. Energy is used in the body to do a number of things, including:

- To grow, repair and replace cells.
- To provide insulation or warmth.
- To protect us from infection.
- To fuel our breathing, heartbeat, circulation, brain activity and movement.

The amount of food that a person's body requires varies according to their age, physical characteristics and their activity levels. For example, a child needs more calories and more energy than an elderly person. Similarly, a very active individual will need more energy, and therefore more food and calories, than someone who is immobile and cannot move to burn off energy.

KUS 8

All of the individuals that you work with will need a good, healthy, balanced **diet**. The word 'diet' does not simply describe what people do when they want to lose weight. Our diet is what we eat on a daily basis. This should include foods from the main food groups and contain a balance of nutrients.

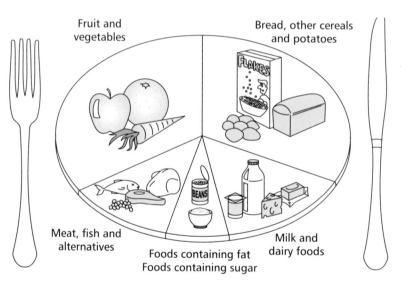

Figure 1
The main food
groups

The nutrients needed for a **balanced diet** are:

- Protein – main sources are meat, fish, nuts, cereals, eggs and milk.
- Carbohydrates – main sources include potatoes, root vegetables, bread, pasta and rice.
- Fats – main sources are meat, dairy products (milk, cream, cheese) and oils used in cooking.
- Vitamins – depending on the particular vitamins (A, B, C, D or E for example), the main sources include eggs and cheese (vitamin A), cereals (vitamins B and E), citrus fruits (vitamin C) or fish (vitamin D).

- Minerals – sources depend on the particular mineral (such as iron or calcium) but include meat, beans, dairy products and fortified cereals (i.e. those that have had vitamins and minerals added to them).

Most human beings will need a diet containing at least some of each nutrient in order to be healthy. We also need fluids to survive and fibre to help with digestion. Ideally, water should be available to all of us at all times. It is recommended that we drink at least two litres of liquid a day. This is about eight large glasses. Liquid can be fruit juice, squash, tea, coffee or other non-alcoholic drinks. All of us probably need to increase the amount of water we drink and reduce our consumption of other drinks especially those containing:

- Caffeine – this is a stimulant and a toxin.
- Carbonated drinks – these can cause dental decay and many contain high levels of sugar. Sugar replacements in diet drinks can cause diarrhoea if consumed in large quantities.
- Fruit juices – these contain high levels of citric acid which can cause problems for our teeth and stomach if consumed in large quantities.
- Alcohol should be limited to a maximum of 21 units a week for men and 14 units for women as it is addictive, a stimulant and can cause harmful reactions with many prescribed medications.

Digestion

Digestion is the physical process of breaking down food and drink into more-easily absorbed substances. The food that a person eats and drinks has to go through the digestion process to become the fuel that enables us to grow, develop and stay alive. It is important that the food an individual eats is part of a balanced diet so that the essential nutrients are absorbed into the body during the process of digestion.

Dietary issues in the care setting

Each of the individuals that you work with should have specific dietary information recorded in their care plan. This should show any special or **therapeutic diets** that they are on and should also give information about personal dietary preferences and dislikes. Special diets are designed for individuals to meet a number of needs. For example, they may be prescribed for health reasons or required because of religious needs or cultural choices.

Despite these general points about different types of special diet, an individual's personal preferences must always be taken into account. Some people stick to their special diet less strictly than others. For example, some Muslims, Sikhs and Hindus, especially the younger ones, will happily drink alcohol. As a care worker, failure to respect the individual's right to follow a particular diet could be seen as discriminating against the person.

KUS 2, 3, 7

Choosing meals

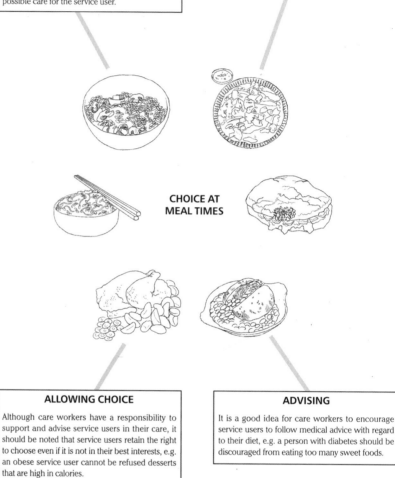

MAKING NOTES

Making notes is an important part of the care worker's job. It is important to keep an up-to-date record of service users' dietary needs and the level of support needed. Sometimes it may be useful to record service users' food intake. These notes should be available to help all staff ensure the best possible care for the service user.

READING

Helping the service user to read and make sense of the menu on offer. You might have to repeat this several times, as there may be several choices on offer.

CHOICE AT MEAL TIMES

ALLOWING CHOICE

Although care workers have a responsibility to support and advise service users in their care, it should be noted that service users retain the right to choose even if it is not in their best interests, e.g. an obese service user cannot be refused desserts that are high in calories.

ADVISING

It is a good idea for care workers to encourage service users to follow medical advice with regard to their diet, e.g. a person with diabetes should be discouraged from eating too many sweet foods.

Figure 2
Monitoring and
planning diets is
very important

Individuals who need special or therapeutic diets are likely to have their food monitored and carefully prepared. If you are involved in this you will need to watch out for the so-called hidden contents of food. Not all foods are what they seem. For example, a vegetarian quiche may have cheese in it. Therefore, this would make it unsuitable for a person who follows a vegan diet. Some popular mint-flavoured sweets contain glycerine. This is a meat product and therefore it is not suitable for vegetarians and vegans. Shopping, cooking and eating out with individuals who have special diets may take extra time because you will need to ensure that their dietary needs, wishes and preferences are respected whilst also ensuring that they receive a balanced, **nutritional** diet.

Table 1 Examples of special diets

Type of diet	Special restrictions
Vegetarian	A vegetarian will not eat meat, fish or products containing these foods.
Vegan	Vegans are also vegetarians but have a stricter approach. They do not eat any food containing animal products (including dairy products like milk, eggs or cheese).
Kosher (Jewish)	A kosher diet is eaten by some (but not all) Jewish people. The kosher diet does not contain pork. Jews are forbidden to eat meat and dairy products together. The preparation of meat must be kosher. This means that the animal has been killed and prepared in a particular way.
Halal (Muslim)	The Muslim faith forbids eating pork or the meat from other carnivorous animals and shellfish. Meat in the Muslim diet must be halal. This means that the animal has been killed and prepared in a certain way. Alcohol is forbidden.
Hindu	Many Hindus are vegetarian. Those who are not will not eat beef. Alcohol is forbidden in the Hindu diet.
Sikh	The Sikh diet does not contain beef or alcohol.

Figure 3
You should support individuals with both their nutritional and medical needs

Table 2 Examples of therapeutic diets

Type of diet	Therapeutic reasons for diet
Anti-allergy diet (e.g. nut-free diet)	Food allergies can be dangerous and even fatal for the people who have them. Nut allergies have been publicised recently and food labelling has now improved in an effort to inform people. Issues for care workers working with individuals who have food allergies do not just relate to the purchase, preparation and serving of food. They must be mindful of foods and treats brought in by visitors.
Low fat	Many adults in the UK suffer from high cholesterol levels. This is related to the excessive consumption of animal fats and may lead to heart disease and obesity. Obesity is now also considered as one of the biggest factors related to poor health and premature death. Restricting fat consumption is one of the recommendations for a healthy diet. Individuals who have gall-bladder problems are also recommended to have a very low-fat diet.
Low sugar	Sugar is often referred to as **empty calories**. It can cause obesity and dental problems. People who have **diabetes** are particularly likely to be on a low-sugar diet.
High protein	Individuals who have been particularly unwell and have lost weight are sometimes given a high-protein diet to enable them to gain weight. High-protein diets are normally offered as six small meals a day so that the individual does not feel uncomfortably full.
Low protein	This diet reduces the amount of protein taken in the diet and is used particularly where an individual has kidney problems.
Weight reducing	Many popular weight-reducing diets are found to be lacking in essential nutrients and lead to poor nutrition. Individuals who need to lose weight for medical or health reasons should have their diet planned and monitored by a qualified dietician to ensure that it is balanced and nutritious as well as therapeutic.
High fibre	A high-fibre diet is sometimes used to help an individual who wishes to lose weight and/or who has digestive and bowel problems.
Soft diet	A soft diet consists of food that is cooked and prepared in a way that will make it easier to chew and swallow. However, this will mean that it has a higher water content and is not as good for the individual nutritionally. It is important to remember presentation when an individual is on this type of diet as **puréed** food can often turn into a grey, unappetising mush.
Coeliac diet	Individuals who have been diagnosed with **coeliac disease** have to maintain a gluten-free diet. **Gluten** is found in wheat and flour-based products. Not following this diet would lead to abdominal pains, discomfort and health problems for the individual.

Make preparations to support individuals to eat and drink

Planning for nutritional needs

KUS 1, 4

Each individual will have had a care plan written as part of their initial assessment when they were admitted to your workplace or when they were assessed in their own home. This will include information on needs and preferences in all areas of their life including dietary needs and preferences. Check the care plan regularly to make sure that there have been no changes to what the individual can eat and drink, or how they will eat it.

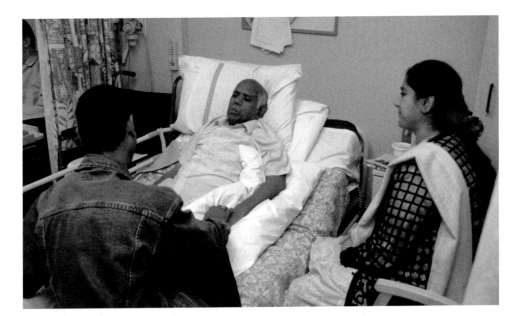

Figure 4
Always respect the individuals right to follow a particular diet

Practical Example

Special dietary issues

KUS 1, 2, 3, 4, 11, 13

Mr Zuman is a practising Muslim. He has had a stroke and has very limited speech and mobility. He cannot undertake any self-care tasks and requires full assistance with washing, dressing, eating and drinking.

He does not eat pork or any other pig product. This includes gammon, ham, bacon and most sausages because of the pork content. He wants to have full consultation in meal planning and in his recent care-planning meeting he asked to be given this opportunity.

He has also asked to be taken out more and wishes to travel to see his family, a two-hour drive away. This will require a train journey and meals while out.

Mr Zuman also requires help to wash in running water before and after mealtimes.

> ➤ *If he is admitted to your workplace or you are responsible for caring for him, how could you help Mr Zuman to ensure that he does not eat anything containing pork?*
>
> ➤ *What plans would you need to make to prepare Mr Zuman for the journey to see his relatives?*
>
> ➤ *Why do you think Mr Zuman needs help with washing before and after meals? Hint: think about his religious beliefs as well as hygiene.*

We base much of our diets around our personal likes and dislikes rather than around our nutritional needs. For example, some of us might eat sprouts only at Christmas or eat too much chocolate or too many cakes! This is much the same for the individuals we provide care for. If an individual has a poor diet, it may be due to them eating what they like or prefer. However, there could be many other reasons for a poor diet. These might include:

- *Financial problems* – lack of money can make it difficult to maintain a healthy, balanced diet. Many people have other payments such as rent or a mortgage that they see as more important than buying food. Parents may report that either they have not eaten or have had a very restricted diet to make sure that their children are able to eat well. Older people on low incomes may have to choose between buying food and paying for heating.

- *Mobility* – if an individual has limited mobility, they may find it difficult to get into the kitchen to cook. Poor mobility may also prevent an individual getting to the shops. They may be unable to exercise which, again, could affect their physical health.

- *Location* – many towns no longer have accessible shops within easy reach for people who do not drive. Carrying shopping on a bus or paying for a taxi makes shopping for healthy nutritious food more difficult.

- *Health factors* – undiagnosed health problems can make eating and drinking difficult. **Stomach ulcers**, **irritable bowel syndrome** or food allergies may cause people to avoid foods that cause them pain rather than seeing a doctor to find out what the problem is. Some people restrict their diets to such a degree that they are in fact malnourished. People who experience **migraines** may avoid foods that are known to trigger an attack. A cold or mild infection may cause an individual to lose their appetite temporarily.

- *Mental-health problems* – depression, stress or anxiety can have a huge influence on diet and eating. Mental-health problems can influence an individual's appetite to the extent that a person may have no appetite or, in contrast, may over-eat. Stress can also cause sickness or nausea, resulting in the individual not wanting to eat.

- *Confusion/dementia* – an individual with dementia or confusion may not remember whether they have eaten or may become fearful of food.

- *Lack of knowledge* – some people may not know what a balanced diet consists of and might not have easy access to information that would allow them to find out.
- *Habit* – eating poor-quality junk food, eating late at night and consuming comfort food can all become habits that are hard to break. This can result in a diet that is unhealthy and which results in a person experiencing weight gain and even malnutrition.
- *Dental health* – poor dental health, ill-fitting dentures or sore mouth/gums will mean that eating may be painful or cause a change in how the food tastes.

As a care worker, there are several key people that you will need to work with in order to plan ways of meeting an individual's nutritional needs. These people include:

- *An individual's family and friends* – the levels of support that the individual needs at mealtimes will depend upon a number of factors. These will include what the meal is, how well the individual is on the particular day and whether the individual likes the meal. If the individual is unable to tell you about their likes and dislikes, you might be able to get this information from friends and family.
- *Dietician* – a dietician will be able to support you in designing a diet and menu plan to meet the particular needs of the individual. A qualified dietician should be able to provide information relating to any special foods that an individual needs or special methods of preparation necessary for them to maintain a healthy diet.

If an individual is unable to eat any food, a dietician will normally remain involved to help provide **enteral nutrition**. This is where the individual is fed directly into

Figure 5
Enteral nutrition
may be required
where a person
is unable to
swallow food
safely

KUS 1, 4, 7, 10, 13, 14

their stomach through either a **nasogastric tube** or a **gastrostomy**. Dieticians may also prescribe build-up drinks to supplement the individual's nutritional intake. These drinks often come in the form of milkshakes and should be offered after or in addition to a meal as giving them before can make the individual feel full and unwilling to eat.

- *Speech and language therapist* (SALT) – at first glance this may seem a strange professional to be involved in eating and drinking. However, a SALT's role concerns the movement of the lips and tongue to make speech clear and understandable. These same movements enable us to eat, drink and swallow. If an individual has had an injury or accident that has affected their face, or has had a stroke, then they will probably receive support from a SALT to help them regain the skills to eat and drink. An individual who has a problem swallowing may be prescribed a thickening powder to add to drinks to reduce the risk of choking on fluids.

- *Occupational therapist* – an occupational therapist could be involved in the design and provision of utensils to help an individual to eat and drink. These might be two-handed cups and special forks, or mugs that make a noise to signal that they are full, for example.

- *Cook* – the cook in your workplace will need to be involved in the design of the menu to ensure the individual receives a diet appropriate to their needs. This involvement may relate to the content or preparation of meals or how the meal is served and presented to the individual.

- *Housekeeper* – housekeeping and cleaning staff are important at mealtimes as they, rather than care staff, are the ones who often give out meals and clear away when everyone has finished. They will see how much has been eaten or drunk, and they need to know whether the individual can have a second helping or a choice of foods. They may also be involved in recording the intake of food and drink for particular individuals.

- *Religious leaders* – if an individual has been put on a special diet this may have an influence on their ability to meet their religious needs and take part in religious ceremonies and festivals. If a Muslim individual has been diagnosed as diabetic this may mean that it is inappropriate for them to fast through daylight hours during the festival of Ramadan. Doing so may have a detrimental effect on their blood-sugar levels and medication. In this situation, a religious leader may be asked to discuss this with staff and the individual to either find a solution or to assure the individual that breaking this tradition for the benefit of their health is acceptable to their faith.

Supporting individual choices

KUS 1

It is important that individuals have a choice of food and drinks. This can be difficult at times, especially if you are catering for lots of people. In this case there is often a rotating menu, offering individuals a choice from a limited list of meals. There must be sufficient choice to meet the needs of individuals from the different religious and cultural groups and for those on special diets.

Menu lists must be accessible to all of the individuals. This may mean that they need to be produced in a range of languages, in Braille, large print and with pictures, to meet the needs of individuals who speak different languages, have lost their sight or who have other disabilities.

As a care worker, it is your responsibility to support individuals in choosing what they eat but also to ensure that they are getting adequate nutrition and a balanced diet. You should also ensure that the nutritional needs and dietary preferences of all individuals are met equally. Unbalanced or restricted menus may discriminate against some individuals. Check, for example, whether all individuals have the choice of vegetarian meals or choices that may be labelled as the 'Asian', 'Chinese' or 'kosher' meal option. If this is restricted to individuals who require these foods due to their faith or ethical beliefs, you may be denying other individuals the opportunity to experience a range of different foods.

As a care worker you must remember that you cannot force individuals to follow their prescribed diet. It is your role to inform, explain and advise individuals about the content of their diet, to highlight the risks, record their actions and report these to a senior member of staff.

Adapted equipment and feeding aids

KUS 7, 12, 13

Individuals may need **specialist equipment** for a range of reasons related to their age, disability or current health status. Specialist items of equipment can be obtained from one of the large retail community pharmacies, from an occupational therapist working for Social Services or the NHS, or sometimes from a dietician. Support groups for individuals with specific disabling conditions and disorders (such as The Stroke Association) often produce leaflets with information about what type of equipment may be useful and where this can be obtained.

If an individual is lying flat in bed due to a spinal injury they will need to be helped by a care worker to eat, and they will need protective clothing such as an apron in case of spillages. A bib is referred to as an apron because it is a more appropriate term to use if the individual is over five years old. Remember issues of dignity when communicating with individuals.

Figure 6
Specialist eating equipment

Examples of specialist equipment include:

KUS 12

- *Plate guards* – these raise the edge of the plate to help the individual to scoop their food onto utensils.

- *Large-handled utensils* – if an individual has lost power in their hands as a result of injury or a stroke, it may be difficult for them to grip the handle of a traditional knife or fork. Some utensils have a strap to secure them to the user's hands and stop them from dropping on the floor.

- *Scoop bowls* – these bowls are shaped so that individuals, especially those with the use of only one hand, are able to load their spoon without chasing the food around the bowl.

- *Heated plates* – these enable the food to be kept at an acceptable temperature for longer, so that if an individual takes a long time to eat, their meal does not go cold.

- *Two-handled mugs* – these help to prevent individuals dropping their drinks.

There are many other items of equipment on the market to enable individuals to eat without extra help. These can now be purchased in a range of materials such as pottery and china as well as plastic. This will help to make the individual feel more comfortable at the dinner table and when eating with other people and ensure that their place setting does not look different from the others.

Preparing for mealtimes

KUS 2, 3, 6, 11, 12, 15

Mealtimes are important social occasions for individuals as well as a chance to maintain good nutrition and enjoy food and drink. There are a number of issues that you should consider when preparing for mealtimes. These include:

- Preparing the care environment.
- The timing of meals.
- Hygiene and health and safety.

Preparing the care environment

Preparing the care environment for mealtimes is an important part of supporting individuals to eat and drink. Eating and drinking should be enjoyable activities and the environment in which this happens influences our enjoyment. There are various things that you can do to make the environment suitable for an individual to eat in. This may be as simple as tidying up a person's room, making sure that the area is free from smells and removing equipment that is not required for mealtimes. Remember that if an individual is unable to get out of bed, they may be eating and drinking in the same place as they sleep, get washed, use the toilet, have medical procedures and spend the whole of their day. This may be an uncomfortable or even an unpleasant environment to have a meal in, so a little bit of tidying and reorganisation may help to make mealtime more enjoyable for them.

The timing of meals

The timing of meals includes both the time of day (or night) when meals are provided and the time that individuals spend having a meal. Individuals who live in residential care settings may be required to have their meals at specific points in the day to fit in with organisational arrangements. If at all possible, individuals should be allowed to choose when they eat and drink. They should not be forced into having meals they do not want. Individuals who receive care in their own home are free to decide when they will have their meals and their preferences should, wherever possible, be accommodated.

The amount of time that is spent on mealtimes can influence the individual's enjoyment and digestion. If the individual is rushed they may not chew the food properly and they could get indigestion. The amount of time required for a meal will depend on the needs of the individual. Always make sure that the person does not feel rushed. Allow them enough time if you are feeding or assisting them with their meal.

Hygiene, health and safety

KUS II

The hygiene standards and safety conditions of the mealtime environment must be monitored to ensure health and safety is maintained for individuals and for yourself. Good standards of food hygiene are required in food-preparation areas such as the kitchen as well as all areas where food is served. It is important that dining areas are hygienic, clean and safe environments.

As a care worker you will come into contact with many substances that could be a risk to individuals' health and safety. At mealtimes you must be aware of hand hygiene. You should wear protective clothing to make sure you do not come into direct contact with food. Sticking your finger in to see if a meal is hot enough is inappropriate and dangerous. As part of health and safety procedures, many care settings provide staff with different-coloured aprons to wear for different tasks. This ensures that their clothing is protected and also highlights if a member of staff has not changed their apron after providing personal care.

As well as observing general food-hygiene principles when preparing and serving food, you should also consider the hygiene and health and safety issues that are relevant to care practice when you feed an individual. The policies and procedures of your care organisation will probably direct you to use gloves and aprons and to provide individuals with napkins or aprons during mealtimes where they are appropriate. Basic hand-washing procedures are also an important part of maintaining high standards of food hygiene and health and safety.

In some care environments it is considered good practice that care workers, where possible, eat with the individuals. This is sometimes referred to as a therapeutic meal because it enables the individual to model their behaviour at the meal table on that of their care workers. However, in other care settings, this shared approach to mealtimes is not possible. Nevertheless, as a member of staff, you can make the meal more enjoyable for individuals by your attitude and manner, especially if you are able to make them feel comfortable and relaxed.

Key points – preparing to support individuals to eat and drink

- An individual's care plan should contain information on their dietary needs and preferences. This should be checked regularly and followed to ensure the individual receives an adequate diet.
- Some people require extra support and specialist feeding equipment to enable them to consume food and drink that is nutritious and which meets their dietary needs.
- Individuals may have personal, cultural or religious beliefs that affect their preferences regarding food and drink. These should be noted in the person's care plan and you should meet these preferences wherever possible.
- Care workers should identify and provide any specialist equipment and protective coverings that an individual needs to use at mealtimes.
- The dining environment, timing and presentation of food contributes to an individual's enjoyment of their meals. You should pay attention to each of these factors in order to make eating and drinking enjoyable and safe.

Element
HSC214b

Support individuals to get ready to eat and drink

Supporting individuals at mealtimes

KUS 10, 13, 15

People who live, either temporarily or permanently, in a residential-care setting will probably have less control over aspects of their daily life than if they were living in

Figure 7
Give individuals a choice of what to eat!

Monday

Melon

Chicken, new pot...
and seasonal veget...

Chocolate tart

Tuesday

Melon

Chicken, new...
and seasonal...

Choc...

Wednesday

Melon

Chicken, new potatoes
and seasonal vegetables

Chocolate tart

their own home. This is partly because care staff may be responsible for activities like mealtimes, cleaning and arranging activities. However, one way of helping individuals to keep some control over their daily life is to ensure that you give them choices wherever possible. Liaising closely with individuals regarding the content and timing of their meals, for example, can improve their experience of care. If you think about the decisions that you make regarding when you eat and drink, you will realise that choice is an important way of giving an individual a sense of control and dignity in their life.

Giving individuals a choice about when they eat and drink is not a common feature of life in care settings. However, imposing strict mealtimes on individuals may not be a positive thing to do, especially when there is a danger that individuals will become **institutionalised** or dependent on care workers and the care organisation to meet their needs. Do you eat at the same time every day? Do you grab a drink when you are thirsty or only drink at 10.30 a.m., with your meals, at 3.15 p.m. etc.? It is worth thinking about the impact of mealtime routines on individuals. Consider ways that these could be altered to give individuals better choices.

Mealtime issues

KUS 3, 4, 7, 10, 13, 14, 15

Mr Stevens uses a wheelchair. You have noticed that over the last few weeks he has become reluctant to come into the dining room for his meals. He has asked to eat his meals in his own room and is now having all meals in his bedroom, only coming out when he has visitors. He says he does not want to be a nuisance and that it is easier for you and him if he stays in his room rather than being hoisted in and out of his chair and taken into the dining room. You have also noticed that he becomes distressed by the table manners and noise of one of the individuals who has recently been admitted. As you walk away from his room one day you notice that he is saying grace before he starts his meal.

➤ *What are the issues raised by Mr Stevens eating in his room?*

➤ *How could you encourage him to rejoin the rest of the individuals?*

➤ *What could you do to make mealtimes more enjoyable for all of the individuals?*

Identifying individual support needs

KUS 6, 13, 15

How much support do the individuals with whom you work need to get ready to eat and drink? This is a difficult question to answer. The only really helpful answer is that each individual will have their own particular support needs. It is therefore important to assess and identify these on an individual basis. Each individual's care plan should contain information about their support needs and you should review this regularly. It is likely that a number of people will have helped to prepare the care plan. This group should have included the individual, their family or carer and other professional workers involved in their care.

The support needs of the individuals you work with will vary from person to person and may vary for the same individual over time depending on changes in their condition and particular needs. The preparations that you will need to make to enable individuals to eat and drink safely and comfortably will vary depending on the setting that you work in and the needs of the individuals. The individual may be able to provide you with this information, but it is important to refer to their care plan. Factors that you should think about when considering an individual's possible support needs include:

- *Religious needs* – some individuals will not be happy to eat unless they have had the opportunity to say grace. This is a Christian ritual that many people still wish to follow. Other religious requirements include, for Muslims, the need to wash in running water both before and after a meal. Does the mealtime set in your workplace conflict with individuals' time for worship?

- *Position* – the posture of an individual is important during mealtimes. They need to be in a comfortable, upright position. This may mean that they need adapted seating so that they can reach their food on the dining table. A physiotherapist or occupational therapist could work with the individual to achieve this. You should also consider the following points:

- If all individuals are going into a dining area, how is the seating arranged?

- Do individuals get a choice of where to sit?

- Is there a table for people who are slower eaters?

Giving individuals a choice of where to sit may make mealtimes more enjoyable. If an individual is expected to sit next to someone they dislike, they may be reluctant to stay at the dining table and may not finish their meal. Individuals who have been affected by a stroke may need to use cushions to help them stay in a suitable position for eating and drinking.

- *Location* – if the individual is unable to leave their room you must make sure that it becomes a pleasant place to eat. This includes clearing equipment and addressing any issues of bodily or food smells.

- *Equipment and eating aids* – if a recommendation has been made that an individual use adapted equipment (such as crockery, cutlery or table mats), this should be made available at each meal. If an individual finds it difficult to use the equipment, you should support and encourage them to get used to it. Other aids that may be necessary to support an individual at mealtimes could include sensory aids like glasses and hearing aids. Without these, the individual may not hear much of what is said at mealtimes. This could result in the person going hungry or feeling isolated at the meal table. If an individual cannot see where their glass of water is they may remain thirsty or be labelled as clumsy if they knock it over.

- *Reluctance to eat* – if an individual is reluctant to come to the dining room you need to find out why. Perhaps they are feeling unwell or uncomfortable, or maybe they are not interested in the meal. If you become concerned about an individual's reluctance to eat you need to report it to senior staff and the situation should be monitored. Some types of medication affect an individual's appetite or cause **nausea**. The doctor or a registered nurse involved with the individual's care should make you aware of this so that you can monitor the situation and take action to remedy it. Often there are other drugs that can be taken to stop the nausea. If an individual is reluctant to eat, you should encourage them but you should never force or pressure them. Offering alternative meals that still meet their dietary needs is one way of maintaining an individual's interest in food.

- *Confusion and memory loss* – individuals who have confusion and memory loss (this is sometimes experienced with dementia) may forget that they have eaten or they may not recognise the signs of hunger. It is important that you work with other professionals to ensure that individuals maintain good nutrition and eat regularly. Charts that show the time and type of meals that have been eaten may be a useful resource. Simply placing food in front of confused individuals or dropping off a prepared meal at their home will not ensure that the meals are eaten. Some individuals will forget or not even be aware that food has been provided for them. This can lead to malnutrition and even starvation. It is sometimes necessary to provide additional assistance for individuals who are confused or who have significant memory-loss problems.

- *Thirst and dehydration* – most people find it difficult to eat with a dry mouth. So it is important to make sure that individuals drink as well as eat regularly. Lack of fluid in the diet is a major cause of constipation. Increasing the amount of fibre in a dehydrated person's diet will have no effect on constipation. To resolve the problem the individual must drink more. However, offering too much fluid before a meal can make the individual feel full and unable to eat, so drinking needs to be carefully balanced. Individuals who are reluctant to drink can be offered foods such as soups and jelly to increase their fluid intake.

- *Recent activities* – eating and drinking may not seem like important activities to an individual who is distressed or upset, who may have just woken up, or who has recently experienced an unpleasant or uncomfortable clinical procedure. In such cases the individual may be reluctant to eat. If this is the case you must make sure that they have a chance to eat later.

Hygiene needs and issues

KUS 2, 3, 4, 6, 11

Hygiene is a very important issue in relation to food and the care practices associated with it. High standards of hygiene are required to promote safe care practice. Simple hand-washing routines are a key way of achieving this. So it is important that all individuals are given the opportunity and support to wash their hands before starting their meal. Your role in this may simply be asking individuals if they want to wash their hands. You may need to assist them to the bathroom, or if the individual is more dependent, you may have to wash their hands for them. Remember to always wash your own hands before serving food or assisting individuals to eat. Avoid touching food that an individual is going to eat.

Toileting needs

If any individuals need to use the toilet before starting their meal, you should assist them. Needing to use the toilet may adversely affect their comfort and their enthusiasm for the meal. Conditions such as irritable bowel syndrome and **Crohn's disease** can also cause discomfort after a person has eaten certain foods. The effects of these foods on the individual and those around them need to be controlled to make mealtimes an enjoyable experience for everyone. If an individual suffers from constipation they may be reluctant to eat as feeling bloated and uncomfortable will make eating an unpleasant experience. Any incidence of constipation must be closely monitored as long-term constipation can cause additional health problems.

Medication issues

You must check before giving medication. Some individuals, such as those with diabetes, may need to take their medication before they eat a meal. Other medication must be taken straight after a meal or with food. The treatment may be less effective if you do not keep to these requirements. Care workers and kitchen staff should work together on this issue.

Mouth care

Poor dental health will make eating and drinking a more uncomfortable experience for an individual and may even mean that they require special food, such as a soft diet. It is important to ensure that individuals receive mouth care and can chew and swallow safely. If an individual has dentures these should be worn at mealtimes to ensure that the individual is able to eat properly. Dentures should also be cleaned and checked regularly to make sure that they still fit, as poorly fitting dentures may cause rubbing and soreness in a person's mouth. If teeth are not cleaned regularly this may result in an unpleasant taste and an uncomfortable feeling in the person's mouth. Cleaning an individual's teeth just before a meal may also reduce their enjoyment of the meal if the food then tastes of toothpaste. If an individual does not have many teeth this may affect their choice of food as chewing hard foods could be impossible.

Providing dietary information

KUS 7, 8, 9, 13

If you are working in a collaborative way with individuals who are receiving care, you will be giving them choices and encouraging them to make decisions about what they eat and drink. One of the consequences of this will be that individuals will ask questions and want dietary information to ensure that their particular food-related needs and preferences are being met appropriately.

In order to respond appropriately to questions and issues raised about the food and drink that individuals are about to consume, you will need to know the menu and be aware of each individual's needs and preferences. If you can tell individuals about the content of their meal, you will be better able to support them. Have you ever bitten into something to find that it is not what you expected? By knowing exactly what the meal is, you will be able to tell the individual and help them prepare for the meal. In contrast, being vague or ill-informed is not helpful. 'It is a mince thingy' is not a useful piece of information to either whet an individual's appetite or give them accurate information about the content.

Often individuals who are on special diets are afraid that they are eating the wrong foods. The consequences for an individual with a food allergy who eats the food they are allergic to could, at worst, be fatal. A person with **coeliac disease** eating food containing gluten will have painful and unpleasant experiences as a result. A Jewish individual eating pork would contravene their religious code and may become very distressed because of this. It is unacceptable to lie to an individual about the content of their food. In fact, this is inappropriate, discriminatory and extremely bad practice.

Figure 8
Gluten-free
products are
now widely
available

Sometimes you may be unable to answer questions or provide the information about food that an individual or their relative requires. In these circumstances it is always best to say that you do not know the answer. Then refer the question to a senior member of staff who may be able to help or, if appropriate, contact a dietician.

Key points – supporting individuals to eat and drink

- Individuals should be supported and encouraged to develop, maintain and use their eating and drinking skills.
- Care workers have a responsibility to ensure that each person has sufficient and appropriate forms of support to enable them to eat and drink safely.
- Hygiene is an important health and safety and cultural issue at meal-times. Every individual should be helped to achieve high standards of personal hygiene (especially hand washing) prior to eating or drinking.
- Care workers should be familiar with the nutritional content of individuals' meals. This should enable them to respond to questions about an individual's diet. Where this is not possible, the query should be referred to a senior colleague.

KUS 2, 3, 4, 7, 13

Help individuals consume food and drink

Identifying and agreeing support needs

The level of support that an individual requires to help them to consume food and drink will vary according to individual needs. Helping a person to eat and drink does not always involve physically feeding them. Sometimes helping an individual to remove cling film from food stored in the fridge, opening jars or bottles, or placing food in the oven for them is sufficient to help a person prepare or eat their own food.

It is important to note that the help and assistance that an individual needs may change on a day-to-day basis. You could be required to help with something as simple as unpacking a person's sandwiches from a lunchbox one day or you could be required to assist fully on another. The precise level of help an individual requires should therefore be assessed on an ongoing basis.

Assisting individuals to eat and drink

Good practice at mealtimes can be divided into three phases.

- Preparation *before* mealtime:
  - Find out whether the individual is hungry. Check if they want the meal. If not, offer an alternative.
  - Know who needs assistance and to what extent – do not just feed everyone, check the individuals' care plans to see what and how much help they need.
  - Check what the individual feels able to do for themselves today.
  - Make sure that the individual is ready to eat. Is there anything that they have to do before they are comfortable to eat? This may be something physical or simply saying grace for example.
  - Make sure that the individual is comfortable, secure and able to stay in that position for the whole meal.
  - Check how hot the individual likes their food; do they want it to cool before they eat it?
- Assistance *during* mealtime:
  - Introduce yourself – do not just start assisting the individual.
  - Only assist individuals to eat and drink when they are unable to do this for themselves. You should not deny individuals their independence just because they are slow feeding themselves.
  - Sit down. Looming over the individual is intimidating and often makes them hurry. Do not bend down to assist the individual as your back will start to ache.

- Take your time. Several people may need assistance, but try not to rush the individual. Patience, time and attention are essential when assisting individuals with feeding.

- Give the individual time to chew, swallow and enjoy their food. Do not hover with the next spoonful. Allow 5 to 10 seconds for each swallow, bite or sip.

- Encourage the individual to eat. This can be done both verbally with prompts such as, 'You are doing well', or non-verbally with smiles and nods to encourage them to take another mouthful.

- Check that the individual is swallowing the food and not storing it in their cheek.

- Wipe around the mouth and chin if necessary during the meal. Use a napkin or wipe for this. Do *not* scrape food off their chin with a spoon.

- Give the individual the chance to have a drink between each mouthful of food as this helps the process of eating.

- Look for signs of discomfort, allergy or pain.

- Give the individual your full attention.

- Do not ask questions when the individual has a mouth full of food.

- Support *after* mealtime:

  - Try to ensure that the individual remains in an upright position for at least 15 minutes after a meal as this aids digestion and reduces the likelihood of choking.

  - When required, make a record of the food eaten and drinks taken. Try to be as accurate as possible about portion sizes.

The presentation of food can also play a part in ensuring that mealtimes are enjoyable occasions. We experience food with all of our senses. We smell it as it is being prepared, we taste it once it gets into our mouths, we feel its texture as we eat it, we see it on the plate and often hear it sizzling as it cooks. How a meal looks on the plate can have a huge influence on whether we want to eat it. Setting the table in an attractive way and making the room comfortable will also help to prepare the individual to enjoy their meal. However, if you are working with individuals with visual impairments or confusion, less is more. When you are laying the table it is better to have only a few utensils on it so as not to confuse the individual with additional shapes to negotiate.

Providing care during mealtimes

As we have already discussed, individuals have different and changing needs for help and assistance during mealtimes. When you do give help it should be practical and appropriate to an individual's needs. Putting a meal in front of an individual may only be the first step. The individual may not be able to eat it unless they are fed or encouraged to feed themselves.

Figure 9
Is the amount
of food
appropriate?

The help that individuals need could vary on a daily basis and will differ for each individual. Your assistance may be as simple as loading the spoon so that they can feed themselves, or making sure that the sandwiches stay on the plate. However, you must remain vigilant to ensure that the individuals are safe and are not experiencing any problems. If an individual needs total support from staff in order to eat, you should follow any guidance given to you by their dietician, speech and language therapist or doctor.

It is also important that you use any prescribed equipment in the right way. Non-slip mats, for example, are a very useful piece of equipment to keep the plate in one place during a meal. They can help an individual who has poor **manual dexterity**. These rubber mats gently stick to both the bottom of the plate and the surface of the table. However, using them on top of a tablecloth renders them useless. Specialist cutlery is also often designed to be used in a particular hand – so make sure that you place the cutlery in the appropriate hand so that the individual can use it effectively. This type of information should be included in an individual's care plan and it is often helpful to use pictures to show the individual how the item should be used.

Tables are normally laid with a fork on the left-hand side and a knife to the right. This does not mean that individuals will use them this way. If an individual prefers to eat with just a fork or holds the fork in the right hand and the knife in the left hand, you do not need to make them change this. Or an individual may prefer to eat with their hands. Remember that not all food needs to be eaten with cutlery and for some individuals finger food can be used very effectively to improve and maintain independence in feeding.

Eating is a social experience and often it is appropriate for individuals in a long-stay setting to go out for meals. It is therefore important to remember a number of points if eating out with individuals:

- Book the table, ensuring wheelchair access if necessary.
- Check the menu and ring ahead if you have any concerns regarding food allergies.
- Most reputable restaurants will be prepared to **purée** a meal if they are asked to.
- Take any medications that the individual needs at mealtimes.
- Take any equipment that is necessary to assist the individual to eat.

Observing and reporting on dietary intake

KUS 15

As a care worker you must make sure that you monitor and report on individuals' eating and drinking. Monitoring **dietary intake** is necessary to ensure safety, but it also provides information that is needed to maintain an individual's records. Many care settings use fluid balance and dietary intake charts to record an individual's consumption of food and fluids. Make sure that you know how these work and that you can record your observations accurately on them.

Name: .... Weight:				
Date of Birth: .... Date:				
Balance carried over ....mls.				
Time	**Oral Fluids In**	**IV Fluids In**	**Fluids Out**	**Total in Mls**
06.00				
07.00				
08.00				
09.00				
10.00				
11.00				
12.00				

Figure 10
A fluid
balance chart

Fluid balance charts record the time that individuals have drunk fluids, what they have drunk and how much. It is not usually sufficient to record 'small glass' or 'large mug'. How much do each of these hold? To ensure accuracy you need to

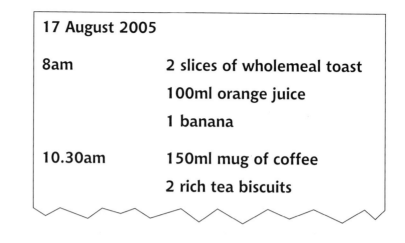

17 August 2005

8am	**2 slices of wholemeal toast**
	100ml orange juice
	1 banana
10.30am	**150ml mug of coffee**
	2 rich tea biscuits

Figure 11
Dietary intake
chart

record the sizes of the usual cups and glasses that the individual uses. On some occasions it is all right to record small sips as this may be all that the individual has swallowed.

Dietary intake charts are used to monitor the food that the individual has eaten over a period of time. Dieticians and other health professionals use these to investigate problems with weight loss or gain and other issues relating to the individual's ability to eat or pass bowel movements. It is important to record the quantity of food supplements that have been consumed. However, these should be recorded *either* on an individual's fluid intake chart *or* their dietary intake chart. Recording them on both will give a false reading.

Although monitoring an individual's intake of food and drink is important, it needs to be done in a way that is supportive of the individual and does not make them feel uncomfortable. As well as monitoring the quantity and range of food and drink that an individual consumes, you should also look out for:

- Symptoms of food allergy.
- Difficulties experienced in eating, especially swallowing food.
- Refusal to eat food.

Food allergies

KUS 6, 9,
10, 14, 16,
17

It is possible that an individual you are working with will have an allergic reaction to the food they are eating. If an individual has any known allergies (such as to nuts or dairy products) these must be recorded clearly in their care plan and in an obvious place in the kitchen area. Individuals must not be offered foods that contain any substance that they are known to be allergic to. Common food allergies are to peanuts, fish, eggs, milk or strawberries, but an individual may be allergic to any food. Signs and symptoms of an allergic reaction vary depending on the food but may include one or more of the following:

- Flushed/red face.
- Tingling of the lips.
- Swelling of the lips and mouth.
- Vomiting.
- Sweating and muscle cramps.
- Rash on the skin.

Symptoms can range from those that are embarrassing and unpleasant to those that are fatal. It is difficult to tell whether a person's allergic reaction will be mild or severe. Therefore, if any of these reactions occurs, you should call for help immediately and get medical assistance from a doctor or, in a community setting, from the ambulance service via a 999 call. Once help arrives you need to tell the doctor or paramedic exactly what the individual has eaten and how much. Give them a sample of the leftover food. Record the details in the individual's file. You may also need to fill in an accident or incident form.

Eating problems

Individuals who use health and social-care services may experience eating problems for a variety of reasons. Sometimes these are due to physical disability. For example, an individual who has experienced a stroke may have particular problems eating and swallowing because of muscle paralysis and brain impairment. Similarly, an individual who has had an injury or operation to their mouth may experience problems chewing or swallowing food. Joint stiffness and **dexterity** problems may also mean that individuals find it difficult to cut up their food.

Refusing to eat

If an individual refuses to eat they should be encouraged and offered alternative food choices. Never force an individual to eat. This situation can be very difficult and frustrating for care workers. However, forcing food into the mouth of an individual is abusive and can cause injury and choking.

Recognising and reporting eating problems

You are helping Ms Carr to eat when she complains that the food does not taste right. She then coughs, splutters and vomits. After cleaning up and tidying Ms Carr, you notice that she is still uncomfortable and is unwilling to eat or drink. She also complains of stomach pain.

➤ *What might be happening?*
➤ *What should you do now?*
➤ *Who should be informed?*

Key points – help individuals with eating and drinking

- Care workers should respond in a supportive way to each individual's needs and wishes for assistance at mealtimes.

- Individuals should be encouraged and supported to feed themselves wherever possible. Only provide assistance with eating and drinking when individuals are unable to do this for themselves.

- Appropriate utensils and specialist equipment should be provided to enable individuals to eat and drink at a pace that best suits them and in a way that is socially acceptable and respectful.

- You have a responsibility to observe and report on problems and changes in an individual's dietary intake.

Unit
HSC214 **Are you ready for assessment?**

Help individuals to eat and drink

This unit is all about your involvement in supporting service users who require assistance with eating and drinking. This unit also links closely to unit HSC21 covering communication, and as this unit involves such close personal care there are also clear links with the principles and values of care in HSC24. It also links closely to unit HSC218 covering personal care. You should consider this when planning with your assessor.

Your assessment will mainly be carried out through observation by your assessor and this should provide most of the evidence for the elements in this unit.

As this unit is about your role in directly supporting individuals who require support with a daily task, there will be ample opportunities for observation by your assessor. However, if such observation might intrude on the privacy of individuals you can plan with your assessor to use the testimony of an expert witness instead of observation by your assessor or as an additional source of evidence.

Direct observation

Your assessor or an expert witness will need to see you carry out the performance criteria (PCs) in each of the elements in this unit.

The performance criteria that may be

difficult to meet through observation or expert witness testimony are:

- **HSC214a PC 4**
- **HSC214b PC 5**
- **HSC214c PC 6, 7, 8**

because they might not always occur. ▶

Preparing to be observed

You must make sure that your workplace and any individuals and key people involved in your work agree to you being assessed. Explicit, informed consent must be obtained before you carry out any assessment activity that involves individuals or which involves access to confidential information related to their care.

Before your assessments you should read carefully the performance criteria for each element in the unit. Try to cover as much as you can *during your observations* but remember that you and your assessor can also plan for additional sources of evidence should full coverage of all performance criteria not be possible or to help ensure that your performance is consistent and that

you can apply the knowledge specification in your work practice.

Other types of evidence

You may need to present other forms of evidence in order to:

- Cover criteria not observed by your assessor or by an expert witness.
- Show that you have the required knowledge, understanding and skills to claim competence in this area of practice.
- Ensure that your work practice is consistent.

Your assessor may also need to ask you questions to confirm your knowledge and understanding of this unit.

Check your knowledge

1. Name three of the main food groups that make up a balanced diet.
2. Identify four reasons why an individual may need a special diet.
3. Which religious groups forbid eating pork?
4. What professionals might be involved in working with individuals to aid eating and drinking?
5. A diabetic individual is refusing to follow their prescribed diet. What should you do?
6. What symptoms might an individual show if they are having an allergic reaction to the food they are eating?
7. Why is the presentation of food important?
8. Why should individuals be able to make choices about what they eat and when they have their meals?

UNIT HSC216
Help address the physical-comfort needs of individuals

This unit describes the role that a care worker can play in minimising an individual's pain and discomfort and ways of promoting rest and comfort. The unit consists of the following two elements:

⌒ *HSC216a Assist in minimising individuals' pain or discomfort*

⌒ *HSC216b Assist in providing conditions to meet individuals' needs for rest*

⌒ Introduction

An individual's experience of physical comfort or discomfort plays an important part in determining their general quality of life. Physical comfort can affect all aspects of an individual's care and has a powerful effect on a person's mood and mental state. For example, being in constant pain can lead to depression and anxiety as well as aggression and irritability. Pain and discomfort can also affect the normal functioning of all the major body systems. Your role as a care worker is to help the individual to be comfortable and become pain free where this is possible.

Understanding pain

KUS 1, 2, 11

'Pain' is a difficult word to define because it means different things to different people. Basically pain is something that causes physical or mental discomfort and suffering. Pain might be felt inside the body (internally) or on the surface of the body (externally). In some ways pain is seen as having a positive role in human health because it provides an important biological safety mechanism. The feeling of pain is a warning that something is wrong, that the body is threatened. So when we feel pain it may cause a quick, protective reaction in order to avoid further harm.

Care workers sometimes find it difficult to assess and respond to the pain that individuals receiving care complain about. This is generally because pain is a **subjective** experience. This means that each person tends to identify, describe and experience pain in a personal way. One person's pain threshold may be different to another person's so it can be hard to judge whether an individual can cope with a particular level of discomfort or pain. So you should always be wary about judging an individual's level of pain. It is possible to make a pain assessment but the individual should, wherever possible, contribute to this so that you can begin to understand how they are actually feeling and experiencing their pain. From a care worker's point of view, you have to accept the individual's description of the pain.

When you care for people who are in pain, your role is usually to help the individual to express their comfort needs and to reduce any discomfort that they may be feeling. In order to respond to an individual's pain it is necessary to understand how pain occurs and to appreciate that whilst some people are able to say they are in pain others prefer not to say anything at all and suffer in silence. In the next section we will look at how pain is experienced, at what influences pain and at how we can help individuals to be as free from pain as possible.

Factors that affect the experience of pain

KUS 2, 3

Pain is complex and there are several theories about how to understand it. One of the most popular is the 'gate theory of pain'. According to this, a person's thoughts, beliefs and emotions may affect how much pain they feel from any physical sensation. The theory claims that when **sensory receptors** in the skin are stimulated they send 'pain' information through open 'gateways' in the nervous system to the brain. The brain processes these pain signals and responds by sending instructions to the nervous system to either close the pain gateway and block further sensations of pain or to leave the sensory gateway open and to react in a protective way. If the brain orders the pain gates to open wider, the pain signal and the experience of pain intensifies.

Figure 1 identifies factors that affect a person's experience of pain.

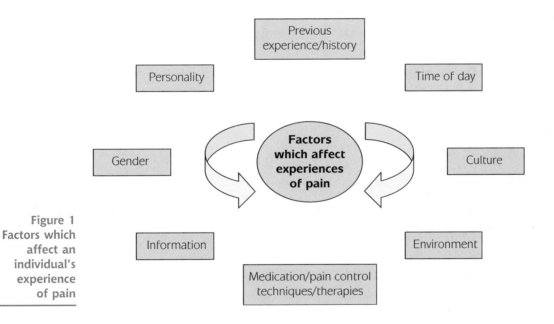

Figure 1
Factors which affect an individual's experience of pain

Previous experiences/history

Anxiety and pain are linked. Individuals who express unusually high levels of anxiety also tend to have lower pain thresholds and complain about pain more often. The stressful effects of unrelieved pain have the potential to increase anxiety levels even more. For example, they may interfere with a person's activities of daily living and could interrupt the individual's normal sleep pattern causing them to have problems sleeping.

Awareness of the links between anxiety and pain has influenced care practice. For example, it is now good practice to make sure that individuals are fully informed about any care procedures and actions that are going to be carried out because this reduces their anxiety and limits subsequent pain. If simple, clear explanations are given, the individual can be more in control of the situation and is better able to manage their reaction to potentially uncomfortable procedures. For example, a person with diabetes who requires several daily injections may cope with this experience better by knowing that the injection will save their lives. If you assist the individual and help them to carry out the task themselves they can choose injection sites that are less sensitive, and so help reduce anxiety and any painful effects.

It is important to talk to the individuals you care for about their previous experiences of pain and about any anxieties that they may have regarding treatments or particular forms of care. An individual's notes may provide some information on these matters. If you can find out about previous experiences of pain you can then work with an individual to identify constructive ways of helping them to deal with their anxieties.

Culture

KUS 3

In some families and cultures, people are brought up not to make a fuss, to be long-suffering, to show strength and **fortitude**, or to be a good patient. In other families and cultures, people are brought up to be vocal and demonstrative, which may include displaying agitation, moaning, crying out, rocking, chanting, calling on God, clicking fingers or slapping themselves. Therefore, it can be difficult to assess an individual if you do not know how they normally express pain. Using a pain assessment tool can help (see Figure 2 for an example). When choosing a pain assessment tool, you should consider cultural requirements as some assessments could lead to offence. The use of a pain assessment chart, for example the McGill Pain Questionnaire which shows the back and front of a naked body, may be shocking and unacceptable to people who observe strict codes of modesty. An alternative pain assessment tool, for example a Faces Pain Assessment, may be useful. If you are aware of an individual's cultural needs and respect that everyone is different, you will be in a better position to help the individual to express their discomfort and to help them be more comfortable.

Time of day

Time of day can affect people's pain thresholds. For example, pain is experienced more often in the morning and last thing at night. An individual may experience morning pain because they have not been able to lie in a comfortable position during the night. Similarly, lying in one position or guarding (where the individual protects the injured site) can cause discomfort because the individual is worried that this will make any existing pain worse. Not moving can lead to joint and muscle stiffness causing more pain. Stress and tension also lead to increased pain.

Pain at night can be due to the stress and strains of the day. Anxiety regarding being in bed, and not having any daytime distractions to take one's mind off the discomfort, can make pain feel worse especially if the individual is unable to get into a comfortable position or feels they cannot talk to someone. This is more evident in home care situations when the individual may not see anyone until the morning.

As a care worker you can help individuals by assisting them to be comfortable, by ensuring that they have had their medication, that their bedding is clean and comfortable and that they are able to call for assistance should they need it. In a hospital or residential care setting, immediate assistance should always be available.

Personality

Research studies have found that people who are **introverted** experience more intense pain but are known to complain less than **extroverts**. Attitudes to pain may be influenced by beliefs that offer a reason for pain.

It is important that you develop a good rapport with an individual experiencing pain so that you get to know how they normally deal with their pain. For example, the individual who is always quiet may need more time and opportunity to express their needs. You can achieve this through conversation and by observing any changes in the individual's body language and their normal way of expressing themselves and relating to others.

Assessing and measuring pain

KUS 5, 6

It is often quite difficult to make an **objective assessment** about how much pain an individual is experiencing. Pain assessment tools, used properly, can make a big difference to this process. They help to give a reasonably accurate impression of whether adequate care and treatment is being provided to deal with the individual's pain. There are a number of different types of pain assessment tools. They include body charts, pain scales that use pictures or numbers and pain questionnaires.

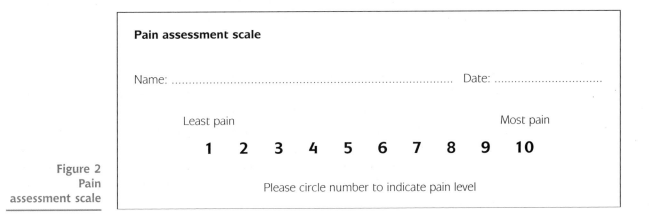

Figure 2
Pain
assessment scale

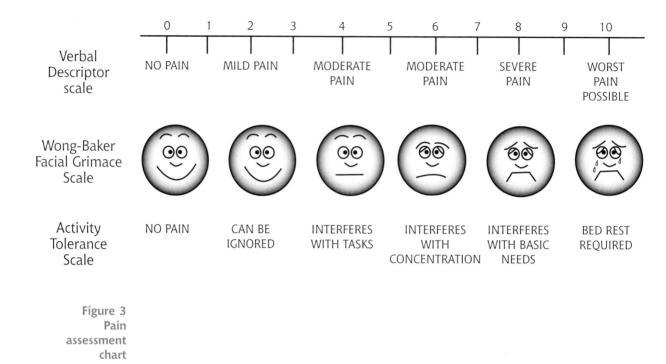

	0	1	2	3	4	5	6	7	8	9	10
Verbal Descriptor scale	NO PAIN		MILD PAIN		MODERATE PAIN		MODERATE PAIN		SEVERE PAIN		WORST PAIN POSSIBLE
Activity Tolerance Scale	NO PAIN		CAN BE IGNORED		INTERFERES WITH TASKS		INTERFERES WITH CONCENTRATION		INTERFERES WITH BASIC NEEDS		BED REST REQUIRED

Figure 3 Pain assessment chart

Element HSC216a

Assist in minimising individuals' pain or discomfort

Observing and identifying discomfort and pain

KUS 8

Observing and identifying discomfort and pain is achieved through regular monitoring and communication between the care worker and the individual receiving care. The individual should feel that they are able to express their needs and that these will be listened to and addressed immediately.

As a care worker you must observe the verbal and non-verbal cues that the individual communicates. Verbal cues may include describing the different types of pain and the location. They may refer to 'sharp', 'throbbing', 'aching' or 'nauseating' pain or discomfort, for example. Non-verbal cues will be observed via the individual's general physical responses and body language. Position and guarding, restlessness and irritability can all be symptoms of discomfort as can changes in skin colour, sweating and abnormal results to measurements, for example raised pulse, blood pressure and breathing rates.

Pain is divided into different categories. A thorough assessment can determine the possible effects and how these may be lessened. As previously discussed, a pain assessment chart can help this process.

Chronic pain

Chronic pain is pain that continues to be experienced over a period of time and is complex. It can become a continuous part of daily life (see Table 1). Chronic pain may be treated by medication, surgery or alternative therapies to relieve the symptoms such as inflammation, swelling, throbbing or aching sensations.

The physical effects of chronic pain can include tiredness, weight loss, sleeplessness and restricted mobility. These effects can also add to the **psychosocial** effects of chronic pain. For example, people in chronic pain may experience low mood, they might reduce their social activity (i.e. they may not want to see family or friends), suffer loss of libido, be unable to concentrate and they could develop memory problems. In some individuals this can lead to low self-esteem and loss of confidence.

There are several types of chronic pain and these can be categorised as follows:

- Superficial pain. This is felt in the skin and underlying tissues.
- Deep pain. This is usually felt in muscles and joints.
- Visceral pain. This may be associated with one organ, e.g. the stomach.
- Neuralgic pain. This affects nerves, e.g. facial nerves.
- Referred pain. For example shoulder pain could be a symptom of heart problems.
- Phantom limb pain. This is experienced as tingling, or pins and needles in an area that has been amputated or is missing.
- **Psychogenic** pain. The individual experiences pain when there is no physical explanation for the cause of that pain.

Table 1 The potential effects of chronic pain

Physical effects of chronic pain	Psychosocial effects of chronic pain

• Tiredness.
• Weight loss.
• Sleeplessness.
• Mobility restrictions due to:
  • Muscle wasting.
  • Loss of strength/tone.
  • Joint stiffness.
 	
Causing disruption to activities such as:
• Self care.
• Bodily functions and activities of daily living.
• Leisure.
• Family activities.
	Decreased:
	• Social activity (friends, family).
	• Libido.
	• Concentration and memory.
	• Ability to plan ahead and set goals.
	• Self-esteem.
	• Self-confidence.
	• Sense of control and usefulness.
	
	Causing:
	• Increased depression.
	• Suicidal thoughts.
	• Hopelessness.
	• Despair, frustration and anger.
	• Fear of pain.
	• Worry about causing further damage.

Acute pain

Acute pain can be brief, lasting a few minutes, or it may persist for several months. It can cause extreme discomfort to the individual and can be potentially life threatening (see Table 2). Acute pain may be remedied through surgery, medication or alternative therapy.

The physical effects of acute pain can include symptoms such as increased heart and respiratory rates, tiredness, infection and raised temperature. Increased adrenalin within the body can also **exacerbate** psychosocial effects. Examples of these effects include sleeplessness, anxiety, fear, disorientation, problems with concentration and memory, and confusion.

Table 2 Effects of unrelieved acute pain

Physical effects of acute pain	Psychosocial effects of acute pain

Increased:
• Heart rate.
• Respiratory rate.
• Infection.
• Fatigue.
• Immobility leading to:
  • Venous thrombosis.
  • Pulmonary embolism.
• Fever.
• Adrenalin/noradrenalin.
	• Sleeplessness.
	• Anxiety.
	• Fear.
	• Disorientation.
	• Reduction in cognitive function (memory, problem solving, thinking, concentration).
	• Mental confusion.
	• Denial or stoicism (i.e. denying the effects).

Monitoring and using the individual's care plan

The individual's care plan will have a detailed record of the care that they require. This will be based on a detailed assessment of their individual care needs. The care plan will be regularly updated to include such things as any recent surgery, injuries, disease, infections or illnesses that may require extra care in addition to the normal activities of daily living. Each area of need should be addressed in the care that is provided for the person.

Practical Example

Care plan

Brian McDonald, aged 70, is admitted for respite care to recover from a fractured hip. He arrives at the care home in considerable pain and has also developed a pressure sore on his sacrum (the wedge-shaped bone at the base of the spine). [See Table 3.]

➤ *Who is responsible for producing Mr McDonald's care plan?*

➤ *Who might be responsible for implementing this care plan?*

➤ *What should you do if an aspect of care is unclear?*

➤ *How should you report any changes in Mr McDonald's condition?*

➤ *Why is it important to note any changes in treatment and care?*

Table 3 Example care plan

Name of individual: Brian McDonald	Date of birth: 8.9.35	Address: The Gables, Harrogate, N. Yorks	Emergency contact: Name: Susan McDonald Number: 0900 123456
Medication: Paracetamol 1000 mg (2 tablets) qds	**Activities of Daily Living Assessment carried out?** Y/N *(Please attach)* **Communicating** **Breathing** **Eating** **Drinking** **Elimination** **Personal cleansing and dressing** **Religion** **Working and playing** **Sleeping** **Expressing sexuality** *(Please circle and read attached assessment)*	**Significant factors Summary** No problems Occasional bronchitis No problems Needs encouraging No problems Self caring with assistance Attends C of E Sundays Likes crossword, newspapers Difficulty since operation No problems	**Other (physical):** Skin: Pressure sore Hair: No problems Teeth: Wears denture plate Sight: Myopia; wears glasses Hearing: No problems Mobility: Restricted by fracture Other (intellectual): Retired teacher Other (emotional): Missing family Other (social): Prefers own company

ASSESSMENT	PLANNING	IMPLEMENTATION	EVALUATION/REVIEW
Week 1:	Date:	Care staff:	Named nurse:
Management of acute pain	Carry out pain scale assessment	Record in care plan Assess outcomes	Review as necessary until pain relieved Hourly, daily, weekly
Medication	GP to review medication	GP to see individual Continue with medication as prescribed by hospital until seen	Make appointment asap Monitor and review daily
Communication	Assist individual to communicate requirements	Call bell within reach Listen to individual Monitor and report any changes in condition Provide telephone for contact with family	Monitor and review daily
Physical	Ensure individual is comfortable	Regular change of position Support aids in bed To include: bed frame, sheepskin, extra pillows	Monitor and review daily
	Therapy	Offer alternative-therapy treatments Physiotherapy x 1 daily	Organise aromatherapy massage Monitor and review daily
	Dressings	Check dressings and plaster for leaks and chafing Change as required using aseptic technique	Monitor and review daily

Responding to an individual's pain

KUS 8

Responding to an individual's pain is a vital part of meeting the physical-comfort needs of individuals. You should be sensitive to the individual's needs and, where possible, anticipate potential causes of discomfort and pain so that these can be minimised. Encourage the individual to express themselves without fear of judgement and reassure them that their comfort will be attended to. If you are unable to respond using simple care measures, an appropriately qualified or experienced person who can carry out more complex pain-relieving treatment should be called. It is important to respond to the individual's immediate needs and requests as this helps to build trust and promotes a therapeutic rapport between the carer and individual. The individual will be confident that the care they are receiving is appropriate and this will help to reduce any anxiety that they may be feeling.

> **Key points – the care worker's role in supporting the comfort of individuals**
>
> As a care worker you are in a unique position to support and assist the individual to achieve maximum comfort. You can assist the individual in the following ways:
>
> - By listening to what the individual says and reporting pain that cannot be controlled by physical movement and comfort aids.
> - Using comfort aids such as pillows, bed cradles and mobility aids to assist the individual to be independent and pain free.
> - By making call bells and other assistance aids available so that the individual can summon help when required.
> - Assisting the individual with care routines to include medication, physiotherapy and/or other types of therapy.
> - Supporting the individual to meet their activities of daily living.
> - Reporting any signs of discomfort to the appropriate nursing or medical staff.

Practical Example

Pain and the carer's role

Peggy Robinson is a 72-year-old diabetic who lives at home with her daughter and grandchildren. She is mainly self-caring, but a leg ulcer has become infected and the district nurse regularly comes in to change the dressing. The most difficult part is when the dressing is removed as it is extremely uncomfortable. The district nurse has noted this and asks Ms Robinson to take her painkillers (analgesia) at least an hour before her visit to help reduce some of this pain. Ms Robinson has become increasingly anxious about her leg. She was a nurse and she knows that she may lose her leg if the infection does not clear up. She confides this information to her care worker who helps her to have a bath during the week, but she does not want to worry her daughter about this. Ms Robinson's daughter has already expressed concerns but does not want to worry her mother.

> ➤ Should the care worker report the information she has been given 'in confidence' to the District Nurse?
> ➤ What measures could ease Ms Robinson's discomfort?
> ➤ Why is it important for the individual to express feelings of discomfort and pain?
> ➤ How can the care worker support Ms Robinson's family who are distressed by her pain and discomfort?

Managing and easing an individual's pain

KUS 8, 10

When an individual is suffering from pain it is unusual for that pain to be only one type. Instead a person's pain may be a combination of deep-rooted pain and surface (peripheral) pain. This is important to know because different treatments or a combination of treatments may be required. In your role as a care worker you should assist the individual with the prescribed treatments and help them achieve physical and mental comfort.

Care should be carried out according to the individual's care plan and will closely follow the activities of daily living that relate to the individual. This could involve supporting the individual with each care need from toileting to working and playing. You will need to judge what the individual can and cannot do. If some activities are difficult to carry out because the individual is in pain, you might request that another assessment is carried out with a view to increasing pain control or that medical staff review the effectiveness of the person's medication and treatment.

Medication

Medication used to treat pain is commonly known as **analgesia**. Analgesic medicines help to keep a person free from pain. The main principles of analgesic prescribing are based on the World Health Organization's analgesic ladder. This is a gradual approach to prescribing, and studies have shown that it improves pain management for 69–100% of individuals.

Different analgesics relieve pain in different ways. Research recommends a **multi-modal** approach to pain management commonly known as balanced analgesia. Pain management based on the analgesic ladder involves the following analgesic groups:

- Non-opioids (non-steroidal anti-inflammatory drugs).
- Opioids (e.g. morphine).
- Adjuvants (e.g. antidepressants, analgesic skin preparations).

As a care worker it is not your responsibility to prescribe medicines, but you will find it useful to know how these are used to treat the individual and to assist the individual with their medication routine. It is important that analgesic medicines are given at the correct time of day and that they are evenly spaced so that the individual can benefit from pain relief throughout each 24-hour period. It is also very important that the individual completes the prescribed treatment and medication. Treatment will be less effective if the prescribed medication routine is not followed.

Pain management is approached from several directions because pain is felt internally and peripherally. Multi-modal medications work at different levels and strengths within the body to counteract the effects of the different types of pain. A simple example of this is when you suffer a paper cut. This is quite painful because the nerve endings in the skin are near the surface and are sensitive and many pain messages are transmitted back to the brain. If you experience a deeper cut you may feel less or no pain as there are fewer nerve endings.

Positioning

KUS 8, 10, 14, 15

Positioning individuals to achieve maximum comfort is another way of helping them to reduce pain. The key to this is to take a person's weight off the affected part of their body. You can do this by, for example, turning individuals over when

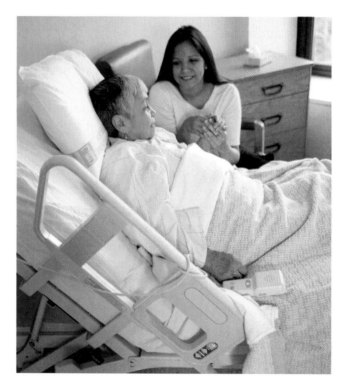

Figure 4
Changing
a person's
physical position
regularly may
help alleviate
their pain

they are lying down. You could turn them at regular intervals, usually two-hourly but this depends on individual needs. Alternatively, in some circumstances you may be able to use equipment that will support the body or the affected part, such as a bed cradle that reduces the weight of heavy blankets on a leg ulcer.

Supporting individuals in pain

Sarah Darling is an 81-year-old lady who has chronic rheumatoid arthritis. She has suffered considerably over the years and is sensitive to any movement. The care staff find looking after Ms Darling very difficult as she is rather particular and always asks for her pillows to be rearranged several times before she is comfortable. If she is moved, and sometimes before she is moved, she will cry out that the carer has hurt her. The pain is worse in the mornings and last thing at night. When Sarah is shown the pain scale chart to assess her level of discomfort she always says it is 9 or 10 even when she appears to be comfortable.

➤ *How could you encourage Sarah to express her feelings of discomfort and help her to feel confident that you know what to do?*

➤ *Sarah's pain is obviously worse in the mornings and evenings. Why is it important to pass this information on to the medical staff?*

➤ *How could key people manage Sarah's comfort and pain control?*

➤ *The residents on either side of Sarah's room are distressed by her cries of discomfort. How can you support these individuals and respect Sarah's rights?*

➤ *What aids could be used to enable Ms Darling to achieve some independence in her mobility?*

There are many simple but effective measures for managing pain. Medication is usually the recommended course of action. However, other non-medical methods can be just as useful. For example, listening to the person, regulating their temperature, reducing their anxiety by helping them to understand the importance and timing of routines, and supporting them to achieve more comfort through stress reduction and relaxation exercises and alternative therapies may all help.

Breathing exercise

This exercise can be carried out anywhere. The care worker can assist the individual by repeating the instructions, or the individual can carry out this exercise independently.

● Sit in a chair, or lay on the bed, or stand (supported if necessary).

- Close your eyes.
- Place both hands on your abdomen.
- Take a deep breath in for a count of five whilst raising the shoulders and feeling the abdomen rise under your hands.
- Slowly breathe out through your mouth for a count of five.
- Repeat three times, raising and relaxing your shoulders and abdomen on each inhalation/exhalation.

Visualisation exercise

Visualisation exercises are useful to help individuals regain some control over situations where they may feel powerless. They help the individual to **compartmentalise** problems or areas that may be difficult to deal with. These exercises can be carried out at any time.

The ball-of-colour visualisation exercise

- Close your eyes and take five deep breaths remembering to exhale through your mouth.
- Imagine you are surrounded by a warm light like the sun shining on your face, or a cool breeze that is gently washing over your body which gives you a wonderful feeling of well-being.
- If this is difficult, try taking five deep breaths remembering to slow your breathing rate while feeling more relaxed and comfortable.
- With your eyes closed, identify and look at the pain. Visualise yourself rolling it up into a small ball.
- Give the ball a colour of your choice.
- The ball may feel very heavy. Try to make it feel lighter so that it floats outside of your body in front of you.
- Remember you are surrounded by warmth and a feeling of well-being.
- Take the ball full of colour and try to make it smaller so that the colour disappears and you are less aware of it.
- You may prefer to take the ball, which is your pain, and throw it far away from you, watching it disappear from view.
- Take five deep breaths remembering to exhale through your mouth, continuing to feel the warmth, love and comfort that is surrounding you.
- Count backwards from 10 and slowly open your eyes, feeling relaxed and reassured as you count.
- Repeat as often as necessary.

Alternative therapies

There are many alternative therapies that can help to ease individuals' symptoms of discomfort and distress. These are becoming much more accepted care practices. It is important that the individual and other care staff agree with the way these are incorporated into the care plan. It is also important that therapies are carried out by qualified people who have detailed knowledge and who are aware of any potential risks and hazards.

Aromatherapy

Aromatherapy can be used in pain management to help reduce anxiety and stress. Used with massage, aromatherapy can help ease muscular aches and pain.

A qualified aromatherapist should be consulted regarding the use of the correct essential and **carrier oils** and the proportions for diluting them for use in massage therapy. However, essential oils can also be used in a vaporiser or in an oil burner to create a relaxing and pleasant environment. There are always health and safety considerations when using essential oils in this way due to the potential fire hazard. Oils and burners should not be left unattended or placed on any surface that is not completely fireproof.

The most common essential oils that promote rest and relaxation are lavender, rose absolut and sandalwood. Essential oils that help to uplift moods are neroli, lemon and geranium. Rosemary oil is beneficial for memory and concentration.

Reporting on individuals' pain and discomfort

KUS 1, 8, 13

Whenever you notice that an individual is experiencing pain and discomfort you should report this. Make a verbal report to your supervisor or the care worker responsible for the individual's care. It may also be appropriate to put your observations in writing so that other care workers are made aware of the situation.

Wherever possible, the individual should be involved in all aspects of their care. It is helpful to ask the individuals that you are caring for about their particular needs and their experiences of pain before you report their condition or hand over their care to other care workers at the end of your shift. You can gain useful information from the individual, and in some cases their family, about:

- The location of any pain: the individual should identify exactly where the pain is being felt. You may record this on a body chart or in the individual's notes.

- The type of pain being experienced: this may change from aching, sharp, dull, crampy or burning pain. It is important to note these changes.

- The intensity of the pain: the individual may describe pain as mild, severe or excruciating. A pain assessment chart will help to show when and how often pain is being experienced.

- The onset of the person's pain: it is very useful to note when the pain started or changed. It may be linked to other events, e.g. eating, exercising or taking medication.

- The duration of the pain: it is important to note how long the pain has been present. If the individual is taking medication then this observation will help to determine whether medication is effective or not.

- Any changes that occur in the person's experience of the pain: the individual's pain may change or move to a different part of the body. Referred pain occurs where a common nerve ending is stimulated and it can affect a completely different area to where the underlying problem is. For example, pain in the lower back area can indicate a kidney infection; tingling and pain down the left inner arm can indicate heart problems.

Your role as a care worker is to pass on these types of information so that the individual can receive the appropriate care and attention. This is an important responsibility. The care worker usually spends the most time with the individual and is therefore in a unique position to note small changes in their condition.

Supporting others

KUS 12

When caring for and supporting individuals it is also necessary to note how an individual's pain may be affecting others. It is distressing to know that someone is suffering and yet feel powerless to support them. Your skills and knowledge will be invaluable here.

Caring for others does not necessarily involve immediate hands-on care and there are many ways that an individual's relatives and friends can support them. These can include taking care of practical daily tasks such as cooking a meal, doing the laundry or mowing the grass. Other activities that can help are listening, encouraging work/play activities, writing letters, reading or just sitting close by. It is very comforting for the individual to know that they are not alone and that they can share their worries and concerns with someone. It is comforting for those who are close to the individual to know that they are needed.

It can be extremely upsetting to witness another person's suffering. Every opportunity should be made for individuals not directly involved in care to discuss and share their concerns with staff. This may mean explaining why some procedures are necessary to help the individual or explaining that some people communicate their suffering in order to release it and let it go.

For children who are witnessing the pain of a relative or friend, it is very important to encourage them to discuss their feelings. This will help to stop them being afraid of care settings or avoiding expressing their own needs. Actively talking and listening, role-playing situations where the child is in charge, and drawing pictures or making things can all help them to express their feelings. If the child is having nightmares or is avoiding situations then it may be necessary to seek advice from a GP or health visitor.

KUS 4, 7, 10, 15, 16

Key points – helping individuals with physical comfort needs

- 'Pain' is a complex experience that can have many causes and which has a negative effect on an individual's quality of life.

- As a care worker you are responsible for assessing and responding immediately to each individual's particular experience of pain and discomfort.

- It is important to take each individual's complaints and their description of pain seriously when assessing discomfort or pain.

- The care and approach needed to deal with a person's pain and discomfort should be detailed in their individual care plan.

- You should always follow the approach identified in an individual's care plan when responding to the person's complaints of pain or discomfort.

- Simple care interventions such as moving and repositioning an individual, providing them with distraction activities, simple complementary therapies and taking the time to listen and be supportive can all help to reduce feelings of pain and discomfort.

- If simple care interventions and psychological support fail to reduce the person's pain or discomfort, the problem should be referred to a senior colleague.

- An individual's experience of pain and discomfort should be reported to other members of the care team and documented in their records in a clear and objective way.

Element HSC216b

Assist in providing conditions to meet individuals' needs for rest

Introduction

Every person has a physical need for sufficient rest and sleep. The amount of rest and sleep that a person needs will probably change over the course of their life. However, it is always important to get good-quality rest and sleep. This is extremely important in maintaining quality of life as well as physical and mental health and well-being. Without adequate rest and sleep individuals may experience confusion, memory loss, **paranoia**, poor concentration, longer recovery time from illness and disease, restlessness and agitation. Your role is to recognise and support the needs of each individual in this important activity of daily living.

Sleep involves physical and mental inactivity from which a person can be roused to consciousness. During sleep physiological changes occur, for example the respiratory and pulse rates reduce and blood pressure drops. There is also less brain activity. However, some activity is experienced as a result of dreaming. During sleep a person may be roused to consciousness through external stimuli such as noise, movement or pain.

Preparing an individual for rest and sleep

KUS 9

Adults vary considerably in the amount of sleep they require, but on average, adults sleep between eight and twelve hours in each 24-hour period. An older person may sleep less and sometimes this causes them to worry. However, this is entirely normal as, due to reduced activity through age and longer periods of rest during the day, the body requires less sleep than it did when they were younger.

The rhythm of sleep is governed by an internal biological 'clock' known as a 'circadian rhythm'. This internal rhythm has a pattern of peaks and troughs of wakefulness and sleep activity. A person's daily pattern of activity as well as their internal body chemistry and external factors in the environment (such as whether it is light or dark, warm or cold) affects the circadian sleep rhythm. A person is most likely to sleep soundly when their temperature is lowest, in the early hours of the morning. People usually wake up when their temperature starts to rise at around 6–8 a.m. As we age, the part of the brain that controls the circadian sleep rhythm loses cells. This can cause noticeable changes in how a person sleeps. They may nap more, have disrupted sleep and wake up earlier.

There are five stages of sleep known as cycles and each cycle lasts approximately 90–100 minutes (see Table 4).

The function of sleep is still not fully understood, but researchers who study sleep generally support the idea that sleep is necessary for:

- Restoration and growth of all body cells.
- Conservation of energy.
- Recovery after illness.
- Healthy brain function.

People who live in care settings, either temporarily or permanently, may have their natural routines and rhythms disrupted by the care-work activity that goes on around them. Busy care settings where a number of people are working all day and all night can interrupt normal circadian rhythms and cause individuals to lose sleep. However, a care setting that recognises people's needs should take individuals' different rest and sleep patterns into account. Each individual's needs should be assessed and recorded within their care plan.

Factors affecting rest and sleep

KUS 3

Factors that influence a person's ability to sleep may include some of the following:

- Age.
- Pain or discomfort.

Table 4 Stages of sleep

Stage 1	The sleeper has closed their eyes or 'dropped off'; there is general relaxation and fleeting thoughts. The sleeper can be woken by small noises or external stimuli. If the person is woken up, this stage is remembered as a feeling of drowsiness. When this stage continues for longer than 15 minutes the next stage is entered.
Stage 2	During this stage, thoughts tend to take on a dream-like quality and there is greater relaxation. The sleeper is asleep but can still be woken easily.
Stage 3	This stage is usually entered after 30 minutes. Complete relaxation occurs and the pulse rate starts to slow down along with other bodily functions. The person is less likely to wake to familiar noises, voices or household sounds. If uninterrupted the next stage follows.
Stage 4	In Stage 4 the sleeper rarely moves and is relaxed. The person is now in a deep sleep. If the individual is prone to sleep walking or is incontinent then it is likely to occur during this phase.
Stage 5	It is during this stage that dreaming is most likely to occur and is characterised by rapid eye movements (REM) causing the eyelids to flutter and sometimes for the body to move in response to the dream. The person may wake easily during this stage as the brain is stimulated and aroused.

- Anxiety.
- Medication (e.g. night sedation).
- Night-time routine.
- Amount of sleep/rest taken during the day.
- Amount of activity/exercise.
- Illness or disease (e.g. Alzheimer's disease).
- Stimulants consumed (e.g. alcohol, caffeine).

The carer's role in assisting sleep and rest

KUS 4, 8, 15, 16

You can promote rest and sleep by recognising the factors that can prevent it. You should note the recommended actions on the care plan and record any changes that may need reviewing.

Sleep

A regular routine and change of day clothes to nightclothes will assist the individual. Some individuals enjoy a bath and a hot drink before retiring. Some individuals like to read a book, watch TV or listen to the radio. The advantage of working with individuals on a regular basis is that routines can be established that will support this activity of daily living. Sometimes when routines are disrupted with changes of staff and unfamiliar routines and surroundings, individuals can become anxious and find it difficult to settle.

In Alzheimer's disease and sometimes with senile dementia, individuals lose the ability to differentiate between night and day. This may cause them to get up and get dressed in the middle of the night or to be extremely restless and wander. It is important to re-emphasise what time it is. In these circumstances it is sometimes possible for individuals to get some sleep during the night. However, in some cases night-time sedation may have to be prescribed to help people to achieve a regular sleep pattern.

Individuals may choose to sleep in a chair overnight. You should ensure that they change position regularly to reduce the risk of pressure sores occurring.

For individuals who are regularly disturbed in the night due to incontinence, medication regimes, illness or disease, it is important that you enable the individual to catch up on their sleep during the day if appropriate. The dilemma occurs when night-time waking develops into a pattern and the individual finds it difficult to settle. Temporary night-time sedation may be prescribed to break the cycle of disruption.

Practical Example

Assisting sleep

William Brown is a 92-year-old gentleman who likes to smoke and to drink a glass of whisky before he retires to bed. He takes several naps during the day and prefers to go to bed late at night and wake up quite early. Over the last few weeks his night-time sleeping habits have changed as he has woken several times in the night to go to the toilet. In the morning he is very agitated and is quite rude to the staff. He also tells them that they make too much noise in the night. The care staff report these changes and he is prescribed night sedation to help him settle. Over the next two weeks Mr Brown sleeps very soundly but now he is incontinent of urine and this further distresses him. His family note that he is not himself.

➤ *What factors are disturbing Mr Brown's night-time routine?*

➤ *Why is it important for the care worker to report any changes in Mr Brown's condition?*

➤ *How can the care worker help Mr Brown to sleep and rest at night?*

➤ *How can the care worker support Mr Brown during the day?*

Rest

Rest can take many forms, from having a catnap to playing games and activities. Rest is important during the day but must be balanced so that the individual still sleeps at night.

Restful activities include reading, listening to music, painting, gardening, watching films, going for a walk, talking, sewing etc. Alternative therapies such as aromatherapy (in which essential oils from plant extracts are massaged into the skin), reflexology (in which gentle pressure on areas of the feet stimulate energy lines and help to balance the body) and Indian head massage are useful for promoting general relaxation and for reducing anxiety or stress levels. These therapies are also useful for managing pain and other physical ailments, but they should be performed by a trained practitioner.

Gentle physical exercise will also promote relaxation and aid sleep. This can be in the form of a dance or music class. Tai Chi, which uses slow movements to gently tone and condition the body, is also becoming very popular as a form of relaxation and exercise. In the East, especially in China, this is a daily routine that helps people of all ages.

The care worker can promote rest by helping the individual to use the available resources and facilities. Rest is also useful throughout the day.

Moving and changing position will assist the individual's comfort. It may be appropriate for an individual to lie down, for example after lunch, in order to promote rest and also to relieve pressure from the sacral area if they are sitting for long periods. Some individuals may choose to take a walk or to go out for some fresh air.

If the individual is able, they might like to go swimming.

Dealing with disturbances

Sleep is affected by many factors. The individual's care plan will reveal their normal sleeping habits. Some people report that they do not normally have problems, whilst others may report that they are light sleepers and require night-time sedation. Most people fall somewhere in between.

Disturbances to sleep can affect a person's recovery period, may make people irritable and can affect concentration and memory. It is important that noise and unnecessary movements are kept to a minimum when individuals are sleeping. Some procedures mean that an individual will be disturbed during the night. The individual may need to use the toilet several times during the night. Pressure area care may mean that an individual is moved at regular intervals.

Some disturbances can be reduced by dimming lights, closing doors quietly and switching the call-bell system to lights only (however, the call bells must not be turned off). Policies should be in place to regulate visiting times and telephone calls late at night or during afternoon rest periods. In a busy environment it may be necessary to ask people to keep their voices down. Some people forget how sound can carry at night. Other measures can include closing or partially shutting windows, turning radios and televisions down slightly or requesting that people use earphones after an agreed time. Mobile phones should not be used in any environment where there are cardiac monitors or where other radio or monitoring equipment is being used in care.

Achieving a restful environment

KUS 7, 8

Rest and sleep can be promoted by paying attention to various aspects of the physical environment as well as the atmosphere and sense of security present in a residential-care setting or a person's own home. Aspects of the physical environment that affect restfulness include the use of colour and space, the kind of décor used and the general comfort of the surroundings.

It is known that some colours are more restful and relaxing, for example pastel shades of blue and green. Soft furnishings that are similar in tone to the surrounding furniture and objects within a setting are more restful than those that are highly patterned and decorated with competing colours and designs. Areas that are clutter-free are more conducive to rest and relaxation. Some people find quiet music that has a regular harmonic sound more relaxing than music that is loud and discordant. Some people enjoy solitude and being able to listen to everyday sounds and weather noises, such as the wind, raindrops etc.

The 'mental environment' relates to the general atmosphere of the care setting and the approachability, professionalism and friendliness of staff. The mental environment can be promoted through rest and relaxation or visualisation exercises or simply being allowed 'to be'. Quite often in care individuals get little respite from constant care and attention. Sometimes they may like to be left alone and given time to themselves to think and reflect.

Figure 5
A quiet area
for relaxation

Reporting on rest and sleep

When carrying out daily care, you should note whether the individual is achieving rest and sleep. Any facts that the individual reports should be recorded in the care plan. If there are factors that can be responded to immediately then you should address these. An individual's care plan should show details of how much sleep the individual normally has and their particular requirements. For example: 'Prefers to sleep sitting up supported by pillows'; 'Enjoys a bed-time drink and to fall asleep whilst listening to the radio'; 'Rises early, prefers to go to bed after 11.00 p.m.'.

If you note any aspects of the environment over which you do not have control, for example noise from building works outside, it may be necessary to report these for further advice and assistance. Sometimes new individuals or new neighbours can upset a normal routine. It may be necessary to allow a settling-in period or someone may have to remind others that they are disturbing the peace. More serious concerns, for example with difficult neighbours, may require other agency intervention such as social services, the council or the police. However, it is always worth trying to communicate concerns in an amicable and non-threatening manner. This may be the responsibility of a senior care worker or other senior member of staff.

Key points – assisting individuals to rest

- Every individual has specific needs for rest and sleep. These change over a person's life but play an important part in their health, well-being and quality of life.
- You should be aware of each individual's normal pattern of sleep and rest and you should note and respond to any factors that disrupt this.
- You can help individuals to achieve a positive and regular sleep pattern by encouraging and supporting a pre-sleep routine that is relaxing and restful.
- Individuals may suffer sleep disturbances for a variety of reasons. A sensitive and supportive approach to this could involve orientating individuals and helping them to use relaxation and any prescribed medication to re-establish a regular sleep pattern.
- A restful physical environment and a calm, quiet and considerate approach from staff are needed to promote and support individuals' sleep at night.
- You should note and report any disruptions or problems that individuals have with sleep or rest. This should then be addressed through the person's care plan.

Unit HSC216

Are you ready for assessment?

Help address the physical comfort needs of individuals

This unit is all about supporting individuals who are experiencing pain or discomfort and helping them to rest and be more comfortable. It is about adjustments that can be made to the individual's position and to their surroundings. This unit links closely to unit HSC21 covering communication and unit HSC22 covering risk assessment and health, safety and security.

Your assessment will mainly be carried out through observation by your assessor and this should provide most of the evidence for the elements in this unit. As this unit involves careful monitoring of the individuals' care plans, the evidence may include reference to these confidential records but they should never be included in your portfolio.

This unit is about your role in directly supporting individuals who are in pain or discomfort and also your work with colleagues and other key people, so there will be ample chances for observation by your assessor. However, if such observation would intrude on the privacy of individuals, you can plan with your assessor to use the testimony of an expert witness instead of observation by your assessor or as an additional source of evidence.

Direct observation

Your assessor or an expert witness will need to see you carry out the performance criteria (PCs) in each of the elements in this unit.

A performance criterion that may be difficult to meet through observation or expert witness testimony is:

• **HSC216a PC 9**

because it might not always occur.

Preparing to be observed

You must make sure that your workplace and any individuals and key people involved in your work agree to you being assessed. Explicit, informed consent must be obtained before you carry out any assessment activity that involves individuals or which involves access to confidential information related to their care.

Before your assessments you should read carefully the performance criteria for each element in the unit. Try to cover as much as you can *during your observations* but remember that you and your assessor can also plan for additional sources of evidence should full coverage of all performance criteria not be possible or to help ensure that your performance is consistent and that you can apply the knowledge specification in your work practice.

▶

Other types of evidence

You may need to present other forms of evidence in order to:

- Cover criteria not observed by your assessor or by an expert witness.
- Show that you have the required knowledge, understanding and skills to claim competence in this area of practice.
- Ensure that your work practice is consistent.

Your assessor may also need to ask you questions to confirm your knowledge and understanding of this unit.

Check your knowledge

1   Identify reasons why care workers sometimes find it difficult to assess an individual's complaints of 'pain'.

2   Identify a range of factors that may influence an individual's particular experience of pain and discomfort.

3   What should a care worker observe and ask about when assessing an individual's particular experience of pain?

4   Explain the difference between acute and chronic pain.

5   What part does an individual's care plan play in attempts to deal with the person's pain and discomfort?

6   Identify three non-medical ways of helping an individual to deal with pain or discomfort.

7   Identify a range of factors that affect an individual's experience of rest and sleep.

8   Describe ways of promoting rest and sleep for individuals receiving care.

UNIT HSC218

Support individuals with their personal-care needs

*T*his unit covers all aspects relating to supporting the personal hygiene, toileting and dressing needs of individuals. There are three elements:

⌒ *HSC218a Support individuals to go to the toilet*

⌒ *HSC218b Enable individuals to maintain their personal hygiene*

⌒ *HSC218c Support individuals in personal grooming and dressing*

Introduction

Providing personal care is an important part of the work of many care workers. In some care settings individuals may simply need guidance and some basic assistance to meet their personal-care needs. However, sometimes individuals are completely dependent on care workers to provide them with appropriate personal care. This can be physically and emotionally difficult as it involves working very closely with an individual and assisting them with tasks that would otherwise be thought of as private and intimate. Before we look at ways of providing personal care it is necessary to consider what personal care involves.

What is personal care?

Personal care relates to hygiene needs, for example care of skin, hair and nails as well as intimate genital hygiene. When you provide personal care it may also involve helping an individual with their toileting needs. Personal care is important when an individual finds it difficult to carry out these intimate but everyday activities due to illness, disease or age. As a care worker you may need to provide some assistance to support an individual to carry out personal-care activities themselves, or you may need to carry out full personal care if the individual is no longer able to do any of this for themselves. Your role as a care worker is to support independence where possible and to note and report any changes in the individual's condition and general well-being.

A detailed knowledge of **physiological** processes and body systems is not necessary in order to provide basic personal care but it may help you to understand why certain care practices are carried out. The two body systems that are most important in this respect are the digestive system and the urinary system.

Understanding the digestive system

In order to understand the process of **elimination** it may be useful to look at the organs involved and at the basic functions of the digestive system. The main organs of the mid and lower digestive system are the:

- Stomach.
- Intestines.
- Colon.
- Rectum.
- Anus.

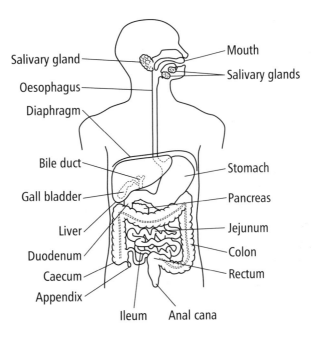

Salivary gland

Oesophagus

Diaphragm

Bile duct

Gall bladder

Liver

Duodenum

Caecum

Appendix

Mouth

Salivary glands

Stomach

Pancreas

Jejunum

Colon

Rectum

Ileum   Anal cana

Figure 1
The digestive system

The digestive system is responsible for processing food so that it can be used by the body. It is also responsible for getting rid of solid waste products. The end product of this natural process is solid waste material known in medical terms as faeces or stools. Faecal matter in adults is usually brown in colour and soft in consistency. The odour that is produced is a by-product of the different types of bacteria that are present in the digestive system. It varies due to the type of diet, food ingested and bacteria present. Faeces are normally made up of 75% water and 25% solid matter. Output varies, but in Western societies adults tend to produce a stool at least once each day. The time taken from **ingestion** of food to **defecation** also varies but is about three days in healthy adults. The process tends to be slower for older people and can take anything up to two weeks depending on the individual's diet and digestive health.

Understanding the urinary system

Elimination includes the processing and passage of liquids. The main organs of the urinary system are the:

- Kidneys.
- Ureters.
- Bladder.
- Urethra.

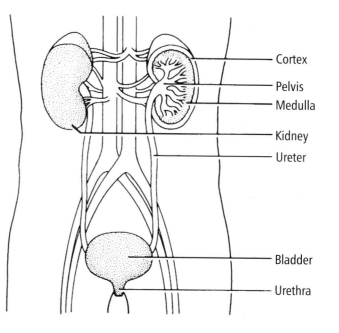

Figure 2
The urinary system

The organs of the urinary system eliminate fluid waste products in the form of **urine**. Normal urine output in a 24-hour period is approximately 1.5 litres. An individual may urinate between five and ten times during this period. Urine production usually slows down during the night. However, because of reduced bladder tone and bladder size, some older people may need to go to the toilet during the night. Urine is composed of 96% water, 2% salts and 2% urea (a nitrogen-based waste product). Urine smells of ammonia after exposure to air and alters in smell and consistency if the person has an infection, illness or trauma. Urine is usually straw coloured but it is darker and more concentrated first thing in the morning and if the individual is not drinking enough fluids or is losing fluids via other means, such as through sweating or blood loss.

Sensitivity and personal care

The aim of personal care is to maintain quality of life for all individuals and for them to feel confident and have their self-esteem needs met. Individuals must be treated with dignity and respect at all times whilst receiving personal care. Therefore, you need to be sensitive when meeting the personal-care needs of individuals. It is important to respect the individual's rights to dignity, privacy and freedom of choice whilst maintaining the person's independence and individuality as much as possible. Sometimes, in the course of what seems to be routine work, some of these aspects of caring are forgotten in the effort to keep up with workloads, achieve the daily tasks set and to make up for shortfalls in lack of equipment, facilities and staff. Acknowledging this may help you to remember the individual's best interests and carry out care appropriately.

Element HSC218a

Support individuals to go to the toilet

Communication and personal-care needs

Communication is an important aspect of care, especially when meeting toileting needs. The words we use to describe needing to use the toilet should be treated with sensitivity. The terminology and other phrases used need to be expressed clearly and without embarrassment, loss of dignity or privacy. Sometimes when an ordinary personal-care activity is taken for granted care staff can be:

- Unaware that they are acting inappropriately by rushing an individual.
- Unaware of the urgency of the situation.
- Patronising by using language they would normally use with children.
- Impatient or appear off-hand.

Assisting a person to communicate their wish to use the toilet or receive help with other forms of personal care is an important part of your role as a care worker. If an individual needs support and assistance with personal care they should be encouraged to express this verbally to the staff caring for them. If they are unable to do this, other methods, such as the use of flashcards, or more commonly call-bell systems, can be used to enable people to communicate. It may also be appropriate, when you know an individual and understand their personal-care needs, to ask the person directly (and discreetly) whether they wish you to assist them to use the toilet or receive other forms of personal care. You can then either assist the individual to mobilise to the toilet, or the toilet (in the form of a commode chair, disposable urinal or bedpan) can be brought to them.

Responding to an individual's toileting needs

Some individuals will need minimal assistance whilst others will require full care.

In a 24-hour period adults will need to pass urine (urinate or **micturate**) about eight times. This means that on average a person will need to go to the toilet approximately every two hours. As a care worker you should promote a person's independence and encourage them to manage their own toileting needs wherever possible. A number of factors influence the extent to which an individual will be able to recognise and manage their personal toileting needs (see Figure 3 overleaf) and be able to meet them independently.

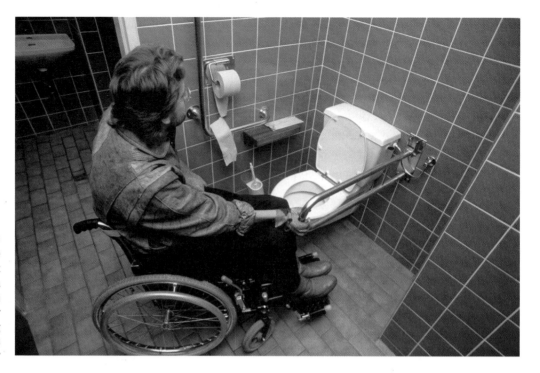

Figure 3
Appropriate
equipment
can enable a
disabled person
to meet their
own toileting
needs

Identifying the potential and actual problems that a person has with elimination requires careful assessment of the individual's needs and requirements. Guidance on this area of a person's functioning should be contained in their care plan and needs assessment. If you have to assess an individual's need for help and support you should consider and find out about issues such as the following:

- Can the person communicate their need to eliminate or do they require some form of communication support?
- What are the person's normal elimination routines and practices?
- Does the person have any problems with mobility?
- Can the person adjust their clothing and carry out post-eliminating cleansing (i.e. use toilet paper, wash)?
- Can the person wash their hands?
- Does illness, injury, disease and/or medication affect the person's elimination directly or indirectly?

Assisting individuals to use the toilet

It is important that the individual knows where the toilet facilities are and which ones they can have direct access to. Embarrassing accidents can sometimes occur in care settings because an individual does not know where to find the toilet rather than because they are unaware that they need to use the toilet. Not being able to find or reach the toilet in time can be humiliating for a person who is otherwise able to manage their **continence**. Therefore, you should consider the location and size of toilet-related signs and notices in care settings and assess the ease of access, space and size of toilets. All individuals should be able to access appropriate toilet facilities regardless of their personal size and whether they use a wheelchair or walking frame to mobilise. You should also pay attention to the availability of ramps, handles, support rails and aids such as raised toilet seats and facilities for washing and personal cleansing. In the home-care environment an occupational therapist may be able to help with assessing the individual's needs. Wherever you are working, you should think about the individual's dignity when assisting them to use the toilet. You can show respect for this by ensuring the toilet door is closed, that the person has all of the privacy they require, and by knocking before you go in to help the person with cleansing or dressing after they have used the toilet.

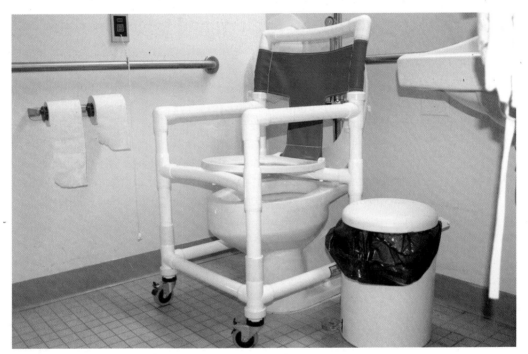

**Figure 4
Aids that help
individuals
to use the toilet**

Most people would prefer to be left alone while they carry out their elimination needs. As a sensitive care worker you should comply with the individual's wishes. Ensure that they have a call bell if required and that they are safe and comfortable. After the person has used the toilet you may, because of their particular condition or health needs, be required to monitor their output using a measuring jug and to note on a chart or in the individual's notes volumes and anything unusual. Any concerns that you have about unusual output should be reported to a more senior member of staff. Where required, you should also assist the person to wash their hands after using the toilet. In some circumstances, particularly where the individual has been incontinent, a full wash and a change of underwear and/or incontinence pad (if worn) may be required. Take care to ensure that the individual is not rushed and they are clean and comfortable. You may need to apply creams to protect the individual's skin from dryness, fungal infections and/or pressure sores. This is an ideal opportunity to check the condition of the person's skin.

If an individual is confined to bed they should be able to summon assistance as required. If they use a bedpan or urinal for elimination, you should help them to achieve a comfortable position to use it. Always be careful to ensure that the individual is not exposed to the gaze of others when eliminating. Draw curtains around the bed or close doors as appropriate. If the individual is on a hospital ward or public area it may take a little longer for them to go to the toilet than is usual. This may be because people feel embarrassed and inhibited about using the toilet when other people are only a few feet away and may hear them. Switching on a radio or television can help to mask toileting sounds and reduce some people's embarrassment. Turning on the taps in the bathroom can also sometimes stimulate urination if a person is having trouble with this.

Managing hygiene and infection risks

After using the toilet and elimination, the individual should be assisted to wipe themselves if appropriate. It is good practice to cover the commode, urinal or bedpan before taking it away for disposal. This helps to reduce potential cross-infection and smells. It also preserves the individual's dignity. If any creams or lotions need to be applied they should be applied at this point. You should also assist the individual to wash their hands. Check bedclothes in case there were any spillages and change them if necessary. An air freshener is useful to prevent embarrassing odours, but do not use this if individuals have chest or lung problems. Clean all equipment after use and dispose of waste products as per care-setting

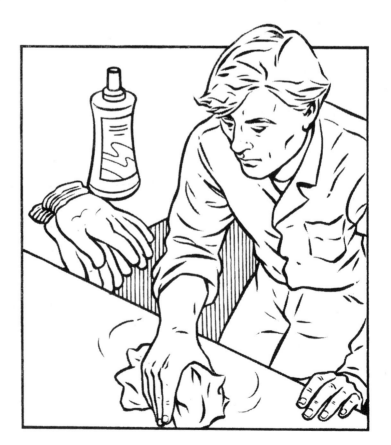

Figure 5
Reducing
infection:
What is he
doing wrong?

procedure and policy. It is good practice to take the shortest route to the disposal point, avoiding areas where other people are present if at all possible, and to dispose of the waste as soon as possible. You should always wear gloves, wash your hands to reduce the spread of infection and dispose of gloves following the local waste-disposal procedure.

Measuring and recording elimination output

Urine output is usually only monitored at the specific request of medical staff. Where this is the case, urine output may need to be monitored carefully using a measuring jug and the results recorded on a fluid balance chart. The individual's normal routine and history should have been recorded in their care plan or you may have noted a change in the individual's usual habits and recorded this.

Urine is commonly tested using a chemically treated plastic strip (stick) that is dipped into the individual's urine. Some diabetic individuals carry out this procedure twice a day to test for glucose. Other potential problems that can be detected using the stick are those identifying pH values (alkalinity, acidity) and whether there is protein, blood or excess minerals present. You should record the findings on the individual's chart or notes and report them to senior staff responsible for the person's care.

Sometimes a sample of urine has to be collected and sent off for more sophisticated analysis in the laboratory. A mid-stream urine (MSU) sample is a clean sample that is taken after the individual has had a wash and is then asked to urinate and stop mid-flow. The individual is then asked to continue so that they provide a clean, mid-stream sample that is collected in a sterile urine container. When this has been done the individual can complete their toileting needs until finished. Always wear gloves when collecting samples like this and clean up any urine that spills over the sides of the container. The sample container must be sterile before use and should be sealed immediately afterwards to avoid contamination. This will ensure that no external bacteria enter to affect the readings when the specimen is analysed. The specimen container should be labelled clearly and then sealed in a plastic bag showing the individual's correct details, the time the sample was taken and the date. If an individual has a **catheter** then a catheter specimen of urine (CSU) will be taken. As a care worker you should receive training before carrying out this procedure and you should follow care-setting policy.

Another common monitoring procedure in addition to observing colour, amount and odour is one of registering fluid balance. A person's fluid balance is normally worked out by assuming that what goes in (fluids, drinks) must come out (through urine, expiration (breathing out) and sweating). A fluid balance chart (Figure 6, overleaf) is normally completed over a 24-hour period for individuals who have become dehydrated or who need their output closely monitored for medical reasons. Everything that the individual drinks has to be recorded on one side of the fluid balance chart and everything the individual excretes is measured and recorded on the other. At the end of the day the balances are added (readings are usually taken midnight to midnight).

Name:			**Weight:**	
Date of Birth:			**Date:**	
Balance carried over ....mls.				

Time	Oral Fluids In	IV Fluids In	Fluids Out	Total in Mls
06.00				
07.00				
08.00				
09.00				
10.00				
11.00				
12.00				

Figure 6
Fluid balance
chart

Monitoring faeces

Once a stool sample has been collected it is usually analysed in a laboratory. As a care worker you should note changes in colour, consistency and appearance and report these to medical staff or a senior colleague. Testing for blood in faeces is usually carried out by trained staff or by a care worker who has had relevant training. Any faeces sample should be collected in an appropriate container that is then labelled and sealed before being sent to a clinical laboratory for analysis. Always wear protective gloves when dealing with faecal matter.

Observing and reporting on elimination problems

The individual who is receiving care may be the first person to note changes in their bowel or bladder habits. As a care worker you should also be observant as changes in elimination habits often indicate problems in other parts of the body. Obvious changes to watch out for include:

- Reduced or increased frequency with which an individual uses the toilet.
- Changes in the quantity of output (called oliguria, anuria and polyuria).
- Blood in the urine (uraemia) or blood in stools (melaena).
- A strong odour or changes in the colour or consistency of urine or faeces (e.g. diarrhoea).

Changes in the pattern or contents of a person's elimination output can indicate an infection caused by bacteria, illness or the onset of diseases such as diabetes or gastroenteritis.

> **Medical terms associated with urine output**
> - Oliguria – this means less than 500 ml of urine formed in 24 hours.
> - Anuria – this means a urine output of less than 250 ml in 24 hours (this is also known as renal shutdown).
> - Polyuria – a volume of urine in excess of the normal (over 2000 ml in 24 hours). This can indicate renal disturbance caused by conditions such as chronic kidney disease or diabetes.

Incontinence

Incontinence is usually associated with the **involuntary** passing of urine but it can also involve the involuntary passing of faeces. Urinary incontinence problems are often linked to infections or irritations of the bladder or urethra. However, in the elderly incontinence may also be caused by:

- **Degenerative** changes or the inability of the bladder and **urethral sphincters** to work properly due to ageing.
- Relaxation of the pelvic floor muscles due to age-related changes.
- Disease, surgery, trauma or loss of awareness resulting in a loss of control over urination.

Urinary incontinence, also known as stress incontinence, ranges from small leaks that occur on coughing or exertion to full bladder emptying. The bladder is a muscle and in some cases it can be retrained to limit or reduce a person's incontinence problems. If the individual is physically and mentally capable, pelvic floor exercises can also be performed. These consist of the individual beginning and then stopping elimination mid-flow for a count of 10 (or possibly less) and then emptying their bladder again. This exercise can be carried out several times a day until the bladder regains some of its normal tone.

Other ways of coping with incontinence include:

- Ensuring that the individual is drinking sufficient fluids. Reducing fluid intake will not necessarily reduce urine output.
- Avoiding caffeine-based drinks which are natural **diuretics**.
- Offering to take an individual to the toilet on a two-hourly basis during the day if they have severe incontinence problems. During the night the frequency of using the toilet can be reduced although the correct frequency of using the toilet will depend on individual needs.

Always change the individual's clothes and bed linen if they are incontinent. This will help prevent pressure sores from developing due to wet skin and uric acid. The person's skin should be washed and dried thoroughly to ensure that it is clean and that they are comfortable. You must also protect yourself and reduce risks of cross-infection by wearing gloves and an apron when dealing with an incontinent person. Bring the linen-waste sack to the bedside so that any soiled linen may be disposed of immediately. This will reduce the transfer of **micro-organisms** to other areas in the setting. Gloves and aprons should be disposed of appropriately in the room. However, if you need to dispose of bodily waste in the sluice area you must wash your hands immediately afterwards and in between dealing with different individuals.

Exercise instructions to strengthen pelvic floor muscles

This exercise can be carried out when a person is sitting, standing or lying down:

- Tighten muscles around buttocks as if to prevent bowels opening.
- Tighten muscles around bladder as if preventing the passage of urine.
- Try to tighten these muscles and hold them for 10 seconds, then relax.
- Do this exercise at regular intervals throughout the day.
- When passing urine, stop and restart a couple of times.

In cases where the individual is incontinent of both urine and faeces (i.e. doubly incontinent), the same procedures should be applied when caring for them. It is good practice to dispose of soiled linen separately from ordinary used linen. Your care setting may use a coloured bag system and have a clear hygiene policy and procedure that indicates what is expected. If you are working at night, be sensitive to the individual's need for sleep and also the need to protect the individual from becoming susceptible to pressure sores and possible infection should they be left in a soiled bed or soiled clothes. An individual's care plan should address these issues and should be reviewed on a regular basis by nursing and medical staff.

Key points – providing personal care

The following are good practice points in meeting the toileting needs of individuals:

- Answering calls for assistance immediately.
- Ensuring that the individual has access to clean facilities and/or equipment to use.
- Asking the individual what they would like in terms of assistance.
- Assisting the individual to use the toilet as appropriate or required.
- Ensuring the individual is not unduly exposed and that privacy is maintained throughout.

- Ensuring that the individual has the chance to wash their hands/genital areas as appropriate afterwards.
- Ensuring that any continence aids are comfortable and appropriate to the needs of the individual.
- Monitoring, recording and reporting any problems or concerns to an appropriate senior member of staff.
- Being aware of cultural differences surrounding toileting practices and personal cleanliness.
- Seek training and advice if you are unsure how to handle any procedures, equipment or individuals with particular needs.
- Not discussing individuals' toileting habits in public areas.

Element HSC218b *Enable individuals to maintain their personal hygiene*

Self-care and support for personal hygiene

Supporting and helping individuals to manage their personal hygiene is a central part of a care worker's role in providing personal care. The way that you help an individual to address their personal hygiene needs requires sensitivity and understanding. For example, it is important to first find out what the individual's personal hygiene requirements are and how much help they may require to meet them. Key areas of concern are:

- Care of the teeth, mouth, skin, hair, nails, feet and genital areas to preserve cleanliness, prevent infections and minimise the risk of pressure sores occurring.
- Understanding cultural requirements and practices relating to personal hygiene and personal care.
- Balancing the normal personal-care practices of the individual against the hygiene and social requirements of the setting.

Managing hygiene and health and safety

Managing hygiene and health and safety and enabling individuals to maintain their personal hygiene needs are important issues. Balancing the needs and requirements of the individual and meeting health and safety needs requires negotiation that will empower the individual but that will also limit the risk of accidents occurring. A risk assessment of the care environment and of the individual's ability to carry out tasks will need to be undertaken. You may be asked to contribute to one or both of these risk assessments, or you may be able to look at existing risk assessments if they are available in your local care setting.

In any personal-care situation it is important that you remember to manage your own personal hygiene and health and safety needs. For example, you may need to read the manual-handling policy and ensure that you follow it. You may need to wear gloves and other appropriate protective clothing. You should dispose of waste and linen appropriately and report any health and safety or hygiene problems to the people who are responsible for them.

The main personal-care role of the care worker is to support the individual in their surroundings. So you may have to carry out personal-care routines that are indicated by the individual's needs assessment or you may have to report that an individual requires a fuller assessment of their self-care skills if these appear to be changing or deteriorating. The main forms of personal care that you may need to assist individuals with include:

- Washing and bathing.
- Hand washing.
- Pressure-area skin care.
- Care of the nails.
- Care of the feet.
- Care of the hair.
- Care of teeth and mouth.
- Shaving.

Washing and bathing

Washing and bathing can be difficult for people for various reasons. For example, the physical and mental effects of old age, mental-health problems and physical disabilities can make simple self-care tasks like washing and bathing more difficult for some people at particular points in their life. People who experience visual impairments, immobility and **dexterity** problems may also require assistance because of these problems. For example, health and development problems that limit a person's vision or their movements can make it difficult for some people to carry out simple but essential tasks such as turning taps on and off, using bath and sink plugs and stepping into and out of the bath or shower. The consequences for a person's ability to meet their own personal hygiene needs can be significant.

Before you decide to assist an individual with washing and bathing you should assess how much of this kind of personal care they are able to provide for themselves. If the person struggles to cope, an occupational therapist may be able to identify appropriate aids, adaptations and items of equipment that the individual can use to maintain some or all of their self-care skills.

If you are assisting an individual with washing and bathing, find out what their preferences are regarding soap and other grooming products. Most people wash with soap and water. However, as the skin ages and loses elasticity, natural oils are lost and the skin becomes dry. Soap can make this worse. Some people may have allergies or specific requirements because of skin conditions or sensitivities that you will need to know about. One solution in these circumstances is to introduce individuals to alternatives such as natural oils and moisturisers that lessen some of the negative effects of ageing or skin conditions. However, you should always check with senior and specialist staff before suggesting or using skin-care products, creams or moisturisers that have not been prescribed for or chosen by an individual.

An individual's preferences in this area may also include whether they would prefer a daily bath or shower. Imposing a bathing regime on individuals receiving care is likely to be inappropriate and certainly undermines their right to choose their own care. However, any conflict between the preferences of the individual and the health and hygiene requirements of a care setting have to be managed carefully. If an individual's preferences or wishes are different from the standards or policies of your workplace, you should consult a senior care worker or your supervisor and obtain guidance on the best way to deal with it.

Hand washing

A person's hands should always be washed after using the toilet, before touching food and after touching animals, surfaces or other people. If an individual is confined to bed you should offer hand wipes or a soapy cloth and towel. Frequent hand washing can reduce natural oils, so it is important to dry adequately between fingers and apply hand cream if required.

You should develop the habit of always washing your hands before and after carrying out any clinical procedure. This is essential when dealing with dressings, open wounds or bodily fluids such as urine or faeces. Wearing gloves helps to protect you from infection but is not a substitute for effective hand washing.

Pressure-area skin care

When a person is laying or sitting in one position for any period of time, the pressure on that point causes the skin to become red, painful (due to reduced circulation) and, if not remedied by movement or skin care, the skin can eventually break down, resulting in a pressure sore. This breakdown in skin is also affected by several other factors (see Table 1 overleaf). Pressure sores often occur over bony prominences, such as the elbows, heels, the **sacral area**, ears, shoulder blades, hip bones (iliac crest), knees and sides of the feet. This is because there is less skin in these areas to cushion the full pressure and weight of the person.

Pressure-area care involves monitoring a person's skin, ensuring that it is clean, dry and in good condition, and moving the individual regularly so that they do not develop pressure sores. Many care settings use specialist scoring tools to identify individuals who may be at risk of developing pressure sores. When an individual has developed a pressure sore, their care and the procedures for managing this should be described in detail in their care plan. You should always follow this plan and request help and further explanation if you think that the care required is beyond your level of competence.

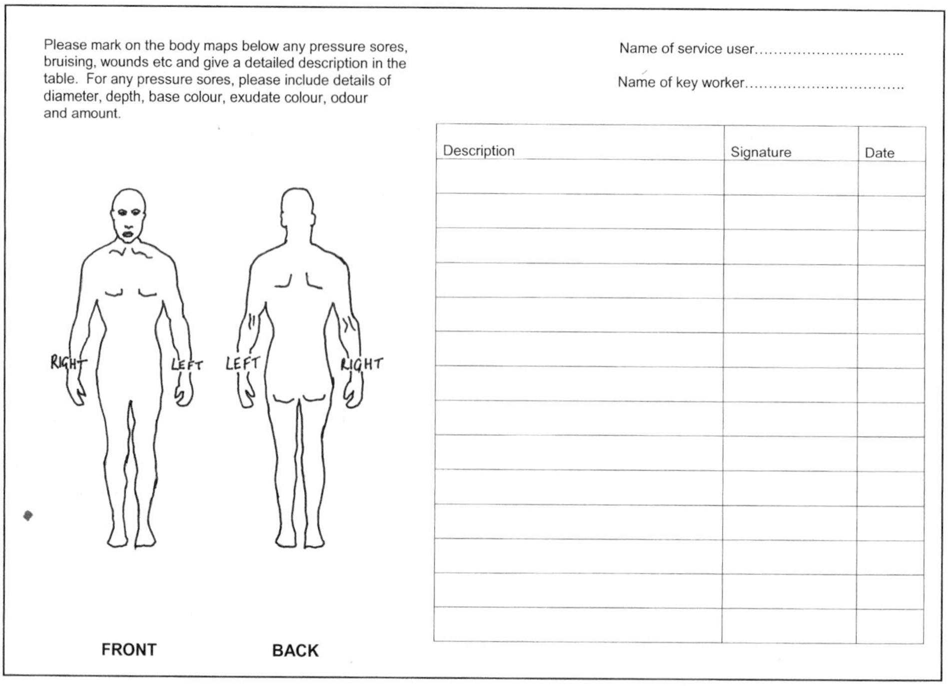

Please mark on the body maps below any pressure sores, bruising, wounds etc and give a detailed description in the table. For any pressure sores, please include details of diameter, depth, base colour, exudate colour, odour and amount.

Name of service user.................................

Name of key worker.................................

Description	Signature	Date

RIGHT   LEFT   LEFT   RIGHT

FRONT   BACK

Figure 7
Example of a pressure area assessment form

Table 1 Factors contributing to pressure sores

Factors	Causes
Friction	Wrinkled clothes, bedclothes; being pulled or dragged over a surface
Moisture	May be due to incontinence; incorrect drying technique; perspiration; illness; dehydration
Compression of tissues	Laying or sitting in same position for any length of time (1–2 hours plus)
Poor skin hygiene	Not washing frequently – especially after incontinence or leakage
Poor general nutrition	Inadequate diet that is either deficient in vitamins or minerals or insufficient in quantity
Age	Wear and tear on the skin; decreased porosity and **elastin**
Reduced mobility or immobility	Difficulty with movement can mean a person remains in the same position for longer periods and so circulation becomes slower; the tissues do not receive as much oxygen
Mental health	Confusion, disorientation or dementia-based illness may mean a person is unaware of actual or developing skin problems or they are unable to report them to others

Care of the nails

With the individual's permission, nails should be kept short where possible as they often harbour dirt that can be transferred when scratching or eating. It is important to maintain individuality and individual choice, but you should consider potential risks of infection to the individual and care worker. Care of the nails also provides a wonderful opportunity for pampering and many people enjoy a hand massage and having their nails manicured and polished occasionally.

Care of feet

Foot care is also very important and the feet are sometimes neglected. It is important that feet are checked regularly as a person may experience considerable discomfort if their toenails are too long and start to grow inwards or if there is infection between the toes or soreness due to inadequate drying after bathing. Poor foot care can lead to problems with mobility and this is an important aspect of individual care. You may be able to get advice from a chiropodist or podiatrist if there are concerns with this aspect of personal hygiene.

Care of hair

Healthy hair is maintained through regular washing and brushing, eating the correct diet and drinking plenty of water. For many people, their daily hair-care routine is part of the way that they maintain their self-esteem. Therefore it is important that you assist the individual with this as much as the individual requires.

Hair should be cut or trimmed and washed according to individual preference. Again, there may be issues in relation to hygiene requirements in the care setting that lead to conflicts with an individual. However, the solution is to negotiate a satisfactory **compromise** with the person or refer the issue to a supervisor or senior colleague to resolve.

Additional issues to consider in relation to hair care include:

- Providing aftercare treatment with oils or other hair-care products where appropriate.
- Enabling visits from or visits to the hairdresser or barber where possible.
- Being sensitive to loss of hair and change of hair colour as people age or lose hair because of health conditions or drug treatments. Individuals cope with this in a variety of ways and can be very sensitive to what they may see as a change in their identity.

Shaving

You should ask the individual what their preferences are regarding shaving. It is easier and quicker to give an electric shave, but some individuals will say that their skin does not feel as comfortable. If you are carrying out a wet shave then the razor must be sharp and it must be used for that individual only. All shaving equipment should be cleaned regularly to stop the blades becoming clogged up and working less efficiently. A blunt blade will cause cuts and bleeding. There is an obvious risk of infection and this must be reduced by individuals using their own shaving equipment. Razor blades should not be shared or used communally. If an electric shaver is to be shared then it has to be cleaned thoroughly between individuals and interchangeable shaving heads must be used.

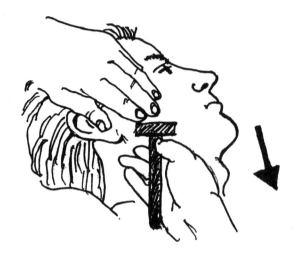

Figure 8
Shaving a male
patient

As we age, hormonal changes can mean that women become prone to facial hair. This should be removed regularly with care and sensitivity. Hair **depilatory** products are not usually recommended for use on the face. Sometimes facial hair is dyed if it is a persistent problem. Always find out which form of care and treatment the individual prefers and comply with their wishes.

Personal hygiene – the genitalia

Individuals should be encouraged and supported to be as self-caring as possible. If a person does require help to manage their intimate personal hygiene, a care worker should ensure that every step of the procedure is explained to the individual. If you are carrying out any intimate care tasks you should always ensure that you have the consent of the individual. This should prevent any misunderstanding.

In females, the genital area requires attention as, if the folds of skin are not cleansed properly, this can lead to the spread of infection. This occurs particularly when micro-organisms from the bowel (such as E.coli) enter the short **urethral passage**. So it is important when cleansing to always wipe from front to back (urethra–vagina–anus) to reduce the risk of infection occurring.

In males who are not **circumcised** the foreskin should be carefully pulled back and cleansed to remove any potential bacterial build-up (such as candida albicans or thrush). You should also note and report any unusual skin discolouration, smell, rash, swelling or discharge as these can indicate fungal or bacterial infections or underlying disease that will require treatment.

Oral hygiene – care of the mouth

Mouth care and dental hygiene is maintained through regular brushing of the teeth and through mouth washing. Dental and mouth-hygiene problems happen largely due to the neglect of basic oral-hygiene procedures.

The build-up of food deposits on teeth can lead to the formation of plaque. If they are not removed, food deposits can cause the teeth and gums to become infected. General wear of the teeth as well as neglect of oral hygiene can also lead to dental caries (holes) developing. As we age, our teeth tend to deteriorate and eventually they may have to be replaced by dentures and/or dental plates. Teeth can also become sensitive and so it may be advisable to use a desensitising toothpaste to reduce the pain. Sometimes a mouthwash may be the only way to maintain oral hygiene. However, careful use of products is important as overuse of strong mouthwashes can also cause gums to become sore. A weak solution of salty water can sometimes be just as effective, but you should always seek an individual's permission before using this to improve oral hygiene.

Adequate fluid intake is necessary to avoid soreness and cracking of the lips and tongue. A moisturising product such as lip balm can help to prevent lips cracking and becoming dry. This should be used regularly to prevent soreness.

Dental hygiene and mouth care is an important aspect of care. Poorly fitting dentures and dental decay can lead to eating and nutritional problems for the individual. You should encourage regular checks to ensure that the individual's dental health and mouth care are monitored and dealt with appropriately.

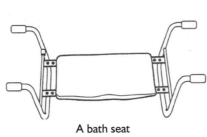

A bath seat

Rails in toilet, bath and shower

A Mobile shower chair

**Figure 9
Personal
hygiene aids**

Practical Example

Personal care

Mrs Saedif Nafeesa is 82 and was admitted to a nursing home for full nursing care following a right-sided cerebrovascular accident (CVA). Mrs Nafeesa is incontinent of urine and faeces and is unable to move the left side of her body. She has a catheter fitted. Saedif has limited communication and requires full care with activities of daily living including personal hygiene needs, eating and drinking, elimination and pressure-area care. A care-plan assessment has been carried out and care workers have been asked to carry out a full bed bath and make Mrs Nafeesa comfortable.

Two care workers are needed to assist Mrs Nafeesa. Before commencing care the care workers put on gloves and an apron. The care workers talk to Saedif and inform her of every action while they carry out personal care to meet her hygiene needs. They start by washing her face ensuring that they use water and soap (as they have checked the care plan and note that she normally uses soap). A light-coloured flannel is used to wash Saedif's face, neck, ears and chest area. At no time is Mrs Nafeesa left exposed or uncovered. A dark-coloured flannel is used for underarms, genital areas, back, legs and feet.

The catheter bag is then emptied as it does not require replacing at this time (the date that it is emptied is written on the side). The bowel chart indicates that Mrs Nafeesa had her bowels opened earlier in the morning.

The water for washing is changed regularly and kept warm so that Mrs Nafeesa does not get cold and the water does not get dirty. During the whole procedure the care workers check for discoloration of the skin, any dry patches or unusual marks and make a note of these on the pressure-area chart. They record that a pressure-area sore is developing in the sacral area and is looking red. A senior nurse is alerted to this and they carry out the current policy for pressure-area care. When Mrs Nafeesa is dry and cream has been applied to her elbows, groin and heel areas she is assisted to put on a nightgown. Her bed is remade and refreshed to ensure that there are no wrinkles in the bedclothes. Friction is reduced by careful use of a sheepskin and a bed cradle.

Mouth care is then carried out and Mrs Nafeesa has her hair brushed and tidied. She is also offered a drink. The care workers note that Mrs Nafeesa is more responsive than on first admission, especially when attempting to hold the cup.

The room is tidied and the soiled linen is placed in the linen bag together with the face cloths and towels that were used to provide personal care. The care workers know that Mrs Nafeesa enjoys listening to the radio at this time so they turn the radio on. They understand that this will also help her to recover her communication skills.

The care that was carried out is recorded in Mrs Nafeesa's notes.

➤ When carrying out personal care for individuals why is it important to ensure that they are completely covered?

➤ The care workers who carry out care for Mrs Nafeesa obtained all the equipment, towels and toiletries they needed before they started. Why is this good practice?

➤ The bowl of water is changed regularly. Give two reasons why this is good practice.

➤ What health and safety practices can you identify that reduce the risk of infection?

➤ The care workers note that a pressure-area sore is developing. Why is it important to report this and record this on a chart?

Enabling self-care

Individuals who require assistance with personal care should be supported to maintain their independent, self-care skills as much as possible. It can be very helpful in promoting self-care if you know which aids and equipment can be used to assist people to provide care for themselves. Aids, equipment and adaptations can improve an individual's quality of life because they give people back some control and choice over sensitive areas of personal care and help to protect dignity and boost self-esteem.

Wherever possible you should ask the individuals you work with to participate in their own care routines. You can achieve this by using verbal and non-verbal communication and by developing an awareness and understanding of how the individual can best function in their home environment or in a care setting. Allowing privacy, placing objects within easy reach, not restricting access to bathroom or toilet areas and providing equipment that is adapted to suit individual needs all help to achieve this. The individual may also be helped to make changes to their routine so that activities can be carried out more simply. For example, it may be more convenient for an individual to sleep downstairs or to have a stairlift installed so that they can get upstairs easily and safely.

Providing support and assistance

It is easier to provide support and assistance to meet physiological and psychological needs if the individual is able to communicate their needs. A detailed assessment of an individual's self-care skills and abilities should be formally written in their care plan. Use this to obtain information and guidance on how best to provide appropriate care and attention. The care plan should be reviewed regularly as the individual's condition can change.

There is a delicate balance to be achieved between enabling an individual to care for themselves and providing sufficient care for them. You should allow plenty of time for the individual to carry out their own personal-care activities. Do not hurry the individual and do not intervene simply because it is quicker to do so. If you take over an individual's care they may lose their self-care skills. The more care that is carried out for an individual the less able the individual will become. However, there may also be times when the individual is able to perform daily activities and times when they would prefer you to help them. It is particularly difficult when the individual is capable of some self-care but refuses to do things for themselves or gives up. A useful tip in striking the right balance between support and direct assistance is to start by asking the individual what they can do for themselves, and then provide assistance where they clearly cannot carry out self-care tasks independently. Less involvement can be beneficial to an individual's health and well-being in the long term.

Observing and reporting on personal hygiene

During the course of care delivery it is your responsibility to note and report any changes in the individual's condition. Meeting personal hygiene needs is an important part of overall care because hygiene and personal-care issues contribute to an individual's overall health and well-being. You should be able to note any changes in personal hygiene needs whilst carrying out activities of daily living.

Pay particular attention to skin, hair, teeth, nails, feet and genital areas, looking out for changes such as swelling, rashes, heat, discoloration, smell and any localised irritations or **infestations**. The behaviour of the individual can also indicate a change in their condition. For example, an individual can become quite confused when they have a urine infection. Irritability and agitation may also indicate potential problems.

It is important that changes are noted and recorded. In all care settings there should be a daily diary or log in which an individual's care can be recorded. A verbal handover or report may also be given to enable staff to act accordingly. It is important that you pass on messages and records to the appropriate people who may then order further examination of the individual and samples or specimens to be taken away for analysis.

Key points – enabling individuals to maintain personal hygiene

- Care workers play an important role in supporting individuals to manage their personal hygiene needs.
- Hygiene and health and safety issues are central for all personal-care routines.
- Risk assessment may be necessary to determine whether an individual can meet their personal hygiene needs safely.

- Washing, bathing, pressure-area care, mouth care, shaving and care of hair are all important areas of personal hygiene care.

- Wherever possible individuals should be encouraged and supported to carry out their own personal hygiene routines so that they maintain their skills and independence in this area.

- Personal hygiene routines provide a chance for you to observe an individual's physical condition and to note and report on any changes or problems that the individual may be experiencing.

Element HSC218c — Support individuals in personal grooming and dressing

The importance of appearance and grooming

An individual's appearance and grooming tend to have a significant effect on their self-image and their self-esteem. Therefore, individuals should be encouraged and supported to maintain their own personal grooming and dressing standards for as long as they are physically and mentally able to do so. This can be difficult for individuals who have physical or learning disabilities or who have an illness that causes them problems managing their needs on a daily basis. However, with your active support and assistance and the appropriate use of dressing aids and the adaptation of clothes to suit an individual's changing needs, they can maintain standards of appearance and grooming that are acceptable to them.

Supporting an individual to dress

Care workers need to focus on a number of issues relating to individuals' clothing and dressing preferences and needs. These include:

- The care of an individual's clothing.
- The adaptation of individuals' clothes.
- Encouraging and respecting an individual's choice of shoes and clothing.

In a communal, residential care situation, care of clothes is very important. Clothes should always be individually labelled and returned to the correct person after careful laundering. This does not always happen because clothes are sometimes mislaid, given to other individuals or are incorrectly washed so that they shrink and wear out more quickly. The clothes of individuals who are incontinent or individuals who have particular trouble feeding themselves tend to undergo more rigorous wear and tear. It is very important to ensure that individuals have a regular supply of clean clothes. This includes socks, tights or stockings. Tights and stockings can become worn or laddered very quickly and it is important that these are replaced regularly. Keeping individuals and/or their carers or relatives informed about the need for these items is an important part of your role as a care worker. Protection of the individual's clothes as a way of maintaining their dignity is also a very important aspect of care.

Clothes may need to be adapted to make them more comfortable or suitable for individuals who have gained or lost weight or who have experienced changes to their physical or mental state that make self-care more difficult. Buttons can be replaced or adapted (enlarged, for example), Velcro can be used to replace zippers and/or buttons, loops can be put onto existing zippers so that the zip can be pulled up, and elasticated waistbands on trousers or skirts can reduce the need to use buttons or zips. The use of a 'helping hand', a metal long-handled gripper device, may also enable an individual with limited physical skills to pick up items of clothing. It can also be used for pulling on socks and tights without having to bend or lean over.

You should respect individual preferences. For example, some people may wear many undergarments including a bra, vest, corset, tights or petticoat, whilst other people wear much less. Personal preferences for particular clothes should be encouraged and respected wherever possible. However, the items may need to be adapted for individuals who have conditions that mean clothes need to be removed or replaced regularly. Correct footwear should be worn to aid mobility and reduce the risk of accidents and falls. Check slippers for loose soles or torn material that may cause trips or slips, and make sure they are cleaned regularly.

Clothing helps us to maintain our identity and body image. For most people the clothes they wear are an outward statement of who they are as individuals. Therefore, it is important that individuals receiving care retain their sense of individuality by having the right to wear their own clothes and to choose the clothes they would like to be dressed in.

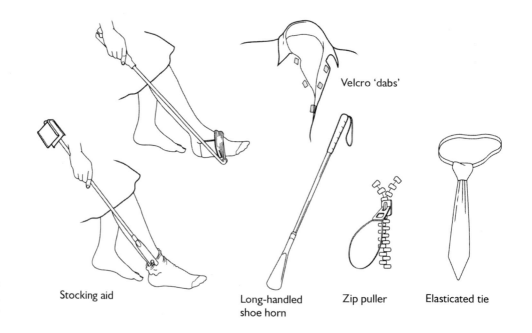

**Figure 10
Dressing aids**

Stocking aid

Velcro 'dabs'

Long-handled shoe horn

Zip puller

Elasticated tie

Promoting and supporting self-care

Individuals receiving care can be helped in a variety of ways to communicate their personal wishes and preferences with regard to grooming and dressing. This is important because a person who is able to express their choices and preferences will maintain greater self-esteem and independence. However, this can also be extremely difficult for those people who are not able to express their care needs clearly because of mental or physical problems. You can use different communication techniques to help more effective communication in these circumstances, including:

- Facing the individual and allowing them to see your face and mouth as you speak.
- Pronouncing words clearly and slowly (not necessarily loudly).
- Using flashcards with pictures of clothes, bath and toilet facilities and menu items for example.
- Allowing enough time for the individual to choose and respond.
- Producing several choices and asking the individual to point to or pick one.

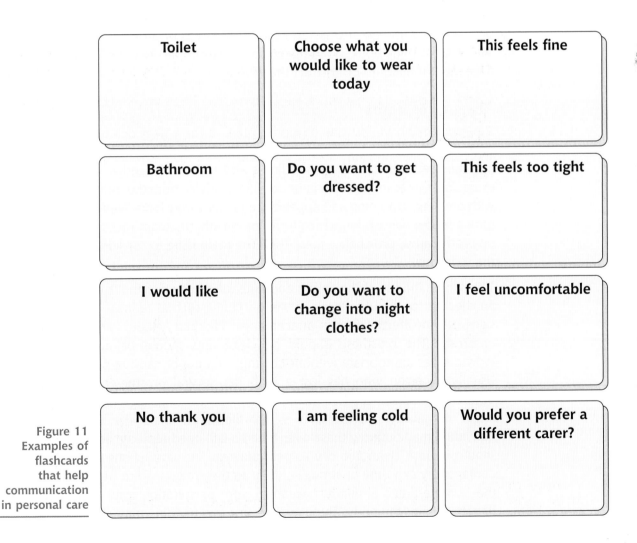

Figure 11
Examples of flashcards that help communication in personal care

Toilet	Choose what you would like to wear today	This feels fine
Bathroom	Do you want to get dressed?	This feels too tight
I would like	Do you want to change into night clothes?	I feel uncomfortable
No thank you	I am feeling cold	Would you prefer a different carer?

Using adaptations, aids and equipment

An individual's ability to manage their personal grooming and to dress themselves independently may be affected by:

- Limited mobility.
- Absence of limbs.
- Sensory deficits.
- Involuntary movements.
- Illness/disease.
- Unconsciousness.

Limited mobility

The assistance provided for a person with limited mobility may be quite minimal. It might involve something as simple as placing clothes, chosen by the individual, on their bed or nearby. The individual may then be able to dress themselves with little or no assistance. They might use dressing aids such as loops through zips and button threaders if necessary. Sometimes individuals may wish to customise wheelchairs with coverings or colourful wraps as a further extension of their personality. Bags can also be attached to the side of a wheelchair and these are useful for carrying books, knitting or cards for example. Be careful to make sure that these do not fall onto or obstruct the wheels.

Absence of limbs

A person may have lost one or more of their arms or legs due to illness or trauma or may have been born without functioning limbs. In such situations **prostheses** may be used in place of missing limbs and to help the individual resume life as usual. Prostheses require specialist care. Seek advice from the individual on assisting with dressing, grooming and appearance (as they may have lived with this for some time already). Or ask for advice from the prosthetics team (occupational therapist, physiotherapist, prosthetics specialist). The main issue to consider is the comfort of the individual.

The skin on the site of the amputated limb (also known as the stump area) needs to be checked for the usual signs of wear and tear such as redness, blisters and other signs of incorrectly fitting attachments. Padding should prevent the above occurring. The prosthesis should be clean and should be adjusted to fit the individual as appropriate without chafing, rubbing or causing pain or discomfort. Usually a person who has lost a limb has several prostheses that are used in different circumstances (for example legs for walking, legs for swimming). This might not always be the case as prostheses are expensive to make and the individual may outgrow these over time so will need replacements. The prosthesis should be kept clean and dry as per guidance and instructions. Prostheses can be damaged by exposure to strong sunlight so they may need to be lightly covered in the summertime. Similarly, sweating and perspiration can occur where the prosthesis joins the body. The use of creams and padding may alleviate this.

Sensory deficits

The main sensory deficit that affects personal grooming and dressing is visual impairment. However, some of the problems associated with this can be overcome by using clothes that are coded and textured to denote colour and the front and back of the item. In the absence of coding, you can describe the clothing so that the individual can make a choice.

Involuntary movements

These may occur due to conditions, such as Parkinson's disease or multiple sclerosis, that affect the functioning of the muscles and nerves. Involuntary movements can range from fine tremors to active arm and leg movements that cause spasm and large movements. If the individual is being dressed when the spasm happens, in extreme circumstances a fracture may occur due to the clothing restricting the movement. Prescribed muscle relaxants and medications should offer some respite from the more vigorous jerks and movements, and this should be reviewed on a regular basis. Awareness of the individual's condition and particular needs can help you with personal cleansing and dressing. Clothes may need to be adapted so that they do not restrict limbs, are easily removed and are comfortable to wear.

Illness and disease

Conditions such as strokes (cerebrovascular accidents), arthritis and Parkinson's disease may make it very difficult for individuals to dress themselves independently. Dressing aids such as button threaders and helping hands (described above) can help some individuals overcome these problems. Your role is to ensure that the individual does not have to struggle alone with this aspect of personal care. Ensure that clothes are placed nearby, that dressing aids are available and that you assist the individual to put clothing on when necessary.

Tips on helping individuals to dress

- When helping an individual to put on a cardigan, shirt or jacket hold the person's hand and gently guide their arm through the sleeves after first putting your own hand through the hand end of the sleeve.

- When helping an individual to put on trousers, sit the person down and while the individual is seated place each of their feet in each trouser leg and roll the trousers up as far as the thigh. The individual can then move over to one side and then the other while the right and left sides of the trousers are pulled up. Alternatively, if the individual can push down on the arm rests of the chair and push themselves upward, you can pull the trousers up and secure them.

- Sometimes it is easier to put a skirt over the individual's head and pull the item down towards the waist. This is much easier if the waistband is elasticated. If you do this (with the individual's agreement) be careful of the individual's face and hair.

- Stockings and support tights can be difficult to put on at the best of times and if worn incorrectly can cause the individual considerable pain and discomfort. It is sometimes easier if (having taken advice) talcum powder is used. This can be rubbed on the legs, and the tights or stockings can be gently rolled up the leg, taking care not to trap any hair or skin. A tube applicator might also be used – the tights are put onto the device and then rolled back down the leg. The obvious flaw is that the toes of the tights will be open ended! However, you could put socks on the individual to keep their feet warm and protected.

The unconscious individual

An unconscious individual will need full care to meet their personal grooming and hygiene needs. This may be an aspect of care that the individual's relative can actively engage in. For example, washing, skin care, oral hygiene, care of the hair, nails and feet, and changing the person's clothing may be areas of care where the individual's preferences and wishes could be communicated by relatives or other key people involved in their care. An unconscious person should always be covered and not left exposed or suffer any loss of dignity. It is usual for light clothing only, such as a cotton nightgown or sheet, to be worn as a way of controlling the person's temperature.

Personal-care needs

Kevin Farrell is an 85-year-old gentleman who lives with his wife Sheila in a sheltered housing scheme. They are mainly independent and self-caring with the aid of a care worker who prepares a daily hot meal.

After a recent fall, Mr Farrell fractured his hip. He made a full recovery, but since he has returned home Mrs Farrell has found it difficult to help him with bathing as she suffers from arthritis. The arthritis makes it difficult for her to dress herself and to assist her husband as much as she used to. She is very worried about this and realises that the care worker will be required to help Mr Farrell with his personal care.

➤ *How can the care worker assist Mr and Mrs Farrell to remain independent in their personal-care needs?*

➤ *Mrs Farrell finds it very difficult to dress herself. What aids could help her to achieve some independence?*

➤ *How can the care worker help Mr Farrell to maintain his privacy?*

Working safely and hygienically

In order to support individuals in personal grooming and dressing, a number of health, safety and hygiene factors need to be considered. If the individual is mostly self-caring:

- Are they able to maintain their own clothes or do they require a laundry service?
- Has the washing machine been serviced lately and are all the electrics in working order?
- Is the telephone number of a service engineer available in case of flooding or equipment not working properly?
- Who cleans the room/house that the individual lives in?
- Does the individual require more help to clean their home or room, or is this a service that is carried out for them?

If you are carrying out cleaning and activities to support daily living:

- Is there a record of equipment that has been health-and-safety checked?
- Is there a label on plugs that shows the date they were checked?
- Is the individual able to summon assistance in an emergency, for example if they have a fall or if they have any concerns?

It is important for the individual to be able to live safely and hygienically in order to reduce the risk of accidents or injury. You should always carry out a risk assessment before providing any assistance and you should ensure that you work safely to minimise any risks that are present in the environment or in relation to the individual's condition or abilities. If you identify hazards that you are concerned about, report them to your supervisor or manager as soon as possible.

Observing and reporting problems and changes

Your role as a care worker is to support independence and also to observe, note and record any changes that might occur relating to this aspect of care. Potential problems such as difficulty using aids and equipment, or clothes becoming too tight and restrictive, or access to the bathroom or toilet becoming limited should be reported immediately to the appropriate person in charge. An individual who is unable to carry out personal hygiene and grooming may be susceptible to a range of risks such as infections, falls or even **hypothermia**. Therefore, it is very important that the individual receives appropriate care and support at regular intervals and at the appropriate time of the day and night. In some instances, such as where a person is struggling to cope with their personal hygiene and dressing needs at home, an increase in support, a move to supported accommodation or admission on a temporary basis to residential care may be appropriate until the person's home environment is adapted and a suitable level of care and support can be provided for them.

Good practice in dressing and maintaining clothes

- Individuals should be encouraged to choose their own clothes.
- Individuals should remain independent for as long as possible and aids should be used to help with dressing.
- Individuals have the right to wear their own clothes.
- Clothes can be adapted with Velcro and hooks to assist self-care.
- If possible, clothes and shoes should be cleaned and, where necessary, replaced with new ones at regular intervals to assist the individual to maintain dignity and individuality.
- Clothes should be checked to ensure that they do not restrict, pinch or damage the individual's skin.
- Clothes should be cleaned and maintained correctly.
- The individual should have their own soap, flannels and towels available.
- The religious and cultural needs of the individual should be respected at all times and the individual should be helped to maintain these.

Key points – supporting individuals in personal grooming and dressing

- Personal grooming and appearance are important aspects of self-image and affect an individual's identity, self-esteem and emotional well-being.
- You have a responsibility to ensure that each individual has a choice of clean and well-maintained clothing.
- Wherever possible, you should support individuals to choose their own clothes and dress themselves.
- Where individuals require aids, equipment or assistance to dress this should be noted in their care plan and provided in a way that meets the individual's wishes and preferences.
- Health and safety and hygiene standards are important issues that should be taken into account when supporting individuals in personal grooming and dressing activities.
- You should note and report changes that affect an individual's ability to manage their personal grooming and dressing independently.

Unit HSC218

Are you ready for assessment?

Support individuals with their personal-care needs

This unit is all about your involvement in supporting individuals who require assistance with washing, bathing, dressing and using the toilet. This unit is linked closely to unit HSC21 covering communication and unit HSC22 covering risk assessment and health, safety and security. As this unit involves such intimate personal care there are also clear links with the principles and values of care in HSC24.

Your assessment will mainly be carried out through observation by your assessor and this should provide most of the evidence for the elements in this unit.

As this unit is about your role in directly supporting individuals who require support with natural aspects of daily living, there will be ample opportunities for observation by your assessor. However, if such observation could intrude on the privacy of individuals you can plan with your assessor to use the testimony of an expert witness instead of observation by your assessor or as an additional source of evidence.

Direct observation

Your assessor or an expert witness will need to see you carry out the performance criteria (PCs) in each of the elements in this unit.

The performance criteria that may be difficult to meet through observation or expert witness testimony are:

- HSC218a PC 12
- HSC218b PC 9
- HSC218c PC 5

because they might not always occur.

Preparing to be observed

You must make sure that your workplace and any individuals and key people involved in your work agree to you being assessed. Explicit, informed consent must be obtained before you carry out any assessment activity that involves individuals or which involves access to confidential information related to their care.

Before your assessments you should read carefully the performance criteria for each element in the unit. Try to cover as much as you can *during your observations* but remember that you and your assessor can also plan for additional sources of evidence should full coverage of all performance criteria not be possible or to help ensure that your performance is consistent and that you can apply the knowledge specification in your work practice.

▶

Other types of evidence

You may need to present other forms of evidence in order to:

- Cover criteria not observed by your assessor or by an expert witness.
- Show that you have the required knowledge, understanding and skills to claim competence in this area of practice.
- Ensure that your work practice is consistent.

Your assessor may also need to ask you questions to confirm your knowledge and understanding of this unit.

Check your knowledge

1   Why is it important to record details of the personal care you have carried out for each individual?

2   How would you resolve conflicts over personal care, for example when an individual does not wish to get dressed or have a wash?

3   How can an individual's beliefs affect their needs and preferences with regard to washing and bathing?

4   When carrying out personal-care needs for individuals, what codes of practice do you need to follow with regard to:
    - Recording, reporting, confidentiality and sharing information including data protection?
    - Health, safety, assessing and managing risks associated with supporting individuals?

5   How can you reduce the spread of infection when meeting the personal-care needs of individuals?

Glossary

Active listening This is the process of receiving and making sense of verbal and non-verbal messages from another person.

Active support Actions that encourage individuals to do as much for themselves as possible in order to maintain their independence and physical ability and encourage people with disabilities to maximise their own potential and independence.

Activities of daily living This term describes the things that a person must be able to do on a daily basis in order to meet their various human needs.

Advocate An advocate is a person who speaks on behalf of an individual when the individual is unable to communicate for themselves. Advocates represent the interests of the individual, often on a voluntary basis, and are not influenced by organisational policy or the wishes of family and friends.

Agenda A list of topics to be covered in a meeting.

Allergen This is a substance that can produce an allergic reaction or cause an immune response.

Analgesia The absence, or the relief, of pain.

Anti-discriminatory practice This is an approach to care practice that challenges instances of prejudice and unfair discrimination and aims to counteract their negative effects.

Appraisal A formal meeting between a staff member and a manager to discuss past and present performance and plan for the future.

Appropriate people In this instance it means the people from whom you need to gain permission before accessing records according to legal and organisational requirements. This could include a line manager or other employees who are responsible for individuals' care records.

Aseptic techniques Methods of carrying out sterile procedures so that there is the minimum risk of introducing infection.

Audit A systematic way of checking that all aspects of care practice have been carried out to the required standard.

Balanced diet A balanced diet contains a range of foods from each of the six main food groups.

Carrier oils Used in aromatherapy, these are the base oils into which essential oils are mixed.

Catheter A tube that is inserted into the body to introduce or drain off liquid. For example, a catheter may be fitted to draw off urine which is collected in a bag outside the individual's body.

Circumcised Having had the foreskin cut.

Codes of practice Documents that provide guidance on ethically appropriate and recommended ways of behaving or dealing with situations.

Coeliac disease A condition where an individual is unable to process carbohydrates and fats in their diet due to an intolerance to gluten.

Collaborate Co-operate with each other.

Compartmentalise To separate something into parts and place in a specific area.

Competence This means being able to do something effectively and to the required standard.

Compromise The settlement of a dispute by mutual agreement in which each party will give in on certain matters.

Confidentiality The protection of information to make sure that it is only accessible to authorised people.

Continence This refers to a person's ability to control their elimination or bladder and bowel functions.

Continuing professional development Ongoing learning and development that usually occurs in the workplace or which is work focused.

Continuity Being continuous and unbroken.

Crohn's disease An inflammatory bowel disorder which can involve chronic diarrhoea and abdominal pain, fever, lack of appetite, weight loss and a feeling of fullness in the gut.

Cross-infection This occurs when an infection, or infectious organism, is transferred from one person to another. It may occur because a care worker fails to use adequate infection-control techniques (such as hand washing) and becomes the carrier of an infection that is then transferred to each individual that they work with.

Culture Patterns of behaviour, customs, art etc. that are passed from one person to another.

Defecation A term used to describe the discharge of faeces through the anus. Other phrases that are used to describe the same process include 'opening your bowels', 'passing a stool' or a 'bowel motion/movement'.

Degenerative Tending to deteriorate or get worse.

Depilatory Something that removes unwanted hair.

Deterrent Something that acts to discourage or put off.

Dexterity Skill in physical movement.

Diabetes A condition where the individual's body is unable to regulate the level of sugar in the blood effectively.

Diet The range of food that a person eats regularly.

Dietary intake What you eat and drink.

Dignity The state of being worthy of respect.

Discriminatory Showing prejudice or unfavourable treatment.

Diuretics Something that increases the need to pass urine.

Diversity The biological, social, psychological, spiritual and cultural differences that occur in assorted people.

Domiciliary care Care administered in a person's own home.

Elastin A protein combined with a carbohydrate found in connective tissue.

Elimination The removal or excretion of waste products from the body.

Empathy Identifying with or understanding another person's situation or feelings.

Empowerment The giving of power.

Empty calories Calories that have a high calorific value but little nutritional content.

Enteral nutrition Special liquid diet taken by mouth or through a nasogastric tube.

Ethical Relating to generally accepted standards of human behaviour.

Ethnic Relating to race or culture.

Evaluation This involves obtaining and then using information to make a judgement about something.

Exacerbate To make worse, e.g. pain is exacerbated by anxiety.

Extroverts Lively, outgoing people who are more concerned with what is going on around them than with their inner feelings.

Feedback Information from other people that sheds light on your ability to do something or which gives their views of your performance.

Fomites Any objects that come into contact with a person who has a communicable disease.

Forfeit Surrender.

Formal assessment This type of assessment is carried out by way of a regulated, structured testing procedure.

Fortitude Courage when suffering pain.

Gastrostomy The creation of an opening into the stomach that allows feeding via a tube. Used when a person is unable to take in food or fluids by swallowing.

Gluten Wheat protein found in flour.

Halal Relating to meat prepared as described by Muslim law.

Hierarchy A system of ranking things in order, one above the other.

Holistic This means considering all areas of an individual's life and how those areas interact to enable the individual to continue to live an independent life.

Holistic care This is care that meets the needs of the whole person rather than care that is targeted at a specific medical or social problem.

Hypothermia A severe reduction in body temperature that can result in death.

Impairment Weakening or damage, especially as a result of injury or disease.

Individualised Tailored to particular needs or requirements.

Individuals This term is used to refer to the actual people requiring health and care services. Where individuals use advocates and interpreters to enable them to express their views, wishes or feelings and to speak on their behalf, the term 'individual' covers the individual and their advocate or interpreter.

Infestations The presence of animal parasites such as lice.

Ingestion Eating or taking food into the body.

Insight Deep, thorough understanding.

Institutionalised This refers to a loss of individuality and independence when a person's skills and abilities deteriorate or are lost because everything is done for them in a care institution.

Intellectual Relating to the mind and intelligence.

Interaction Activity that occurs between people that results in communication.

Introverted A person who is inward looking, quiet and concerned with their own thoughts and feelings.

Involuntary Unintentional, something which is out of a person's control.

Irritable bowel syndrome A condition where the individual experiences disordered bowel function, pain, urgency to empty bowels and/or constipation.

Key people The people who are most important in respect of an individual's health and social well-being. They may include partners, relatives and friends of the individual.

Key worker The person who works most closely with an individual.

Kosher Fulfilling the requirements of Jewish law.

Labelling This involves being negative about people who belong to particular groups in society.

Legislation Law.

Lifelong learning This term is used to describe the process of continual learning and professional development.

Makaton A language programme for people with communication and learning difficulties.

Mandatory study or training Study or training that must be undertaken at particular intervals to meet legal or organisational requirements. It usually includes training relating to fire safety, moving and handling, and food hygiene.

Manual dexterity Skill in using the hands.

Marginalised Prevented from accessing social resources or enjoying equal rights in society.

Mentorship A mentor is an adviser or a guide. The support and professional relationship that a mentor offers is known as mentorship.

Micro-organism This is a general term used to refer to viruses, bacteria, fungi and other very small life forms.

Micturation The passing of urine.

Migraine A severe headache often experienced with nausea, vomiting and/or visual disturbance. Migraines may be triggered as a result of consuming particular food or drink such as coffee, chocolate or cheese.

Minimal prompts Features of behaviour like brief, subtle nods of the head and affirming words like 'yes' or short phrases such as 'go on' that are used by a listener to prompt and encourage a person who is speaking.

Mobilise To move around.

Multicultural A society made up of people from several different cultures or ethnic groups.

Multidisciplinary Involving two or more areas of professional expertise.

Multi-modal Using several different forms or modes.

Multitask To carry out lots of different activities at the same time.

Nasogastric tube A tube that is passed into the stomach via the nose.

Nausea An unpleasant sensation of sickness that can cause a person to vomit or believe that they are about to vomit.

Neurological Relating to the nervous system (i.e. the brain and nerves), especially those aspects that affect sensory and mental functioning.

Non-verbal communication Ways of communicating without using words. This is often associated with aspects of body language such as the use of gestures, eye contact and touch.

Nutritional Containing the nourishment required to maintain life.

Objective Unbiased, not influenced by personal opinions or feelings.

Objective assessment An objective assessment is one where the facts are viewed and recorded as seen. Language used in reporting or recording is usually formal and in the third person. For example, 'On observation, the client's face was red, his pulse and breathing rates were raised and he was sweating.' Whereas a subjective description might say, 'I thought he looked angry and upset.'

Paramount Most important; something that should be put first or ahead of other considerations.

Paranoia A mental disorder; the symptoms include the person thinking that they are being persecuted.

Perineal area The tissue between the anus and the external genitals.

Peripheral Around the area rather than at the centre. Peripheral pain is pain felt around the general area, for example the back rather than directly at the kidney.

Personal development plan A plan for your own professional development. It is usually written after you have had an appraisal or performance review or have carried out a personal evaluation of your knowledge and skills.

Pessimistic Expecting the worst outcome.

Physiological This refers to the physiology or working of the body.

Prejudice A preconceived opinion, feeling or attitude of dislike concerning another individual or group of people. Prejudices are usually unfavourable, unreasonable and unfair judgements which are not based on accurate information or fact.

Priority needs Needs that require attention more urgently than other needs.

Prostheses Artificial limbs that replace missing body parts, e.g. a leg or arm.

Protocols Defined sets of rules that are applied in particular situations. A wound-care protocol, for example, would define exactly how a particular type of wound should be treated.

Proximity Physical closeness. It refers to the amount of physical space between people.

Psychogenic Originating in the mind.

Psychological Relating to the mind.

Psychosocial Psycho means of the mind; social relates to interactions between yourself and other individuals. So psychosocial relates to human interactive behaviour.

Purée Liquidise; turn a solid into liquid.

Rapport A harmonious relationship.

Referral The process used to obtain access to care services.

Reflection This involves conscious thought or meditation on a topic, issue or experience. A person who is reflective tries to think about something in a clear and balanced way.

Risk assessment This is the process of judging how likely it is that a hazard may actually cause harm.

Sacral area An area of the lower back.

Self-esteem A good opinion of oneself.

Sensory receptors Nerve endings within the skin that respond to external stimuli such as hot, cold, touch etc.

Skill A special ability or expertise that a person has or which they develop through training and practice.

Social exclusion This occurs when people are denied access to full citizenship and participation in normal social and economic activity.

Specialist equipment Things that are designed specifically to help in a particular situation. A broad range of specialist equipment is available to help individuals who have difficulty feeding themselves. This includes specialist crockery and utensils, table mats and cooking aids. An occupational therapist or dietician should be able to identify and provide specialist equipment for individuals who require it.

Standards An accepted example or benchmark.

Stereotype/stereotyping A standardised idea of a type of person or social group of people. The range of differences that exist within any group of similar people is ignored. Thinking about people in this way is called stereotyping.

Stomach ulcers A condition causing pain and discomfort in the stomach often associated with stress.

Stroke The medical term for a stroke is a cerebrovascular accident. This is sometimes abbreviated to CVA.

Subconscious Concerning the part of the mind that is not aware of influences, actions etc.

Subjective Influenced by personal feelings or opinions; not impartial.

Subjective experience Experience that can only be described from our own perspective and knowledge.

Supervision The overseeing of the work of a person. This provides an opportunity for a person to discuss work-related issues in order to gain support, develop their learning and improve their standards of practice.

Therapeutic Beneficial to health.

Therapeutic diets These are diets that are designed and prescribed for specific medical purposes. Gluten-free diets, for example, have a therapeutic effect on the health of people who have wheat allergies.

Unfair discrimination Unfair discrimination involves treating a person less favourably than others because of prejudice about their race/ethnicity, age, religion, gender, sexual orientation or disability.

Urethral passage The tube that runs from the bladder to the external skin, through which urine passes.

Urethral sphincters Ring-shaped muscles that close the urethra.

Urine The fluid secreted by the kidneys and excreted through the bladder and urethra.

Values Moral principles that guide our behaviour. They usually affect the way that people treat others (honestly, fairly and respectfully, for example) or expect to be treated themselves.

Vital-signs monitoring This involves recording an individual's pulse, blood pressure, respiration and body temperature.

Index

Page numbers in *italics* indicate figures or tables